GANDHI

Twentieth-Century Political Thinkers
General Editors: Kenneth L. Deutsch and Jean Bethke Elshtain

GANDHI

Struggling for Autonomy

RONALD J. TERCHEK

ROWMAN & LITTLEFIELD PUBLISHERS, INC.
Lanham • Boulder • New York • Oxford

ROWMAN & LITTLEFIELD PUBLISHERS, INC.

Published in the United States of America
by Rowman & Littlefield Publishers, Inc.
4720 Boston Way, Lanham, Maryland 20706

12 Hid's Copse Road
Cumnor Hill, Oxford OX2 9JJ, England

British Library Cataloguing in Publication Information Available

Library of Congress Cataloging-in-Publication Data

Terchek, Ronald, 1936–
    Gandhi : struggling for autonomy / Ronald J. Terchek.
      p. cm. — (Twentieth-century political thinkers)
     ISBN 0-8476-9214-0 (hardcover : alk. paper). — ISBN 0-8476-9215-9
(pbk. : alk. paper)
    1. Gandhi, Mahatma, 1869–1948—Political and social views.
2. India—Politics and government—1919–1947. 3. Nationalists—
India—Biography. I. Title. II. Series.
DS481.G3T43   1998
954.03'5'092—dc21
                                            98-22847
                                                CIP

Printed in the United States of America

∞ ™ The paper used in this publication meets the minimum requirements of
American National Standard for Information Sciences—Permanence of Paper
for Printed Library Materials, ANSI Z39.48–1984.

To
Kristin and Daniel

CONTENTS

ACKNOWLEDGMENTS

G andhi often talked about the importance of acknowledging our debts, and in the course of writing this book, I have accumulated many. One of my greatest debts is to Thomas Pantham who has been a helpful critic, a source of invaluable insight, and a warm and gracious host on several occasions. V. R. Mehta has been a stern and invaluable critic, reminding me of Gandhi's strong roots in the Indian tradition and his deep spirituality. Bhikhu Parekh has taught me much, in both his writings and in our conversations.

I have also learned much in my conversations from Ashis Nandy at the Centre for the Study of Developing Societies in New Delhi, Partha Chatterjee in Calcutta, and Naresh Dadhich in Jaipur. Mahendra Kumar, editor of *Gandhi Marg*, Manoranjan Mohanty of Delhi University and V. T. Patel at Karnatak University have also been thoughtful guides. Nitis Das Gupta of the University of Calcutta has been generous in his comments. I am also indebted to Christian Bay's early encouragement to pursue Gandhi as a serious figure in political theory. Kenneth Deutsch has been an early and helpful reader of my work on Gandhi.

John Dunn and Carole Pateman provided helpful reactions to the materials on Gandhi's economic theory based on a paper given in Ottawa. Edward Jacobitti, Amarjit Singh, and Anthony Parel have, in very different ways, helped me sort out my thoughts. Karol Soltan, Ken Conca and Don Piper have been helpful critics. David Cochran and Thomas Conte have assisted me with my research. Srimati Kamala and the Gandhi Memorial Center and Library have expedited my research. None, of course, is responsible for the errors that appear in this book.

Students, both in lectures and seminars as well as conversations at the Universities of Baroda, Delhi, and Jaipur and the University of

Maryland have been a source of stimulation. The Department of Government and Politics and the Graduate School of the University of Maryland have generously assisted me in my trips to India. The Center for Teaching Excellence also provided support to develop a course on Gandhi, an exercise which sharpened my determination to make Gandhi accessible. The students in the course demonstrated that idealism and hard work are alive and well in the academy.

Mary has been a source of support and encouragement not only in helping me with this manuscript but through our lives together. She has continually encouraged me to write a book that remains faithful to Gandhi and speaks to a world that, although different from his in many ways, still houses the issues, dangers, and opportunities Gandhi finds in his. More than that, she has shown that love can be boundless.

Gandhi reinforced lessons that Kristin and Dan taught me about the importance of each person honestly seeking the truth in his or her own way. They have also shown me that goodness and love have common threads but are expressed in different ways.

INTRODUCTION

My language is aphoristic, it lacks precision. It is therefore open to several interpretations.[1]

There is more than one way to think about Mahatma Gandhi. He is widely recognized as the preeminent theorist of nonviolent civil disobedience, the leader of India's successful campaign for national independence, and an architect of modern Indian self-identity.[2] He also challenges the deep inequalities he finds in India and offers a powerful defense of autonomy alongside a comprehensive critique of Western modernity and modernization. Throughout his life, he seeks a nonviolent, cooperative society based on mutual respect and assistance. Animating all of his work and politics is an abiding commitment to the integrity and worth of everyone. Armed with this standard, he attacks colonialism as well as untouchability because each subordinates the individual. In this spirit, Gandhi challenges modernity and modernization because he sees each disabling men and women, and he confronts violence because it treats people as means to be used for the benefit of the powerful.

Many discussions of Gandhi emphasize that he seeks a peaceful world, a stable society, and a coherent, spiritual life. In this book, I will introduce a Gandhi who sees these goals as desirable but elusive in the modern world and who argues that struggle and resistance are the requirements for a self-governing life. Gandhi thinks this is so because of the unsettling effects he attributes to modernity and modernization, which he does not expect to dissipate after a prolonged struggle. He recognizes that the modern world is here to stay, but he refuses to let it have its own way in determining the character of contemporary society. For his part, he resists both an optimism that modernization and modernity need only be reformed and a despair that nothing effectively can be

1

done to harness their dark side. Instead, Gandhi offers materials to struggle with both ancient and modern enemies of autonomy in order to make a place for the integrity of individuals in their local settings.[3]

READING GANDHI

Gandhi has been read through a variety of lenses. Countless studies celebrate his life and work and seek to extend his message to readers.[4] Several commentators concentrate on his theory of nonviolence.[5] Others focus on Gandhi as a moral and political theorist who is a participant in a continuing conversation about such critical issues as how we understand power and justify its uses, why politics must pay attention to moral issues, what serves to enhance or obstruct a moral life, and how we are implicated in the politics and practices of our government and society.[6] Still others enlist him to challenge modernity and modernization and to show their often hidden costs to community and individual freedom.[7]

Although I build on many of these studies, my primary focus is different. Central to my reading of Gandhi is his deep and persistent commitment to the autonomy of everyone. Gandhi's understanding of autonomy is tied to his expansive view of power, which he locates in the state, economy, and society as well as in each individual. Fortified with his reading of power, Gandhi holds that everyone can and should take charge of his or her own life.

I also read Gandhi as the consummate problematizer of conventional ideas about power and politics as well as of modernity and modernization. In this role, he casts doubt where most people find certainty. Rather than accepting violence as regrettable but necessary, he challenges its legitimacy; instead of holding that political independence from Britain is the sole criterion of freedom for India, he asks Indians to purge their country of indigenous patterns of domination. And in defending tradition as a foundation for autonomy, he continually challenges what he takes to be its defects in order to reform it.

GANDHI'S TEXTS

Gandhi's writings are disarmingly simple: many appear as regular newspaper pieces in *Young India* and *Harijan,* and others come from his voluminous correspondence and speeches.[8] These texts frequently address matters of everyday importance to Indians in the early and middle parts of the twentieth century and often seem atheoretical and remote from the concerns of many readers today. Writing for ordinary Indians, he frequently employs metaphors and engages in homilies to teach about the nature of power and empowerment as well as to remind Indians of their own strong traditions. In this way, he seeks to mobilize the Indian public on behalf of his campaigns of nonviolent civil disobedience against British colonialism, untouchability, and communal discord. Relying on a simple vernacular, he questions much that has been taken for granted in both India and the West, particularly the ideas that violence is an effective way to achieve justice and that modernity and modernization spell progress.

Not all of Gandhi's texts are written. In an extraordinary way, he transforms symbols and his own life into commentaries about many of the matters he wants to convey most urgently. He offers telling narratives with his embrace of the spinning wheel and his habit of spinning several hours everyday; his own austere life at the ashrams; his readiness to terminate civil disobedience campaigns when some Indians engage in violence; his many expressions of love and his self-discipline; and his years in British jails on behalf of independence. His commitments and actions complement his *Autobiography* and his other written texts. The way he lives his life and the symbols he mobilizes serve to authenticate his written arguments for many of his contemporaries in ways that language, by itself, can not.[9] Standing alongside his written texts about love and nonviolence, for example, is the life Gandhi authors for himself which exudes these qualities. In what follows, I will occasionally turn to his actions, although I rely primarily on Gandhi's written texts to unfold his political theory.

Texts are notoriously open to highly diverse interpretations, and Gandhi's are no exception. Many early commentaries on Gandhi take his criticisms of modernity and modernization literally and find the only correct way of reading him is to see him arguing that India must return to a simple agrarian economy and a simple society. While not disputing Gandhi's steadfast commitment to a rural economy and an uncomplicated community, I argue that a parallel and helpful way of reading his texts is to see him offering not only criticisms of the dominant organizing principles of the era but also providing idealized alternatives to them which he wants men and women to enlist in their struggle to protect their own autonomy.

Gandhi raises issues that often seem out of place in any serious discourse in the late modern world. This is particularly the case when he turns to modern views of the world that are highly optimistic and individualistic and that celebrate the power of reason, the promise of science, the benefits of economic growth, and the inevitability of progress. Providing one of the most vocal, trenchant, and unrelenting criticisms of the modern age, Gandhi advances traditional standards and practices as alternatives, some of which seem archaic, such as his defense of a village economy and his celebration of spinning as the universal employer of India. Rather than advancing a literal reading of Gandhi's texts, we can take them as oppositional to the phenomena he is criticizing. The impersonality of the city is juxtaposed with the need for community; the unemployment he associates with economic modernization is contrasted with the full employment he sees in traditional vocations; and the instability and discontent he finds residing in economic mobility is contrasted with the stability and satisfactions he finds in traditional society. He offers his alternatives not as passive refuges from the modern world but as active challenges to its most self-confident themes. Wanting to enlarge the discourse to include neglected, often incommensurate positions, Gandhi hopes not to settle the conversation but to open it up, not to offer solutions but to point to the paradox and irony embedded in any answer. In speaking to the modern condition in his arresting and unorthodox way, he seeks to make certain that autonomy and a commitment to nonviolence do not become expendable standards but are vital principles that are used to judge institutions.

Gandhi often exasperates many Westerners; he seems divorced from their reality, deaf to the sounds they hear in the modern world, and blind to the benefits they associate with modern science and technology. And, of course, the charge is accurate in many important ways. His reality differs from the dominant Western version; he hears sounds and sees sights from the vantage point of someone who lives not only in a non-Western country but also in a colony of a Western nation. In mounting his criticisms, Gandhi problematizes what is settled in the modern West and which seems poised to transform India.[10] When Gandhi gazes at recent scientific and technical accomplishments, he sees many of the same things Westerners do: increased productivity, efficiency, and greater control over nature. For many, these phenomena are positive goods that mark the progress of the human race. But Gandhi links them to the worst features of the age: new forms of poverty and inequality; unemployment; a growing alienation and a ceaseless restlessness; and more destructive forms of violence and a readiness to use them. For him, these problems cannot be corrected by marginal change, more rational policies or additional scientific discoveries. Calling into question the entire Enlightenment project, he seeks to cast doubt on the certainties embedded in the foundations of modern thinking: philosophical, political, social, economic, and scientific. For Gandhi, the issue is not who will win control over modern institutions and practices, but about questioning their efficacy and moral justifications regardless of who controls them.[11]

He means to challenge both traditional and modern forms of determinism. As he sees it, the premodern world constructed its own brand of fatalism which taught that what happened to people lies beyond their comprehension and control. For all of its rationalism and science, Gandhi finds that the modern world has created its own brand of fatalism, one that assumes that reigning institutional arrangements cannot be otherwise and it is our task to adjust to them. For his part, Gandhi rejects all forms of fatalism. He continually tells his readers that they cannot make the state, culture, or history responsible for what happens to them; they, and not others, must be in charge of their lives. In what follows, I read Gandhi as someone who celebrates an autonomous life and warns about the threats posed by hierarchy, indignity, and violence and, in the process, tells his audience they are not helpless but can struggle against such dangers.

GANDHI'S DEBTS

The late nineteenth and early twentieth centuries are a time of intellectual and political ferment in India. Some Indians desire a greater voice in their own governance, and they work for a limited home rule on the subcontinent. Others, such as Gandhi,[12] reject this ameliorist approach and seek complete independence from the British Empire. At the same time, they are deeply troubled about the displacement of Indian traditions (or what they often call "Indian civilization") by the ideology of modernity and the institutions of modernization. Although they frequently disagree among themselves about the extent and nature of the threat and how to respond to it, they particularly quarrel with those Indians who embrace modern modes of thinking and carry modernizing aspirations. At the same time, they confront those Indians who steadfastly cling to a dogmatic, ritualistic reading of their tradition.[13] This is a period when many of the most important issues in political philosophy resurface in India: arguments abound about the nature of knowledge, cosmology, and metaphysics; the meaning of identity; the role of tradition in addressing the dignity of persons; the nature of the state and state-power; the interrelationship between civil society and politics; and the role of violence in social and political relations.[14] In each of these debates, Gandhi is a prominent and articulate contributor and charts important, new areas for theory and practice.

Given his own wide-ranging readings in Indian and Western texts and his frequent, generous comments about how much he learns from them, it is sometimes difficult to determine how much Gandhi is indebted to Hinduism and how much to other traditions.[15] We know he was born and raised a Hindu and has strong affinities to Jainism with its antipathy to taking any form of life.[16] He also spends several years in Britain studying law, which he later practices in the British courts of South Africa.[17] All the while, he reads and discusses Indian and Western texts in philosophy, religion, and politics.[18]

Whatever his debts to Western theory, virtually all scholars agree that Gandhi must be primarily understood within the Hindu tradition;[19] however, there is considerable controversy about what this means. V. R. Mehta sees him primarily as a Hindu thinker who uses other traditions to amplify what he finds inherent in his own.[20] Margaret Chatterjee holds that Gandhi's understandings are mainly Hindu but that he also relies on the teachings of Jains, Buddhists, and Christians.[21] Bhikhu Parekh finds him remaking Hinduism to fit his own commitments to nonviolence and his version of *swaraj*.[22] Others, such as Raghavan Iyer, argue that in developing his theory of nonviolence, "Gandhi was, in fact following the footsteps of the Buddha in showing the connection between the service of suffering humanity and the process of self-purification."[23] For his part, Gandhi believes he is deeply indebted to Hinduism but that he has also learned much from Jainism and Buddhism as well as Christianity.[24] Whatever his debts, he continually returns to Hinduism.

But it is *his* Hinduism: Gandhi reconstructs it, challenging some long-time practices, reforming others, and interpreting the spiritual life to be a life of service.[25]

Sorting out his debts to Western theory is just as difficult.[26] We find similarities to many of Gandhi's ideas in Western texts and can point to the way he employs various Western vernaculars to advance his ideas. However, when he uses Western concepts, he frequently transforms them.[27] Both Gandhi and Enlightenment thinkers, for example, celebrate speech over coercion as a way of arriving at solutions, but Gandhi insists there is no purely neutral or objective form of speech, that there is a multitude of valid discourses, and that those who have previously been silent (or silenced) must not only have a chance to speak but deserve to be heard, themes denied or neglected by most Enlightenment writers. Moreover, their common commitment to the integrity of individuals takes on very different forms of understanding. For Gandhi, Enlightenment conceptions of individualism separate persons from their tradition and from one another, and he offers a theory of autonomy designed to empower individuals within their tradition and community.

Care must be taken when using Western conceptual categories to understand Gandhi's texts because Gandhi seldom recognizes such categories. My occasional efforts to use a comparative strategy to illuminate his thinking is not to determine whether Gandhi is similar to or borrows from one or another Western theorist but to notice how Gandhi is engaged in a debate about freedom, equality, and self-government that is no respecter of time and place and which continually reappears in political theory.

The last word about Gandhi's debts should aptly come from Gandhi himself. In discussing his reading in many traditions and how they contribute to his understanding of *ahimsa* or love as a way of understanding and acting in the world, he signals his tendency to synthesize and reconstruct diverse theories to make one of his own:

> Though my views of *ahimsa* are a result of my study of most of the faiths of the world, they are now no longer dependent upon the authority of these works. They are a part of my life and if I suddenly discovered that the religious books read by me bore a different interpretation from the one I had learnt to give them, I should still hold [my own] view of *ahimsa*.[28]

EXCURSIONS TO OTHER TEXTS

From time to time, I discuss Gandhi's texts in tandem with other texts. Here, I do not intend to determine debts but rather to engage in what Fred Dallmayr has called comparative political theory.[29] In an age of political interdependence when old barriers fall, it is important to think about both what is distinctive and what shared (or universal) in political theories that are authored in very different cultures. There is a tendency for some commentators to emphasize the former and make each culture unique. When this occurs, the texts of each distinctive culture are unable to speak to readers in other cultures who bring a radically distinctive way of thinking and seeing the world. On this reading, the West and India possess their own particular world views as reflected in their religion, philosophy, and social practices. For others, texts can be transported across time and space and made to speak with equal intimacy and authenticity to readers anywhere at anytime. On this account, nothing is essentially lost when texts are asked to do the same work abroad that they do at home. We are, after all, part of the same humanity with the same basic needs.

The first approach dwells on the particularity of texts and builds barriers to understanding what the members of different cultures share; the second universalizes texts and discards what is local, that is, pretends that no differences count. For someone like Dallmayr, texts ought not be approached as if they were either inaccessible or totally available. In very different ways, exclusivist and universalist readings simplify and distort what is inherently a complex endeavor. In what follows, I often read Gandhi's texts as exercises in comparative political theory. In doing so, I show where Gandhi engages in a dialogue about issues that have concerned others while at the same time disclosing what is distinctive about his work. It turns out that Gandhi often shares much with various important Western writers. To make this argument means that binary understandings of East and West must be suspended, particularly the idea that there are monolithic Western and Eastern (or Indian) positions about many of the issues that appear and reappear in political theory.

The writers I recruit for conversations with Gandhi offer understandings of what is important that are significantly different from what we usually encounter in most contemporary Western discourse. For example, I will enlist a group of Western writers who recoil at the ascendance of modernization, but I will not rely on the usual critiques of Tolstoy and Ruskin as do most commentators on Gandhi. Rather, I reach for Rousseau, Toinnes, Weber, Nietzsche, and Tocqueville to show that Gandhi's concerns have often been represented in important texts of the Western canon. In a different setting, I recall the republican arguments of Aristotle, Machiavelli, and Rousseau on behalf of a coherent, cooperative community to draw parallels with Gandhi's concerns about an integrated cosmos and the dangerous disintegration that follows a preoccupation with individualism and materialism.

These excursions into comparative theory are not meant to make writers interchangeable or have them repeatedly intersect. Rather, I mean to show that Gandhi is no esoteric writer but is often a participant in a continuing debate in political theory. In doing so, I see him calling up standards of the good that were once vital or at least intensely defended in the Western canon but have become neglected or lost in their former home. With this move, I show that Gandhi's suspicion of the rationalism and universalism that we associate with modernity had earlier parallels in the West, which saw them as dangerous to other standards of the good embedded in the Western canon.

A comparative approach to political theory highlights matters that do not know geographic boundaries. In doing so, it provides materials that can challenge ideas and practices that have become so much taken for granted that they are seen as true or natural and in need of no defense. Such a stance, however, compounds problems when the reigning theoretical paradigm contributes to some of the most serious problems facing a society. Then fresh, alternative ideas are necessary to address pressing issues such as conflict, environmental decay, and acute poverty, and Gandhi offers his own unique contribution. To the extent that modernity has contributed to many of our most urgent problems, it is helpful to consider perspectives that depart from many of the assumptions and axioms bound to modernity. Such an exercise is especially promising when alternative languages retain some of the standards of the good important in modernity, particularly regarding the fundamental equality and rights due everyone.[30]

In moving fragments of texts across time and place, it is important to remember what is distinctive about them and what cannot readily be transported today.[31] The views of many Hindus, Jains, and Buddhists, for example, that all life, not just human life, is sacred has no prominent place in Western thought. However, because some of what is true for one culture is not true for another, it need not mean that cultures have nothing to learn from each other. Moreover, writers of texts, even when they universalize, almost always have an eye on their own culture and its promises and problems as well as the resources that strengthen and dangers that threaten what is good. For this reason, many of Gandhi's practical suggestions, such as spinning, are meant to apply to the India of his time. To the extent they speak to other traditions and conditions, it is as morality tales that alert readers to obstacles they confront and teach them they can be in charge of their own lives.

GANDHI'S COSMOLOGY

The goal of classical philosophy is to find wisdom—that is, knowledge about who we are and how we should conduct ourselves. Today, we do not talk much about wisdom or even knowledge but rather about information. For someone like Gandhi, this last term epitomizes much that is wrong today. He sees people eagerly acquiring fragments of information, as kings once collected conscripts, and in each case the purpose is much the same: to master new territory. But, Gandhi wonders, how can we master the world if we are not sure of who we are or our place in the world? For him, the world can never be adequately described by its observable attributes but must always include a place for the interrelatedness of its parts and must make the worth and integrity of autonomous men and women its place of pride.

One way Gandhi radically departs from most modern writers and readers lies in his cosmological impulse. He is animated by a view of humanity that stresses its unity and interdependence and denies we can understand the world by segmenting it into narrowly drawn compartments. From his perspective, we are not alone or detached from the whole but are an integral part of the universe. In offering a cosmological reading, Gandhi seeks to undermine the assumptions of the Enlightenment with its starkly individualist understanding of the human condition.

His cosmological perspective calls attention to the debts we owe others: our parents, teachers, neighbors, fellow citizens, clerics, and the many other people—seen and unseen—who contribute to the vitality of our institutions and to our ability to meet our daily needs. Gandhi's perspective also recognizes our debts to our tradition and the ordinary and extraordinary contributions earlier generations have made over time to the best we have today. These are enormous debts, and we cannot repay them all, nor should we be expected to do so. But in repaying what we can, Gandhi thinks that we show we are part of a world, inter-dependent over time and space, that is better because others have made the effort and because we will make our own contributions. However, Gandhi appreciates that not all we inherit from the past is harmoniously integrated into the cosmos. For all of their many contributions to the present, earlier generations often distort what they have received or allow moral principles to decay, and Gandhi makes it the responsibility of the present generation to challenge distortion and decay by purging its own tradition of its accumulated deficiencies.

He does this in several ways in his reconstruction of Hinduism. His reinterpretation of the *Gita* emphasizes the inexorable conflict between good and evil. For him, its violent passages signal the necessity to challenge fatalism and passivity and to reassert the autonomy of everyone through nonviolent confrontation. When he works to abolish untouchability as an affront to the autonomy of persons, he turns to Hinduism to supply him with moral materials for his assault. On his reading of a healthy tradition, people have not only standards of the good life but also institutional practices that enable them to attend to their multiple needs and duties while remaining honest to their principles. Because any tradition can decay, he wants the members of a flawed tradition to repair it not only for the sake of returning to the core of the tradition but also to provide an effective way to confront the many expressions of domination, both ancient and new, that appear in any society. For Gandhi, a decayed, corrupted tradition is no match to confront injustice; therefore, he seeks to cleanse tradition of its vestiges of corruption to become an effective weapon in the struggle.

GANDHI AS A PROBLEMATIZER

Things are not always what they seem. What often is understood as good sometimes turns out to carry unexpected, unwelcome consequences. Freedom, for example, frees men and women from superior, arbitrary power and enables them to make choices. They are free to make choices that promote their moral development or that reflect a preoccupation with comfort and pleasure; they are free to extend themselves socially or isolate themselves from others; and they are free to move beyond their interests or be defined only by their interests, as if nothing else mattered. To notice the problematic nature of freedom is hardly a justification to abandon freedom but shows the many possible consequences of freedom, both the bright and dark ones.

I take Gandhi's texts as efforts to interrogate some of the practices and ideals we take for granted, particularly our views of modernity, conventional politics, and the necessity for violence. In challenging their worth and justice, Gandhi seeks to expose their heavy costs in the lives of ordinary persons. Focusing on his commitments to autonomy and his continual challenge to the standard answers of the modern age serves to help locate Gandhi in a continuing conversation about freedom and power. His abiding commitment to autonomy and his problematizing impulse are at the heart of Gandhi's project. Running throughout his texts is a strong subversive thread. Gandhi wants, for example, to challenge modern celebrations of neutrality, science, and technology because he sees them depoliticizing what should be contestable.

This can also be seen in his efforts to challenge the necessity, legitimacy, and efficiency of violence and thereby undermine its justificatory foundations. For Gandhi, autonomous individuals ought to make choices freely, that is, they ought not be compelled to behave as they do to avoid some costly penalty. On his reading, the pain visited by violence makes many persons captives to fear and dependent on the powerful. For all his severe objections to violence, Gandhi does not question the need for conflict or the need to resist injustice and domination strenuously and publicly. Rather, he rejects the idea that violence is an acceptable mode of proceeding. He wants victims to resist both their victimizers as well as their own tendency to think that their only alternatives are quietly acquiescing or striking back violently. For him, the required virtue in the face of injustice is courageous, nonviolent action.

THE REMAINDERS OF MODERNITY

Arguing that any mode of knowledge is incomplete, Gandhi continually asks about what is neglected. What do we ignore when we see what we see? You and I, for example, encounter the same street scene, and you find activity, color, and buoyancy while I see frenzy, gaudiness, and triviality. Or you see convention and I see injustice. In his discussions of remainders, Bernard Williams helps to clarify the blank spaces in our accounts. Remainders consist of the moral imperatives that we do not consider because they are not part of the specific normative frame that we use when we encounter a particular situation. The problem is not solved, or even eased, by turning to an alternative moral position because every morality is incomplete.[32] Whatever frame we use, much remains unseen and unattended.

Gandhi finds that colonialism, violence, decayed traditions, modernity and modernization, and conventional democratic practices create an incredible range of remainders; he sees them omitting goods that appear and reappear in countless traditions speaking to the dignity of persons. Should such omissions persist, individuals will be judged by their contribution to conventional goods and, if they make no contribution, they become dispensable. Gandhi calls on the core of traditions to reintroduce principles that have become remainders today and to serve as a guardian of autonomy in its struggle with domination and violence. Accordingly, he seeks to make the world open to multiple logics and multiple discourses to advance standards that have been discounted or forgotten in the modern project.[33] As a problematizer, Gandhi continually questions many of the principles we take as good and many of the "facts" or theories we take as true. In raising the questions he does, he tries to show that we will never be able to address, much less challenge, the dangerous sides of our truisms if we unreflectively accept them.

In challenging conventional certainties, Gandhi continues a long tradition in political thought: Socrates surely does so in ancient Athens, Rousseau when he attacks arbitrary rule, and Mill when he confronts the middle-class conformity of his generation. More recently, Reinhold Niebuhr and Hannah Arendt[34] have undermined conventional understandings of politics to make it ironic and fluid. Today, the problematizing impulse is strongest among postmodernists in their quarrel with modernity.[35]

Postmodernism has entered the vocabulary as a term used to convey a distinctive style of thinking that confronts both modernism and traditionalism, celebrates diversity, unearths the unstated and unacknowledged assumptions and axioms of earlier theory and practice, and challenges the hegemony of reigning paradigms—particularly those claiming to be based on the principles of neutrality and impartial rationality. For many, postmodernism is a rebuttal to modernism; for others, it is simply the latest stage of modernism. In what follows, I show that Gandhi's problematizing encounters with domination and violence often share much with postmodernism.[36] However, I do not propose to make him a postmodernist but to disclose how Gandhi interrogates various forms of domination in order to deprive them of their self-certainty as well as to enlarge discourse to include previously excluded voices.[37]

To try to make Gandhi into a postmodernist would be misleading. His complex Hinduism, for one thing, makes it difficult to enroll him as a member of any other particular tradition, approach, or persuasion. Attempts to categorize Gandhi as a postmodernist also need to contend with Gandhi's idea that a truth exists, that its essential meaning can be partially discovered and morally applied, and that people can learn to live together in peace and with dignity. For their part, postmodernists tend to deny the existence of settled truths and emphasize domination rather than harmony. Moreover, Gandhi will make love the center of his theory of social action and relations, something that is clearly absent in postmodernism. Nevertheless, both claim that most conventional settlements rest on manipulation and hierarchy and need to be exposed and resisted.

In what follows, I show how Gandhi engages in some of the important debates of the century. In doing so, I enlist Gandhi in a conversation designed to protect and enhance the autonomy and equality of persons in a world that is often hostile to such goods. In drawing parallels and contrasts between Gandhi and others, I hope to add dimensionality to a writer who challenges some of our most basic modes of thinking and whose thinking often begins at a radically different place than does conventional modern thought. I also hope to convey Gandhi's vision of a world that is moved by love and is hospitable to autonomy.

NOTES

1. Gandhi, M. K. "Discussions with Dharmadev," *Collected Works* (Delhi: Publications Division, 1972), 53, 485.

2. Jawaharlal Nehru, the first prime minister of India, observes that Gandhi's

"teaching was fearlessness and truth and action allied to these. . . . So suddenly, as it were, that black pall of fear was lifted from the people's shoulders, not wholly of course, but to an amazing degree" (*The Discovery of India* [Oxford: Oxford University Press, 1946], 36). Paul Power calls the period from Gandhi's return to India until his death as "The Age of Gandhi in India" (*The Meanings of Gandhi* [Honolulu: University Press of Hawaii, 1971], 59). For a discussion of his mobilization of the Indian independence movement, see Dennis Dalton, *Mahatma Gandhi: Nonviolent Power in Action* (New York: Columbia University Press, 1993), and Lloyd Rudolph and Susanne Rudolph, *The Modernity of Tradition* (Chicago: University of Chicago Press, 1967).

3. I also explore some of the apparent contradictions in his writings, particularly those concerning nonviolence, the role of the coercive state, and the appropriate place for modernity and modernization in India. I do this to show that Gandhi does not offer formula to enlist in his struggles but a continued reexamination of his own positions to protect autonomy under a variety of circumstances.

4. One of the earlier writers to popularize Gandhi in the West is Romain Rolland; see his *Mahatma Gandhi* (London: Allen and Unwin, 1924). Louis Fisher is also an important popularizer, making Gandhi accessible to many Westerners. See his *Gandhi: His Life and Message for the World* (New York: New American Library, 1982) and *The Life of Mahatma Gandhi* (New York: Harper and Row, 1981). Also see Vincent Sheean, *Lead Kindly Light* (New York: Random House, 1949). More recently, Richard Attenborough's film *Gandhi* attracted large audiences in both India and the West.

5. See N. K. Bose, *My Days with Gandhi* (Calcutta: Nishana, 1953); Dalton, *Mahatma Gandhi*; Gene Sharp, *The Politics of Nonviolent Action* (Boston: Porter Sargent, 1973); Arne Naess, *Gandhi and the Nuclear Age* (Totowa, N.J.: Bedminister Press, 1965); and Joan Bondurant, *Conquest of Violence* (Princeton: Princeton University Press, 1964).

6. See Raghavan N. Iyer, *Moral and Political Thought of Mahatma Gandhi* (New York: Oxford University Press, 1973); D. M. Datta, *The Political Philosophy of Mahatma Gandhi* (Madison: University of Wisconsin Press, 1953); Bhikhu Parekh, *Gandhi's Political Philosophy* (Notre Dame: Notre Dame University Press, 1989); Thomas Pantham, "Post-Relativism in Emancipatory Thought: Gandhi's Swaraj and Satyagraha," in *Multiverse of Democracy,* ed. D. C. Gheth and Ashis Nandy (New Delhi: Sage, 1997), 210–29; V. R. Mehta, *Foundations of Indian Political Thought* (New Delhi: Manohar, 1992); Dennis Dalton, *The Indian Idea of Freedom* (Gurgaon: Academic Press, 1982); Naresh Dadhich, *Gandhi and Existentialism* (Jaipur: Rawat, 1993); and Jayantanuja Bandyopadhyaya, *Social and Political Thought of Gandhi* (Bombay: Allied Publishers, 1969).

7. See Rajni Kothari, *Footsteps into the Future* (New York: Free Press, 1974)

and *Poverty* (Atlantic Highlands, N.J.: Zed Books, 1993); Ashis Nandy, *Traditions, Tyranny and Utopia* (Delhi: Oxford University Press, 1987); and Partha Chatterjee, *Nationalist Thought and the Colonial World: A Derivative Discourse* (Delhi: Oxford University Press, 1986). These writers are not "Gandhians," but each borrows from Gandhi in his understanding and critique of modernity.

8. Not including supplementary volumes and indexes, there are ninety volumes in *The Collected Works of Mahatma Gandhi,* each ranging from 400 to 600 pages (New Delhi: Publications Division, Ministry of Information and Broadcasting, 1958–1984).

9. In her biographical study, Judith Brown finds Gandhi is "an ingenious and sensitive artist in symbols"; see her *Gandhi* (New Haven: Yale University Press, 1989), 385. Also see Rudolph and Rudolph, *Modernity of Tradition.*

10. Gandhi's complaints are primarily with modernity and not with the West as such. This is clearly spelled out in his *Hind Swaraj.* This is Gandhi's most frequently published work, printed in many editions and found in numerous collections. In what follows, I will refer to chapters in this work. For a scholarly treatment of the text, see M. K. Gandhi, *Hind Swaraj and Other Writings,* ed. Anthony Parel (New York: Cambridge University Press, 1997).

11. See *Hind Swaraj,* ch. 19.

12. Initially, Gandhi accepts British rule and wants Indians to find a dignified place in the Empire. He becomes quickly disillusioned, rejects any vestige of colonialism, and works for Indian independence.

13. See Mehta, *Foundations*; Bhikhu Parekh, *Colonialism, Tradition, and Reform* (New Delhi: Sage, 1989); and Dalton, *Indian Idea of Freedom.*

14. For an extended discussion of this debate, see Mehta, *Foundations*; Dalton, *Indian Idea of Freedom*; and *Political Thought in Modern India,* ed. Thomas Pantham and Kenneth Deutsch (New Delhi: Sage, 1986).

15. See Parekh, *Colonialism, Tradition, and Reform,* 11–33, 100, 108–120; and Iyer, *Thought.* For Gandhi, Hinduism is "the most tolerant of all religions known to me. Its freedom from dogma makes a forcible appeal to me inasmuch as it gives the votary the largest scope for self-expression. Not being an exclusive religion, it enables the followers of that faith not merely to respect all the other religions, but it also enables them to admire and assimilate whatever may be good in the other faiths" (*Young India,* October 20, 1927).

16. Jainism exercised its greatest influence in India in Gujerat, the state where Gandhi was born. Many of the friends of the Gandhi family were Jains who often visited the Gandhi household.

17. His close association with Jains during his boyhood, his long periods away from India, and his many Christian, Jewish, and Moslem friends lead Parekh to observe that Gandhi "remained a marginal man all his life." See his *Colonialism, Tradition, and Reform,* 267.

18. See Ananda M. Pandiri for an exhaustive compilation of books read by Gandhi and the times and places he reads them. *A Comprehensive, Annotated Bibliography on Mahatma* (Westport, Conn.: Greenwood Press, 1995), 1: 275–309. It turns out that his numerous imprisonments provided Gandhi with the time to read extensively both Indian and non-Indian works.

19. Hinduism cannot be easily categorized in Western terms not only because it is a highly complex set of spiritual outlooks and practices but more especially because it operates from a radically different cosmological foundation than do Western religions and philosophy. See Troy Organ, *Hinduism* (Woodbury, N.J.: Barron's, 1974). In considering Hinduism, there is the danger of making simple (and simplistic) comparisons between Western monotheistic religions and the polytheism of Hinduism, of concentrating on an alleged dualism in the West and unity in India, or in making Western religions assertive and Hinduism fatalistic. What we find in Hinduism are categories that often do not fit readily or coherently into Western ways of thought. The Hindu belief in a moral harmony, for example, often stands alongside a conception of the divine as often playful but sometimes destructive. Rather than embark on a synopsis of Hinduism, I will refer to relevant concepts when they aid in understanding Gandhi.

In looking at Gandhi's relationship with Hinduism, we do well to remember Margaret Chatterjee's observation that it is impossible to talk about a unified Hindu tradition. See her *Gandhi's Religious Thought* (London: Macmillan, 1983), 94. Alongside the Brahmanical tradition—which is itself internally diverse and which Gandhi frequently challenges—is a folk tradition which Chatterjee finds to be the source of Gandhi's Hinduism. See her *Gandhi's Religious Thought*, 27–28. On the importance of the folk tradition for Gandhi, see Nandy, *Traditions*.

20. Mehta, *Foundations*, 211–29.

21. For the claim that Gandhi is heavily influenced by Jainism, see Stephen Ray, "Jain Influences on Gandhi's Early Thought," in *Gandhi, India, and the World*, ed. Stephen Ray (Bombay: Nachiketa Publishers, 1976), 14–23.

22. Parekh, *Colonialism, Tradition, and Reform*.

23. See Iyer, *Moral and Political Thought*, 49. Nicholas Gier holds that "Gandhi's principles of nonviolence can be best interpreted using Buddhist philosophy." Nicholas Gier, "Gandhi, Ahimsa, and the Self," *Gandhi Marg*, 15, 1 (April 1993), 25.

24. Speaking to a group of Buddhists in 1924, Gandhi claims "Buddha did not give the world a new religion: he gave it a new interpretation. He taught Hinduism not to take but to give life" (May 18, 1924, in Raghavan Iyer, ed. *Moral and Political Writings of Mahatma Gandhi* (Oxford: Oxford University Press, 1986), 1: 476–77). A few years later he writes, "I do not regard Jainism or Buddhism as separate from Hinduism" (*Young India*, October 20, 1927).

25. Gandhi reconstitutes Hinduism so radically that it is not recognizable to many devout Hindus, some of whom strenuously object to his efforts. For a discussion of Gandhi's radicalizing of tradition see Parekh, *Colonialism, Tradition, and Reform*. See also Nandy, *Traditions, Tyranny and Utopias*.

26. Several commentators have noticed that Gandhi transports important Western ideas into his rendering of Hinduism. For example, he places heavy emphasis on what he calls the "inner voice" or conscience, a concept that has no analogues in traditional Hinduism, according to Iyer (*Political and Moral Thought*). Parekh (*Gandhi's Political Philosophy*) argues that Gandhi's use of love as the touchstone for conduct conflicts with the Hindu emphasis on detachment. For both Parekh and Iyer, Gandhi frequently builds on Christian, not Hindu, conceptions to develop his theory.

27. See Thomas Pantham, "Gandhi's Intervention in Modern Moral Political Discourse," in *Gandhi and the Present Global Crisis* (Shimla: Indian Institute of Advanced Study, 1996).

28. *Modern Review,* October 1916, in Iyer, *Writings,* 2: 212.

29. Fred Dallmayr, "Introduction: Toward a Comparative Political Theory," *Review of Politics* 59 (Summer 1997): 421–27 and *Beyond Orientalism* (Albany: State University of New York Press, 1996), ch. 6.

30. To the extent that modernity and modernization are highly implicated in the degradation of the environment, it may not be sufficient to call on them to solve the problem on their own. Rather, it is helpful to turn to alternative ways of thinking and acting, and Gandhi provides his voice to this effort.

31. For a discussion of the way fragments are moved about and then used in contemporary political theory, see Ronald Terchek, *Republican Paradoxes and Liberal Anxieties* (Lanham, Md.: Rowman and Littlefield, 1997), ch. 1. In chapter six of that work, I show that efforts to move selected fragments of Adam Smith's works, namely his theory of markets, to the late modern world without working with Smith's commitment to autonomy and his sociological assumptions distort his project as well as his text as a whole.

32. Bernard Williams, *Problems of the Self* (Cambridge: Cambridge University Press, 1973), 172–83.

33. One of the descriptions Agnes Heller assigns to modern society is that it is the disposable society. Gandhi fears, most of all, that people are becoming disposable.

34. Reinhold Niebuhr, *Moral Man and Immoral Society* (New York: Scribners, 1932); and Hannah Arendt, *The Human Condition* (Chicago: University of Chicago Press, 1958).

35. Gandhi parallels the style of much postmodernism. Consider Pauline Rosenau's description of the postmodernist mode of presentation and purpose: "Post-modernists in all disciplines reject conventional, academic styles of dis-

course; they prefer audacious and provocative forms of delivery, vital and intriguing elements of genre or style and presentation. . . . Such forms of presentation shock, startle, and unsettle the complacent . . . reader. They are explicitly designed to instigate the new and unaccustomed activity of a post-modern reading." *Post-Modernism and the Social Sciences* (Princeton: Princeton University Press, 1992), 7.

36. Thomas Pantham sees Gandhi as "an anticipation of some aspects of the present-day poststructuralist deconstruction of the foundational 'binary-opposition' of the political theory of post-Enlightenment modernity." See his "Gandhi, Nehru, and Modernity" in *Crisis and Change in Contemporary India*, ed. U. Baxi and B. Parekh (New Delhi: Sage, 1995), 100.

37. See Huiyun Wang, ("Gandhi's Contesting Discourse," *Gandhi Marg* 17 [October 1995], 261–85) for a discussion of postmodern themes in Gandhi. For further explorations along this line, see also Nicholas Gier, "Gandhi: Pre-Modern, Modern, or Post-Modern?" *Gandhi Marg* 18 (October 1996), 261–281.

1

GANDHIAN AUTONOMY

"No man can be sovereign because not one man, but men inhabit the earth."[1]

Animating all of Gandhi's work is his consistent respect for and tenacious defense of the integrity and worth of persons; this commitment to autonomy inspires all of his other projects.[2] His justification of nonviolence and his frontal assaults on colonialism, untouchability, and modernization are built on this commitment. When he challenges the decay he finds in his own tradition, it is that he sees it stifling thought and robbing many of their dignity.

Autonomy stands at the center of Gandhi's political philosophy. It is his greatest good and precedes in importance his other political and social goals. He sees individuals carrying a moral project that is related to who they are. As such, Gandhi claims, they not only deserve the freedom to pursue their moral projects honestly but they have the duty to do so. Each individual knows best, on Gandhi's account, what that person's moral project is and how it is expressed in action. For him, this means each person should be free from both domination and violence.

In developing his theory of autonomy, Gandhi invests persons with both a moral and biological nature. This means that individuals have basic needs that must be met and, if they are not, Gandhi expects persons to be stuck with the issues of survival.[3] Hungry, homeless, destitute persons are unlikely to concern themselves with moral projects and ought not be condemned for failing to do so, according to Gandhi. Addressing the needs of the most vulnerable members of society is an essential requirement for Gandhi's society of autonomous moral agents. Escaping acute necessity is a prelude for Gandhian autonomy, not its goal.[4]

He expects any moral project to be accompanied with self-discipline and sacrifice and calls on the moral agent to resist the inevitable pull of desires that visit everyone. For him, individuals who are directed by their desires are not autonomous. Then the reflective, moral self does not rule the person; the passions do. For this reason, Gandhi holds that we can be slaves not only of others but also to our own weaknesses.

Gandhi's conception of the autonomous, self-governing agent is simultaneously more demanding and generous than conventional renditions of autonomy. For him, no one is given leave to force others to do what they would not otherwise have done. Moreover, he claims that by what we do and leave undone, we sanction social and political practices that empower or debase ourselves and others. By extension, Gandhi argues, we are complicit and therefore responsible for the injustice that we tolerate or ignore. His agent stands in an interdependent cosmos, neither above nor outside the rest of the universe.[5] There, he imagines all individuals are fundamentally equal, diversity is respected, and the quest for domination is replaced by cooperation. Gandhi's autonomous agents can never be understood apart from their community, where he expects them to be active participants concerned with not only their own self-governance but also the autonomy of each other.

The prominence of autonomy can strikingly be seen in his program for *swaraj* or self-rule for India. His vision of a free India roams far beyond decolonization and the installation of an all-Indian government voted into office by Indians.[6] It is to be a place where the many forms of subordination that hamper freedom have been dissolved and individuals are self-governing.[7] For this to happen, Gandhi repeatedly insists, the country must rid itself not only of British rule but also traditional forms of domination, such as untouchability, as well as tame the forces of modernity and modernization which, he believes, leave millions of Indians unemployed and destitute. For Gandhi, any independence worthy of its name must be comprehensive: not only must the Indian nation be self-governing but so must each of its members. According to Gandhi, complete Indian independence "means the consciousness in the average villager that he is the maker of his own destiny"[8] Gandhi's swaraj comes only when Indians learn to rule themselves, individually and collectively.[9]

GANDHI AND FREEDOM:
AN INITIAL DISCUSSION

Whether it is John Locke assuming individual rights in a state of nature, Kant asking individuals to separate themselves from their contingencies and enter the realm of pure reason, or John Rawls locating individuals behind a veil of ignorance to find a rights-based conception of justice, the foundation of most Western conceptions of individual rights is the rational individual.[10] Locke, Kant, Rawls, and many other liberals work with an abstracted person in order to discover what is due to a person without regard to background considerations. In doing so, they assume that abstracted persons are equal and interchangeable with every other abstracted person. Critics find problems with such a move because it leaves people without attachments, commitments, duties, or a moral identity. Moreover, individuals are said to lose their distinctiveness as a particular human being.[11] However, liberals are reluctant to jettison their position precisely because they see it as an effective way to universalize rights and show that everyone is entitled to be a rights-carrier. In reply to their critics, liberals insist that before we can talk about duties and commitments, we first need to speak about men and women who deserve to be free regardless of their background.[12]

For many, the justification of equal rights is the crowning achievement of Western political theory. Rights are assigned to each person independent of other considerations, including the demands of the state or convention. Gandhi has trouble with this construction of rights, not because he opposes freedom but because he finds the accepted reading of rights is incomplete and misleading. At the same time, he accepts many of the claims of rights-based theories: most notably he works with the basic assumption that everyone is equal and deserves to make moral sense of his or her own life and that other considerations cannot trump these goods. Gandhi claims, for example, "The individual is the one supreme consideration."[13] It turns out, however, that his celebration of freedom is very different from conventional liberal ones. He encumbers agents with duties, assigning them responsibilities to lead a moral life and attend to the good of their community. Moreover, he champions those at the periphery, emphasizing the basic rights of untouchables, women, the unemployed, and others who have been the objects of domination and humiliation. The rights he has in mind, however, are not exhausted with the usual list of liberal rights but speak to the rights of individuals to meet their basic needs in dignity. Gandhi also departs from standard expressions of rights when he holds that freedom should not be taken to mean that individuals should be left alone to make their way in the world. Rather, he wants them to have the freedom to cultivate the love and service he believes characterize the best feature of human nature.

Before we take up his differences with liberalism, it is important to notice where his language frequently parallels liberal conceptions of rights as when he insists that women should "enjoy the same rights as men."[14] Or when he writes that "there is no such thing as inherited or acquired superiority. . . . I believe implicitly that all men are born equal."[15] For Gandhi, "every human being has a right to live and therefore to find the wherewithal to feed himself and . . . to cloth and house himself."[16] On his account, everyone deserves to be free to make fundamental choices and to be free from obstacles that make those choices costly or dangerous.[17] He tells us that because he believes in the "inherent equality of all men that I fight the doctrine of superiority which many of our rulers arrogate to themselves."[18] Here and elsewhere, in good liberal fashion, Gandhi rejects the proposition that ascriptive properties, such as gender, birth, class, caste, education, or nationality, can justify unequal treatment and disqualify some as moral agents.

However, he has a host of serious disagreements with the liberal conception of freedom. The empowerment of individuals that emerges in the liberal version of rights is partial in two senses. What is protected are specified, formal rights, and what is ignored is thought to be unimportant. This Gandhi denies. What is important to him are not lists but how people are treated. Are they humiliated or dominated? Are they denied realistic opportunities to make a living for themselves? Gandhi also is troubled by accounts of rights that fail to pay attention to how the institutional practices and asymmetrical distributions of power in civil society affect the capacity of individuals to frame or make choices. In response to this omission in much of the rights literature, Gandhi challenges practices in civil society and by the state that constrain and discipline the self and force choices of a particular sort.

Gandhi holds that freedom is necessary for moral growth but he also knows that people can abuse their freedom and should be able to. For Gandhi, "We must have the liberty to do evil before we learn to do good."[19] The reason is not that Gandhi expects people to use their freedom recklessly but rather to use it in ways that make sense to them, to experiment with it, and to recognize their mistakes and correct them. More importantly, he knows that a moral life is something a person freely chooses; people cannot be made good or moral by others.[20] Freedom is the beginning, not the end of Gandhian autonomy. The person who appears to be good out of fear or advantage is not, on his account, moral.[21] On Gandhi's account, "A moral act must be our own act." Otherwise, "there is no moral content in our act."[22]

Working with such premises, he argues that to be human means a person deserves liberty as well as to live in a society where everyone else is free.[23] As he understands matters, it is important to pay attention to both the individual and society. His question, "If the individual ceases to count, what is left of society"[24] is meant to call attention to the ideal complementarity of self and society and to the idea that a society where citizens are not free cannot be a good society.

THEORIES OF AUTONOMY

Western conceptions of autonomy both borrow heavily from the literature of rights and move beyond it. Both rights–carriers and autonomous persons are said to deserve to be free and equal, both are credited with rational capacities, and both are enjoined from directly harming others. However, rights come with no instructions on their use: for some, rights become a license to make money and invite a possessive individualism;[25] for others it is a demand to be left alone; and for still others it means practicing one's religious beliefs, cultural identity, or political convictions. For their part, theorists of autonomy want to provide a guide for free men and women, and they do so by investing in individuals the capacity to act on moral principles.

Generally, theories of autonomy assume that people are ultimately responsible for the moral character that grows out of their choices. Many of these considerations are lost in theories of rights that make individuals superior to other considerations, including their community, tradition, or other goods.[26] Moving beyond a materialistic, acquisitive conception of rights, theorists of autonomy ask whether the standards people choose speak to their biological and material needs (or "first-order preferences") or whether they go beyond necessity and comfort and are directed to a moral life that recognizes the responsibilities we have to others (or "second-order preferences").[27]

In theories of autonomy, rational persons are said to be able to separate themselves from their attachments and reflect on who they are and what they are becoming. In this sense, they can decide whether their previously chosen standards accord with the kind of person they want to be. If, on self-reflection, they determine they are becoming something that is antithetical to their own aspirations, they can change their behavior or, if they find their old standard has become unacceptable, they can select a new one.[28] With this in mind, Gerald Dworkin holds that autonomy is "the capacity of persons to critically reflect upon, and then attempt to accept or change, their preferences, desires, values, and ideals."[29]

How do we form our preferences? Where do we get the materials to form our moral principles? Joel Feinberg wants people to be morally independent in order to exercise their "capacity for reflective self-determination."[30] Apart from this kind of generality, little attention is given to where people get and how they develop their standards or what, aside from their own weakness, deflects them from pursuing their moral standards. Moral learning seems haphazard and random in these theories, and there is little acknowledgment that some people live in situations that are hostile to developing the moral standards that autonomy theorists promote. Moreover, with the notable exception of Joseph Raz, most theorists of autonomy give little attention to the role of institutions or the way resources or vulnerabilities affect the choices available to individuals.[31] Gandhi would be particularly impatient with the glaring omission in most theories of autonomy to think concretely about how individuals meet their multiple needs and perform the many duties they carry. The moral development and reflection Gandhi expects for the autonomous person come after people have been able to meet their elementary needs and are not hostage to hunger and destitution.[32] Moreover, he situates persons in vibrant, local traditions that provide them with moral materials to frame choices and judge their conduct.

Gandhi would find conventional theories of autonomy to be inadequate, particularly with their tendency to conflate the cognitive and rational properties of individuals and their neglect of how and where people collect the moral materials for judgment. He also departs from conventional theories that bring duties into the discussion late rather than early and ignore the institutional obstacles that confront some people when they pursue their moral choices. In addition, Gandhi would distance himself from the strong suspicion in most theories of autonomy that tradition thwarts self-reflection because it is said to direct rather than facilitate choice.[33]

Gandhi further complicates conventional theories of autonomy when he pays attention to individuals as equal members of a harmonious and interdependent cosmos rather than as abstracted selves. On his account, people cannot become complete or achieve the good outside of an association with others based on mutual respect and cooperation. When he turns to community, he requires one that is open and tolerant of diverse conceptions of the good as well as one whose institutional practices do not routinely disable ordinary men and women who seek to pursue their conception of the good. Gandhian diversity and unity can be protected only by recognizing each. To emphasize one at the expense of the other distorts the very things he wants to safeguard. A self that is unconnected to others cannot develop as a whole self,[34] but efforts to dictate unity cannot do any more than impose a formal sameness. Moreover, he holds that in doing harm to others, one damages oneself. Seeing us all linked in a cosmic unity, those who hurt others assault their own integrity. From Gandhi's perspective, we harm a part of ourselves when we harm others because they are "ourselves in a different form."[35]

On the face of it, it appears that freedom is necessary for autonomy.[36] For Gandhi, freedom is unnecessary at the theoretical level and essential for autonomy at the practical level. Theoretically, he finds that anyone can courageously confront repression and pursue individually chosen moral projects.[37] His work is infused with countless arguments and examples that show that fearless persons can govern themselves without asking the permission of the powerful and are prepared to suffer pain to do so. They assert their integrity when they refuse to deny their moral commitments, regardless of the punishment. His own life as a member of colonial India reveals a person who thinks he is not formally free but also thinks he is autonomous and acts that way. His call to every Indian to resist British colonialism is an expression of autonomy without political freedom.[38]

At the practical level, however, Gandhi holds that freedom is essential for autonomy. He finds people have both a moral and biological nature and they are inescapably tied to the latter as long as they live. What happens to them can impose extraordinary costs to moral choice, and many, indeed most, do not disregard these costs. Worrying about meeting their elementary needs, for example, they accept a life that has been organized for them elsewhere. Rather than leave ordinary people to their vulnerabilities, Gandhi challenges the forces of domination and control and makes the development of a moral life depend as little as possible on living in a society with stark inequalities and repressive practices.

GANDHIAN DUTIES: A PRELIMINARY LOOK

In defending an autonomous life, Gandhi speaks to individuals not only about what they are due but also about the duties they owe each other.[39] For him, "The true source of rights is duty. If we all discharge our duties, rights will not be far to seek."[40] In making duties come first, he markedly departs from liberalism with its concentration on individual rights. In liberal theory, duties are linked to a reciprocity principle. If we want to claim something as a right for ourselves, we are expected to acknowledge that the same claim validly applies to everyone. To hold that my claim applies only to me or those like me and that I have no duty to recognize parallel claims in others is to argue for a privilege, not a right.[41] Gandhian duties are not reciprocally derivative from rights; nor does he accept the view that obligations principally rest on mutual, voluntary consent.[42]

At first glance, his argument that duties are primary seems to reveal a deep conservatism. The reason we might think so has to do with the way duties have generally been treated in modern political theory. For someone like Hobbes, they represent a restriction on freedom; for Burke, they frequently seem to serve to justify discipline and the unequal distribution of rights and obligations. Gandhi separates himself from these positions. By insisting that everyone has duties and that rights are derivative from duties, he claims that if certain rights-claims deny others their ability to perform their duties, then the claim must be denied.[43]

When Gandhi thinks about people, he does not reach for abstracted persons or for the wisest and most virtuous; he focuses on ordinary people, and one of the things he finds that makes ordinary people ordinary is that they are inescapably tied to necessity and carry multiple needs and duties. For Gandhi, they have a duty to work in order to meet necessity: no one has a claim for food and shelter and no one has a claim to deprive others of work. The duty to work to meet necessity, as Gandhi sees matters, gives each individual a corresponding right to work.

For him, the very fact of living imposes duties on us to meet our own elementary needs as well as attend to the needs of those who are entrusted to us. Gandhi's human beings are not sovereign as are Locke's rational agents in the state of nature who appear with no social relations, traditions, institutions, or friendships. Rather, Gandhi sees individuals united in time and space in a cosmos where they are ultimately affected by what they *and others* do. Because we depend on others for all sorts of things that are essential to our biological survival, Gandhi wants those who have been able to subdue necessity to see that they have a duty to assist those who have not.[44]

Gandhi's highest duty is to act morally, regardless of the consequences. As he puts it, "Fate may be good or it may be bad. Human effort consists in overcoming adverse fate or reducing its impact. There is a continuous struggle between fate and human effort. Who can say which of the two really wins?"[45] Regardless of who wins, Gandhi insists, each agent must do what that person believes is morally fitting.[46] This argument appears again and again in his work; nonviolence, for example, is not to be pursued because there is a guarantee that each application will work but because it is the moral way to proceed. Gandhi wants duties to permeate each person's life, whether expressed in routine activities or in heroic expressions. In approaching duty in a non–consequentialist way, he means to deprive agents of tolerating evil because they think they cannot change matters.

GANDHI'S DUALIST READING OF THE HUMAN CONDITION

Gandhi's theories about the roles of love and unity in politics are highly optimistic and idealistic, and it might appear that he brings the same buoyancy and enthusiasm to his discussion of the human condition. However, this is not the case; he introduces us to highly complex human beings.[47] Sometimes he contrasts their developmental capacities with their repetitious, biological needs; sometimes he differentiates their moral potentialities from their pride; sometimes he speaks of how good and evil reside in each individual; and sometimes he talks about the capacities for violence and love that he sees residing in everyone. These dualisms serve to show not only that self-governance must contend with external factors that can debilitate autonomy but also that individuals must struggle with themselves to be autonomous.[48]

One of the features that Gandhi finds is human about human beings is that they have both biological and moral natures and that they need to be concerned with each. Because so many of his best-known writings are concerned with promoting the latter and because he continually complains that people are apt to pay too much attention to the former, it is inviting to assume that Gandhi expects ordinary people to transcend their biological natures. Nothing is further from Gandhi's intent. For him, ordinary men and women cannot escape attending to their biological requirements: they must eat and sleep, they must be warm when it is cold, they should be expected to care about their health, and they should pay attention to taking care of those who depend on them.[49] But that is not all that Gandhi sees defining human beings who, he argues, have more than biological needs. This can be seen in the distinction he draws between the "brute" in each of us and the developmental capacities of everyone.[50] Gandhi claims

> the essential difference between man and the brute is that the former can respond to the call of the spirit in him, can rise superior to the passions that he owns in common with the brute, and therefore, superior to the selfishness and violence, which belong to the brute's nature and not to the immortal spirit of man."[51]

It turns out that no matter how far a person develops morally, Gandhi thinks that no one ever escapes the vulnerabilities that describe the violence and selfishness of the brute. What this means to him is that people must continually make choices about what they will be. As he understands matters, "Man must choose either of two courses, the upward or the downward, but as he has the brute in him, he will more easily choose the downward course than the upward, especially when the downward course is presented to him in a beautiful garb."[52]

Gandhi sees people, with their multiple needs and duties, continually making and remaking their own lives through their choices and action.[53] "One is called upon continually to make one's choice between one duty and another," and these choices are not always easy.[54] What is morally appropriate at one time may not be so later. With this in mind, Gandhi holds that "Life is not one straight road. There are so many complexities in it. It is not like a train which, once started, keeps on running."[55] A moral choice once made, on Gandhi's account, often produces results that are unexpected and unwelcome; this is why he wants individuals to reflect about whether their choices harm others. However, Gandhi realizes that many frequently do not care and favor themselves because of their pride.[56] Making themselves the center of their universe, the proud take their individual good to be the only reliable way of judging, and Gandhi wants individuals to resist this weakness.[57]

He also knows that a narrow possessiveness or selfishness is not the only form that pride can take; it can sometimes flow from generous sentiments when people believe they know the good and think this gives them permission to impose it on others, regardless of the views of others or the costs assessed on them. Realizing that some of the worst crimes against humanity are undertaken for principled reasons, Gandhi finds that "Few men are wantonly wicked. The most heinous and most cruel crimes of which history has record have been committed under the cover of religion or other equally noble motive."[58] When coupled with power, moral pride attempts to become superhuman, forgetting the inevitable fallibility that marks everyone's encounters with the truth.[59] Just as Gandhi wants people to struggle with those who would dominate or harm others, he wants them to confront their own moral pretentiousness:

> Man is a fallible being. He can never be sure of his steps. What he may regard as an answer to prayer may be an echo of his pride. For infallible guidance man has to have a perfectly innocent heart incapable of evil. I can lay no such claim. Mine is a struggling, striving, erring, imperfect soul.[60]

Wanting individuals to see that any construction of the good must include a place that recognizes the worth of others, Gandhi finds the proud are ready to use other human beings as a means to achieve their purpose. Reminiscent of Kant, he denies that people can be treated as tools or obstacles that can help or hinder us in our particular quest, whether noble or narrow.[61] When others are seen as "things" that are useful or a hindrance, then they have no inherent worth of their own. This is what Gandhi finds typically happens with conventional politics, violent situations, hierarchical relations, and much of the modernized economy where standards other than the inherent dignity of human beings become the criteria by which men and women are judged.

For Gandhi, everyone needs to guard against pride, personal attachments, and moral overconfidence. These vulnerabilities are part of his reading of the human condition, but so is the capacity to move beyond them.[62] For him, the "primary virtues of mankind are possible of cultivation by the meanest of the human species," and no one need be stuck on a narrow conception of the self.[63]

> So long as man remains selfish and does not care for the happiness of others, he is no better than an animal and perhaps worse. His superiority to the animal is seen only when we find him caring for his family. He is still more human, that is, much higher than the animal, when he extends his concept of the family to include his country or community as well. He climbs still higher in the scale when he comes to regard the human race as his family.[64]

Seeing moral development as part of the life process, Gandhi declines to judge the worth of persons on the basis of where they are presently; rather, he asks what they can voluntarily become. This is why he calls himself "an irrepressible optimist. My optimism rests on my belief in the infinite possibilities of the individual to develop."[65] Building on this view, Gandhi holds that "For realizing the self, the first essential thing is to cultivate a strong moral sense."[66]

Another dualism Gandhi discovers in the human condition is what he calls "good and evil." He holds that "Every one of us is a mixture of good and evil. Is there not plenty of evil in us? There is enough in me. . . . The difference that there is between human beings is the difference of degree."[67] What does Gandhi have in mind when he talks about evil? Evil is not merely a lack of goodness for Gandhi as it is for many thinkers, although it is that.[68] He finds it also a real force. This can be seen in his unique reading of conflict in the *Gita*. In discussing the great battle between the forces of evil and goodness, he holds that Duryodhana and his supporters stand for the Satanic impulses in us, and Arjuna and others stand for the God-ward impulses. The battle-field is our body. The poet-seer, who knows from experience the problems of life, has given a faithful account of the conflict which is eternally going on within us.[69]

When he speaks of evil, Gandhi concentrates on what he takes to be evil practices rather than people. The capacity of individuals to do or tolerate evil, from his position, stems from a variety of causes. Some people are blind to the ways they hurt others; some are caught in mindless habits; some cannot free themselves from their immediate attachments; some live in fear; and some are tied to meeting their basic necessities and oblivious to the world around them. For Gandhi, the issue is not whether an agent intends to be cruel but whether the agent's conduct causes cruelty. As he sees it, evil is expressed in social practices, and it "succeeds only by receiving help" from us. It "always takes advantage of the weakest spots in our nature in order to gain mastery over us."[70] In Gandhi's account, the expression of the dualism of good and evil is a manifestation of the violence of the brute and the capacity for love or nonviolence that he sees residing in every human being.

In his quest to defend autonomy, Gandhi challenges both external and internal assaults. With the first, he is attentive to the harm that can come from institutional practices. With the latter, he reminds his readers that they can be the reason they do not rule themselves but allow their weaker natures to rule instead.

AHIMSA AND *HIMSA*

When Gandhi works with dualities such as those between the biological and moral, moral development and pride, and good and evil, he is on familiar ground. However, he offers yet another duality that is unique in political theory, namely the conflict between *ahimsa* or love and *himsa* or violence. Seeing love as the highest expression of human development, Gandhi finds that it holds the world together but when love fails, chaos, domination, and strife follow.[71] "In its negative form," Gandhi writes, ahimsa "means not injuring any living being, whether by body or mind, or bear any ill to him and so cause him mental suffering."

Positively, ahimsa means an unbounded love for all.[72] Its opposite, himsa, means doing injury to others and "does not need to be taught. Man as animal is violent, but as spirit is nonviolent."[73]

Most treatments of love emphasize its intimacy: it is something that requires sharing time and space. Therefore, the number of people any one person can love is thought to be limited and, on this account, cannot include people we do not know. For his part, Gandhi wants us to love everyone and understand that "love has no boundary."[74] Being blind to interest and danger, lovers do not ask about advantage or risk. On Gandhi's account, "Love gives because it must; it is its nature. It therefore does not calculate whether there is a corresponding gain. It is unconscious of giving and more so of the taking. Love is its own reward."[75]

Gandhian love requires moral agents to be strong, or as he puts it, fearless.[76] People are not true lovers if they hold back because they fear they will be rejected or hurt. As I show in an extended discussion of ahimsa in chapter six, such people mimic the coward, and on Gandhi's account, no coward can be a real lover. At the same time, Gandhi believes love will be returned; he expects the lover to move the loved one. In Gandhi's understanding of human nature, everyone has the capacity to love, to respond to love, and to return love. For Gandhi, lovers give meaning to their lives through their love. To convey their love, they rely on language but not only on language; lovers express their love through action and caring and in this way speak to "the heart" in ways that language, by itself, cannot.

> Love and exclusive possession can never go together. Theoretically, when there is perfect love, there must be perfect non-possession. The body is our last possession. So a man can only exercise perfect love and be completely dispossessed if he is prepared to embrace death and renounce his body for the sake of human service.
>
> But that is true in theory only. In actual life, we can hardly exercise perfect love, for the body, as possession will always remain with us. Man will ever remain imperfect, and it will always be his part to try to be perfect. So that perfection in love or non-possession will remain an unattainable ideal, as long as we are alive, but towards which we must ceaselessly strive.[77]

Gandhian love not only competes with the indifference, hatred, and violence of others but also with the weaknesses that reside in every individual. To acknowledge our vulnerabilities to violence, Gandhi argues, is necessary if this part of our nature is to be tethered. And, he goes on to argue, violence must be confronted continually and love can prevail in each contest. However, he insists, there is no final triumph of love over hatred; each success is followed by another test.

GANDHI'S TRUTH

What we think is important today is not always what earlier generations thought important. Today, most of us favor reason, rights, representative democracy, economic growth, scientific inquiry, and social mobility. For earlier generations, different categories are important: faith, truth, duty, stability, and security. We are suspicious of many of these latter terms because some evoke a certainty we no longer claim or because some connote a stasis we do not welcome. For his part, Gandhi frequently allies himself with the latter concepts and returns to them again and again. He uses words such as faith, truth, and duty to mount his challenge to injustice and domination, and in doing so, he often alters their conventional meanings. This can be seen in his conception of the truth.[78]

Gandhi tells us truth is God. This means several things to him. One is that the truth transcends our biological natures and rises above the forces of gravity. He sees individuals, whether Hindus, Christians, Jews, Moslems, or atheists, overcoming their self-interest and approaching the truth through their moral projects.[79] Gandhi's God is the expression of the deep, internal principles that morally define and animate persons, even when they are not religious.[80] For Gandhi, the truths found in the great religions as well as the moral commitments of individuals differ in important respects, but they essentially share the same moral core in respecting the dignity of persons and understanding the best life as one that moves beyond hatred or necessity and aims at ahimsa and morality.[81] He holds that

> The rules of morality, laid down in the world's great religions, are largely the same. The founders of the religion have also explained that morality is the basis of religion. . . . if morality is destroyed, religion which is built on it comes crashing down.[82]

That Hindus, Moslems, and Christians have their own ideas of what that standard should be—indeed, that different Hindus, Moslems, and Christians have different conceptions of the good—presents no problem to Gandhi. He finds "True morality consists not in following the beaten track but in finding out the true path for ourselves and fearlessly following it."[83] He does not promote a moral uniformity but an honest commitment to each person's conception of a transcendent truth. When Gandhi writes that "Devotion to the Truth is the sole reason for our existence,"[84] what he has in mind is that to be fully human, people must be honest to what they take to be true, that is, they must be honest to themselves, even if it leads to their own suffering.[85] In this sense, Gandhi sees people subverting their humanity when they act in ways that are contrary to their deepest understanding of what is true.

WORKING WITH FRAGMENTS OF THE TRUTH

Gandhi holds that it is impossible to know the truth fully. By his account, different traditions include fragments of the truth but its totality remains elusive to any one person or tradition; our grasp of the truth stems as much from love as from knowledge; its best expression comes not with withdrawal but with action; and it requires not the conquest of nature but the discipline of the self. Gandhi's truth, then, bears little resemblance to a self-confident claim to comprehensive knowledge.[86] For him, every person "is right from his own standpoint, but it is not impossible that every one is wrong. Hence the necessity for tolerance, which does not mean indifference towards one's own faith but a more intelligent and purer love for it."[87]

Gandhi denies that the incompleteness of truth leads to moral relativism. He expects people to judge and reach moral conclusions about the world they encounter. Although he wants to treat human beings as equals, he argues, the principle of equality "can never apply to their morals. One would be affectionate and attentive to a rascal and to a saint; but one cannot and must not put saintliness and rascality on the same footing."[88] He goes on to argue, however, that respecting different approaches to the truth is itself an embodiment of the truth.[89] The incomplete grasp of the truth by any tradition or person teaches Gandhi about human fallibility and the need for humility.[90] To claim a comprehensive knowledge of the truth gives the claimant a warrant to enforce and apply the truth that no fragment can bestow.[91]

By his account, claims to a comprehensive truth exceed the limited human capacities to know and control. This is why Gandhi pays attention to the means people employ to achieve the good and denies that some future good can exonerate the pain and suffering it exacts in the present.[92] His emphasis on means also reflects his skepticism about perfectionist views of the good. This can be seen in his argument that people take their moral project seriously at the same time they know that its fulfillment remains elusive. To admit that our best efforts cannot completely succeed is to introduce a moral restraint on our conduct with others. Trying to convert or educate others is critically important to Gandhi, but the very imperfections inherent in human action make him reject efforts to compel anyone to live by moral standards determined by others.

Gandhi's truth always speaks to the autonomy, equality, and dignity of persons and resists domination and humiliation. Armed with this understanding of the truth, he has no trouble condemning colonialism, untouchability, and other institutional practices that he believes inhibit the autonomy of others. The real location of Gandhi's truth is to be found in life, with its plurality and unity: "If I could persuade myself that I should find [God] in a Himalayan cave, I would proceed there immediately. But I know that I cannot find Him apart from humanity."[93] For this reason, the final expression of Gandhi's truth is not an idea or meditation but comes through action.[94] To find the truth and leave it unpracticed is an empty exercise for Gandhi, who wants men and women to act on their understanding of the truth.[95]

GANDHI'S INNER VOICE

Gandhi summons his conscience or what he sometimes calls his "inner voice" to enable him to judge what is proper and what is not.[96] Believing that a person's conscience is expressed in the vernacular of a specific culture,[97] he also claims that the core of each person's conscience reflects a rudimentary sense of good and evil.[98]

> There are times when you have to obey a call which is the highest of all, i.e. the voice of conscience, even though such obedience may cost

many a bitter tear, and even more separation from friends, from family, from the State to which you may belong. . . . This obedience is the law of our being.[99]

Gandhi's conception of conscience as an internal property in all human beings stands in marked contrast to writers such as Hobbes and Locke who argue that there is no inherent standard of right or wrong lodged within individuals and that our conceptions of good and evil are learned, not innate. According to Hobbes, we are composed of myriad desires and aversions, with each person constructing a personal schedule of good and evil. For his part, Locke argues that every infant's mind is an empty cabinet waiting to be filled with moral understanding. Gandhi refuses to accept the view that people are exclusively molded by external factors. Environmentalism plays an important role for Gandhi, but it is always guarded and never cancels his view that people carry internal standards that allow them to respond to injustice and monitor their own behavior.

His understanding of conscience is, in rudimentary ways, similar to that of the Scottish Enlightenment, which assigns innate moral sentiments to everyone. In this account, everyone has an internal monitor (or to use a term Adam Smith occasionally uses, an "inner voice") that enables agents to distinguish good from evil. Three features in Smith's theory of the sentiments carry rough parallels with Gandhi's.[100] In the first place, both Gandhi and Smith believe the sentiments are not automatically expressed but struggle with a person's desires and interest. With training and courage, the sentiments can guide conduct and teach people to favor their sentiments over their interests when the two conflict.[101] Second, both hold that the sentiments are expressed in different ways in different cultures. Someone like Adam Smith finds that no single culture comprehensively embodies all of the sentiments but each culture reflects its own principles, which enable human beings to harness their raw egos and live harmoniously with one another. Finally, Gandhi and Smith see that the universal attribution of the sentiments democratizes moral knowledge in the most profound way. A person's claim to moral knowledge is not contingent on an individual's background, particularly on some proscribed religious training or formal education. In other words, everyone can know right from wrong and respond to cruelty and injustice.

However, Gandhi clearly parts company with Smith's argument that commercial society holds the best prospect for the expression of the sentiments. The very location Smith thinks conducive to the flourishing of the sentiments, the secure middle-class household, is predicated on modern assumptions that Gandhi finds objectionable. Moreover, Smith expects people to rely on instrumental reason in markets and on the job and then shift to the benevolent sentiments when they enter their domestic precincts. However, this leads to a segmented personality, something Gandhi finds is fated to be incoherent and unable to employ consistent standards in the many roles the person occupies.[102] Finally, Gandhi would find Smith's conscience speaks incompletely when it warns about injustice and asks us not to contribute to the pain of others directly. For his part, Gandhi takes these messages as the initial prompts of the conscience but next wants it to urge people to see the ways they indirectly harm others and then act on this moral knowledge. Gandhi wants the voice of conscience to challenge domination wherever it appears.[103]

When Gandhi hears his "inner voice," he has to determine who is speaking and whether what is said is reliable. To do this requires an intense interrogation with what one hears to determine whether the message addresses convenience or conviction. He finds that "The 'Inner Voice' may mean a message from God or the Devil, for both are wrestling in the human breast."[104]

To hear what others have not heard and to see what others have not witnessed and then to act in ways that are often socially disruptive not only invite the charge of privileging the subjective but of exonerating irresponsibility. Gandhi accepts this possibility, admitting that "there is no remedy against hypocrisy." However, he argues that an appeal to conscience "must not be suppressed because many will feign it."[105] According to Gandhi, it is possible to guard against hypocrisy as well as self-deception in several ways. In the first place, he tells his readers that his own "inner voice" is initially accompanied with doubt and he expects people to employ their moral and rational resources to scrutinize and be ready to challenge the message they hear. Second, Gandhi argues that we are more apt to reach reliable judgments if we are self-disciplined. Third, he expects that his inner voice is not contrary to basic moral standards.[106] On no account, he insists, can the conscience deny such basic principles as the dignity and essential equality of all persons.

Finally, Gandhi expects persons to express their conscience in nonviolent public action and be prepared to suffer on behalf of their convictions.

Many do not hear an "inner voice" and busy themselves with the contingent world. Shutting their "ears to the 'still small Voice,' " they allow personal attachments and aspirations to serve as their compass or conformity to social conventions to become their anchor.[107] For this reason, the danger he detects in contemporary society is not the possibility that many will hear their consciences counseling them to resist all authority, but is the reality that many, seeing subordination and humiliation (or even being the objects of subordination and humiliation), do not hear their "still small Voice" telling them that this is wrong and needs to be challenged nonviolently.

Gandhi enlists his theory of conscience in his arguments on behalf of *satyagraha* or civil disobedience.[108] He expects the *satyagrahi* to be honest to their deepest convictions and ready to suffer on behalf of their commitments. Gandhi goes on to argue that those who witness this suffering will be prompted by their conscience and be converted. He has this in mind when he says that "if you want something really important to be done, you must not merely satisfy reason, you must move the heart also. The appeal of reason is more to the head, but the penetration of the heart comes from suffering. It opens up the inner understanding of man."[109] Here and elsewhere, Gandhi argues that everyone has a rudimentary conscience which the suffering of the satyagrahi can awaken.[110] For him, voluntary suffering rouses what had been dormant and creates dispositions that place people on the same moral plane.

INSTITUTIONS, PERSONAL RESPONSIBILITY, AND HONESTY

In emphasizing personal responsibility and in acknowledging the costs assessed on moral conduct by institutional practices, Gandhi's conception of moral autonomy departs radically from much conventional thinking on autonomy. He can readily agree with those, such as Locke, who hold that men and women reach their highest moral level only when they act as free agents and that only as free agents are they capable of making moral sense of themselves. To talk about Locke's virtuous person, for example, is to talk about someone who is morally reflective. For Locke, we alone are responsible for our conduct; our choices and actions reflect our understanding of what is good and evil. That many people may be mistaken is axiomatic for Locke, but this does not lead him to argue that people should be forced to become good. Virtue can only come through voluntary choices and actions.

However, Gandhi is unwilling to accept Locke's moral individualism.[111] For the latter, the actual conditions that await men and women are irrelevant to the ways they develop morally. For his part, Gandhi recognizes that the costs involved in pursuing a person's moral principles are often high and that many refuse to pay the price; and he is not ready to condemn ordinary men and women who fail to rise to the highest sacrifice. He continually seeks to design institutional arrangements that lessen the costs to ordinary people of meeting their moral responsibilities. In his ideal society, men and women are not constantly placed in morally tragic situations in which the only way to follow the good is at continued high personal sacrifice.

When Gandhi says, "Where the people want to be upright but cannot be so, hypocrisy will naturally increase," he is not talking about people who are naturally selfish or dishonest.[112] Rather, he is speaking about people who want to be honest but "cannot be," and we need to ask what he has in mind with the phrase "cannot be." His answer is not that some people are unable to make moral choices or develop morally; rather, he has in mind the heavy costs assessed by institutional practices. Although Gandhi's ideal agents can theoretically reject these costs and are prepared to suffer in order to remain honest to their own deepest convictions, he wants to take account of the vulnerabilities of ordinary people. He does not mean to leave them on their own because they do not measure up to his ideal.

To leave the matter here, however, does not solve the riddle of people wanting to be honest but acting dishonestly. The clue comes in Gandhi's recognition that ordinary people understand themselves through their particularities. This can, for him, lead to a shallow conception of the self, and Gandhi has no trouble condemning such a construction. However, he also realizes that not all attachments are narrow and that individuals carry multiple needs and duties. To act honestly when honesty is severely penalized is to invite harm not only to agents but also to those who depend on them. Indeed, without some of their accumulated responsibilities, agents might be more honest because only they and not others are injured.[113]

This argument will be amplified in the later discussion of Gandhi's theories of economics; here I want to emphasize his position that, at the level of everyday living, ordinary men and women find that the institutional practices they routinely encounter matter to them and influence their choices. For this reason, Gandhi pays attention to actual institutional practices to see whether they make honesty to the self costly or not.

WHO RULES THE SELF?

Gandhi's version of autonomy does not depend on the sovereign individual as conventional theories do. Emphasizing the interrelatedness of individuals in a cosmic order, Gandhi finds the human condition is characterized by interdependent persons who have multiple needs and duties. He concludes that because these multiple needs and duties are an inescapable part of what it means to be human, people deserve to be free to meet their needs and duties.[114] In pursuing their duties, Gandhi wants moral agents to know that they can never be certain they will achieve their goals. The problematic comes not only from the inevitable contingencies of life but also, according to Gandhi, from an unfathomable God who "often dashes the cup from our lips and under cover of free will leaves us a margin so wholly inadequate as to provide only mirth for Himself at our expense."[115] Gandhi does not allow uncertainty to give way to despondency; rather, he holds that it is only through our affirmation of what is right that we give meaning to our lives. As autonomous agents, we pursue the right, in his account, even if this risks suffering; in this way, "we learn to rule ourselves."[116]

Gandhi's autonomous persons, wanting to govern themselves, resist any source of domination, whether in a corrupted tradition or in the modern world. With the former, a distorted reading of texts is in control; with the latter, the standards of efficiency and productivity dominate, and people lose control of what is important to them. Working with this understanding, Gandhi holds that no text and no economic process can claim to possess a truth that displaces the autonomy of individuals.

The human beings that Gandhi surveys are choice-makers.[117] They can choose to be autonomous, even in the face of overwhelming obstacles and at heavy personal costs. Or they can be ruled by external forces, governed by fear, fatalism, timidity, or conformity. No one, Gandhi insists, deserves such a life, but he knows that people cannot escape the world in which they live and that some of its properties seriously threaten their autonomy. Because these obstacles are frequently tied to the ways individuals meet necessity and their multiple responsibilities, Gandhi continually returns to the way individuals are treated in their local situations.

Autonomy, for Gandhi, requires two sorts of struggle, one internal and the other external. With the first, he wants agents to pursue their higher, developmental, active capacities rather then their merely biological nature. With the latter, he asks individuals to challenge the forces that dominate and humiliate. But life is not only struggle for Gandhi. In his idealized, cooperative community, autonomous agents are fulfilled as they go about the rhythm of their lives—in the ways they meet their multiple needs and duties as spouses, parents, friends, workers, neighbors, and citizens.[118] As self-governing agents, their sense of themselves is not measured by change or mobility but by a satisfaction that they are the beneficiaries of and contributors to the good life in their own local cosmos.

NOTES

1. Arendt, *The Human Condition*, 234.

2. Although other writers occasionally speak of the importance of autonomy in Gandhi's work, they do not make it the central, driving force. For example, see Iyer, *Writings*, 3: 8.

3. Gandhi knows that many inflate a variety of desires into the category of needs. That this is a widespread deception, according to Gandhi, is no reason to deny the concept of basic necessities.

4. *Young India*, February 2, 1926.

5. See *Young India*, December 4, 1924.

6. See *Hind Swaraj*, ch. 19.

7. "I am not interested in freeing India merely from the English yoke. I am bent upon freeing India from any yoke whatsoever" (*Young India*, June 12, 1924).

8. *Young India*, February 13, 1930.

9. *Hind Swaraj*, ch. 14.

10. In theories of rights, a valid right is due to everyone and other considerations, except abridging the rights of others, cannot be used to cancel rights. Critics of rights have argued that this often means that individual rights-claims take precedence over other values, such as a general good or a conception of justice.

11. Communitarians find liberalism leaves agents without any social or civic duties. These critics find that the rights-carriers who appear in liberal theory are materialistic individualists. Among the most notable communitarian critics of liberalism are Alasdair MacIntyre in *After Virtue* (Notre Dame: Notre Dame University Press, 1981); Michael Sandel in *Liberalism and the Limits of Justice* (New York: Cambridge University Press, 1982); and Charles Taylor in *Sources of the Self* (Cambridge: Harvard University Press, 1989).

12. Even though many liberals do not return to a state of nature, the effort to remove agents from their setting in order to draw conclusions about equality is prevalent in contemporary liberalism. John Rawls locates individuals behind a veil of ignorance where they do not know their attachments or background; Ronald Dworkin takes individuals on a desert island with his insurance scheme in *Taking Rights Seriously* (Cambridge: Harvard University Press, 1978). For his part, Bruce Ackerman places his agents on a spaceship journey to a new planet in *Social Justice and the Liberal State* (New Haven: Yale University Press, 1980). Once background characteristics are disregarded, liberals find no fundamental difference among individuals and, therefore, no justification in treating people unequally.

13. *Young India*, November 13, 1924.

14. *Young India*, September 10, 1931.

15. *Young India*, September 29, 1927, in Iyer, *Writings*, 3: 498–502. In the same article he says that "he who claims superiority at once forfeits his claim to be called a man."

16. Speech, *The Leader*, December 25, 1916, in Iyer, *Writings*, 1: 356.

17. There is some controversy as to whether Gandhi draws his conceptions of freedom from ancient Hindu sources or from modern theories. Thomas Pantham argues that "throughout his life, Gandhi remained deeply appreciative of, and committed to, the civil liberties guaranteed by modern liberalism"; see his "Gandhi, Nehru, and Modernity," 112. Jayantanuja Bandyopadhyaya, for one, holds that "From the point of view of the Indian tradition, the Gandhian concept of freedom has been a revolutionary contribution. In the vast body of classical Indian literature, there is practically no reference to the secular freedom of the individual. One's station in society and the general work of life were determined at birth by caste, and the relationship between the king and the subjects was at best conceived as being analogous to that between the father and children.

Nowhere is there any recorded thought on the political rights of the individual" (*Social and Political Thought of Gandhi*, 82). For a discussion of the tension and reinforcement between Western and Indian conceptions of freedom see Dennis Dalton, *Indian Idea of Freedom*, ch. 1.

18. See *Young India*, September 29, 1927.

19. *Young India*, October 25, 1921.

20. *Young India*, July 9, 1925.

21. Gandhi asks how he can "compel anyone to perform even a good act? Has not a well known Englishman said that to make mistakes as a free man is better than being in bondage in order to avoid them? I believe in the truth of this. The reason is obvious. The mind of a man who remains good under compulsion cannot improve, in fact it worsens. And when compulsion is removed all the defects well up to the surface with even greater force" (*Harijan*, September 29, 1946).

22. *Ethical Religion*, ch. 3 in Iyer, *Writings*, 2: 55. In the same chapter, Gandhi asks, "How can a man understand morality who does not use his own intelligence and power of thought but lets himself be swept along like a log of wood by a current?"

23. "No society can possibly be built on a denial of individual freedom. It is contrary to the very nature of man." *Harijan*, February 1, 1942.

24. *Harijan*, February 1, 1942.

25. C. B. Macpherson, *The Political Theory of Possessive Individualism* (Oxford: Oxford University Press, 1962).

26. The claim has recently been advanced that there has been an explosion of rights-claims and that some claims thinly hide individual interests and demands for preferential treatment. See Mary Glendon, *Rights Talk: The Impoverishment of Political Discourse* (New York: Free Press, 1991).

Critics fear that the concept of rights has become so relaxed and loose almost anything can plausibly be advanced as a rights-claim. When rights become another name for interests, there is the danger that those with greater resources and influence will have their claims recognized as valid and those without power will flounder, unrecognized and unattended. However, this contradicts a basic axiom of virtually all theories of rights, namely that a right should be independent of power. See Terchek, *Republican Paradoxes and Liberal Anxieties,* ch. 8.

27. Harry Frankfort, *The Importance of What We Care About* (New York: Cambridge University Press, 1988), 12–16.

28. In theories of autonomy, persons are said to govern themselves through their reasoned choices. For this reason, Joel Feinberg finds unreflective adults are not autonomous; see his *Harm to Self* (New York: Oxford University Press, 1986), 28.

29. Gerald Dworkin, "The Concept of Autonomy," in *The Inner Citadel*, ed. John Christman (New York: Oxford University Press, 1989), 60.

30. Feinberg, *Harm to Self*, 33–34.

31. See Joseph Raz, *The Morality of Freedom* (Oxford: Clarendon Press, 1986). One of the most arresting features of most theories of autonomy is that they are decontextualized and we encounter abstracted individuals, much the same kind that many critics find in liberal theories of rights.

32. See *Young India*, March 18, 1926.

33. One of the stark differences between Gandhi's views of autonomy and many conventional ones can be seen in Gandhi's efforts to tie autonomy to tradition and Feinberg's effort to separate the two. According to Feinberg, "We inherit our moral commitments, . . . but with luck, . . . we can minimize our commitments and thus achieve a greater amount of *de facto* moral independence" (*Harm to Self*, 39).

34. See *Young India*, March 21, 1929.

35. Letter to Narandas Gandhi, July 28–31, 1930.

36. For Robert Young, "One must be free to be autonomous" ("Autonomy and the Inner Self," *Ethics* 17 [1980]: 78). Several other Western theorists argue otherwise. Harry Frankfort claims that "to deprive someone of his freedom of action is not necessarily to undermine the freedom of the will." "Freedom of the Will and the Concept of a Person," 70.

37. This is the major thrust of Gandhi's interpretation of the *Gita*.

38. Gandhi holds, "We are the creators of this position of ours, and we alone can change it. We are fearless and free, so long as we have the weapon of Satyagraha in our hands." *Satyagraha in South Africa* (Ahmedabad: Navajivan Publishing House, 1950), 147.

39. Gandhi pushes the connection between rights and duties in still another way. As Margaret Chatterjee argues, Gandhi encourages "the dispossessed to speak up for their rights as well as put their own house in order" (*Gandhi's Religious Thought*, 148).

40. *Young India*, January 8, 1925.

41. While accepting the principle of reciprocity, Gandhi does not make it the basis of duties. He observes, "I am a lover of my own liberty and so I would do nothing to restrict yours" (*Young India*, January 21, 1927).

42. Brian Barry argues that the present generation cannot obligate itself to a future generation because it is impossible for us to enter into a contract with people who do not already exist. From his perspective, if there is no contract, there is no obligation. "Circumstance of Justice and Future Generations" in *Obligations to Future Generations*, ed. by R. I. Sikora and B. Barry (Philadelphia: Temple University Press, 1978), 204–48.

43. *Young India*, March 26, 1931.

44. See *Navajivan*, July 1, 1928, in Iyer, *Writings*, 2: 72.

45. Note to Gope Burbusani, March 16, 1945, in Iyer, *Writings*, 2: 82.

46. This is the major principle Gandhi takes from his reading of the *Gita*. See *Discourses on the Gita* (Ahmedabad: Navajivan, 1946).

47. "I believe in the essential unity of man and for that matter of all that lives. . . . When we descend to the empirical level, we descend to the world of duality. In God there is no duality. But as soon as we descend to the empirical level, we get two forces—God and Satan, as Christians call them." *Young India*, January 21, 1926.

48. Gandhi writes, "I am an *advaitist* (or monist) and yet I can support *dvaitism* (duality)." *Young India*, January 21, 1926.

49. See *Young India*, March 18, 1926.

50. "We are, perhaps, all originally brutes. I am prepared to believe that we have become men by a slow process of evolution from the brute." *Harijan*, April 2, 1938.

51. *Socialism of My Conception* (Bombay: Bharatiya Vidya Bhavan, 1957), 270. For Gandhi, the "possibilities" for moral development are "the same for everyone" (*Harijan*, May 18, 1940). Rejecting "the theory of the permanent inelasticity of human nature," Gandhi insists that everyone has "the capacity of nonviolence." *Harijan*, June 7, 1940.

52. *Harijan*, February 1, 1935.

53. "It is our actions which count. Thoughts, however good in themselves, are like false pearls unless translated into action." Letter, September 11, 1932, in Iyer, *Writings*, 2: 81.

54. Gandhi, *For Pacifists* (Ahmedabad: Navajivan Publishing House, 1938), 64.

55. Chandraskhanker Shukla, *Conversations of Gandhi* (Bombay: Vora & Co., 1949), 10.

56. Gandhi holds that everyone is corruptible and says that he wears "the same corruptible flesh that the weakest of my fellow being wears and am therefore as liable to err as any" (*Young India*, February 16, 1922).

57. See *Young India*, September 25, 1924.

58. *Young India*, July 7, 1927.

59. For a critique of moral pretentiousness in politics, see Niebuhr, *Moral Man and Immoral Society*.

60. *Young India*, September 25, 1924.

61. On Gandhi's similarity with Kant on this matter, see Pantham, "Gandhi's Intervention in Modern Moral-Political Discourse."

62. On conquering pride, see *"Satyagraha*—Not Passive Resistance," September 2, 1917, in Iyer, *Writings*, 3: 51–52.

63. *Harijan*, May 30, 1936. Elsewhere, he holds that every person has "the capacity of rising to the greatest height ever attained by any human being irrespective of race or colour." *Young India*, May 9, 1929, in Iyer, *Writings*, 2: 471.

64. *Ethical Religion*, ch. 7, in Iyer, *Writings*, 2, 65.

65. *Harijan*, January 28, 1939. Earlier, he finds "Life is subject to constant change and development." *Young India*, October 25, 1928, in Iyer, *Writings*, 2: 219.

66. "Letter to Minilal Gandhi," November 24, 1909 in *Collected Works of Mahatma Gandhi*, 10: 70. Ten years later, he writes "Men of ordinary abilities . . . can develop morally." *Young India*, November 5, 1919.

67. *Harijan*, June 10, 1939.

68. "Truth and untruth often co-exist; good and evil are often found together." *Young India*, November 13, 1924.

69. *Harijan*, December 8, 1946, in Iyer, *Writings*, 2: 262.

70. *Young India*, November 24, 1920.

71. In Hinduism, ahimsa commonly refers to compassion and detachment, but in Gandhi's hands it is extended to include a universalizing love and action to combat injustice.

72. *Modern Review*, October 1916, in Iyer, *Writings*, 2: 212.

73. *Harijan*, August 11, 1940, in Iyer, *Writings*, 2: 250.

74. Letter, May 2, 1935, in Iyer, *Writings*, 2: 296.

75. Letter to Esther Menon, February 28, 1932, in Iyer, *Writings*, 2: 295.

76. *Modern Review*, October 1916, in Iyer, *Writings*, 2: 213.

77. *Hindustan Times*, October 17, 1935, in Iyer, *Writings*, 3: 598.

78. For a further discussion of Gandhi's conception of truth, see Bondurant, *Conquest*, 15–23; Iyer, *Thought*, 149–76; and Paul Kuntz, "Gandhi's Truth," *International Philosophy Quarterly* 22 (Summer 1982): 141–55.

79. "God is conscience. He is even the atheism of the atheist. He transcends speech and reason. . . . He is also terrible. He is the greatest democrat the world knows, for He leaves us unfettered to make our own choice between evil and good." *Young India*, March 3, 1925.

80. Gandhi continually makes a distinction between a moral and spiritual life on the one hand and a religious one on the other: "Let us take two men, one who believes in the existence of God, yet breaks all His Commandments; and another who, though not acknowledging God by name, worships Him through his deeds and obeys His laws, recognizing in the divine laws, their Maker. Which of these two men shall we call a man of religion and morality? Without a moment's thought, one would emphatically reply that the second man alone is to be considered religious and moral." "Ethical Religion," ch. 5, in Iyer, *Writings*, 2: 62.

81. For Gandhi, any conception of the truth will include a commitment to autonomy (or truths about the basic dignity of persons), equality (or the truth of nonsubordination), and nonviolence.

82. "Ethical Religion," ch. 5, in Iyer, *Writings*, 2: 62.

83. Letter to Mirabehn, May 2, 1927, *Collected Works* 23: 283.

84. Gandhi, *From Yeravda Mandir* (Ahmedabad: Navajivan, 1932).

85. *Young India*, February 5, 1925.

86. "I think it almost impossible to decide which out of the many interpretations of religious works represents undiluted truth. . . . Imperfect man, therefore, should humbly believe that as one's truth is dear to one, so others' truths are bound to be dear to them. Hence everyone should follow his own path and others should not hinder him from doing so. People will then follow, of their own accord, that path which is found from experience to be the smoothest." Letter to Santosh Maharaj, July 2, 1927, in Iyer, *Writings*: 1, 86.

87. *From Yeravda Mandir.*

88. Letter, March 16, 1932, in Iyer, *Writings*, 3: 505.

89. See M. K. Gandhi, *All Men Are Brothers*, ed. Krishna Kripalani (New York: Columbia University Press, 1958), 76.

90. "I believe that all the great religions of the world are true, more or less. I say 'more or less' because I believe that everything that the human hand touches, by reason of the very fact that human beings are imperfect, becomes imperfect." *Young India*, September 22, 1927.

91. "If we had attained the full vision of the Truth, we would no longer be mere seekers, but become one with God, for Truth is God. But being only seekers, we prosecute our quest and are conscious of our imperfection. And if we are imperfect ourselves, religion as conceived by us must also be imperfect. . . . Religion of our conception, being imperfect, is always subject to a process of evolution and reinterpretation. . . . And if all faiths outlined by men are imperfect, the question of comparative merit does not arise. All faiths constitute a revelation of Truth, but are imperfect, and liable to error. Reverence to other faiths need not blind us to their faults. We must be keenly alive to the defects of our own faith, and must not leave it on that account but try to overcome these defects" (*From Yeravda Mandir*, 55). Here, as elsewhere, Gandhi wants to localize truth. For him, we can always find real injustice at home and, therefore, he reasons, we need to apply our truth where we can have an effect, that is, locally.

92. *Young India*, December 26, 1924.

93. *Harijan*, August 26, 1936.

94. Tagore sees Gandhi as "essentially a lover of men and not of mere ideas, which makes him so cautious and conservative in his revolutionary schemes." R. K. Prabhu and Vavindra Kelker, eds., *Truth Called Them Differently (Tagore-Gandhi Controversy)* (Ahmedabad: Navajivan Press, 1961), 134.

95. Gandhi, *For Pacifists*, 64.

96. *Harijan*, July 8, 1933. According to Iyer, "No thinker before Gandhi [in India] had laid so much emphasis on the notion of conscience as the basis of all social and political action. It could be safely contended that this notion really

came to him from the West" (Iyer, *Thought*, 132). Iyer holds that Gandhi borrows the idea of a sovereign conscience from Socrates (*Thought*, 128–32). Gandhi translated Socrates' *The Apology* into his native Gujarati under the title *The Story of a Satyagrahi*.

97. Truth "is what the voice within tells you. How then, you ask, do different people think of different and contrary truths? Well, seeing that the human mind works through innumerable media and that the evolution of the human mind is not the same for all, it follows that what may be truth for one may be untruth for another" (*All Men Are Brothers*, 71).

98. In universalizing the elementary moral capacities of persons, Gandhi means to show that everyone is able to respond positively to the suffering of the *satyagrahi*. He believes that the capacity for feeling anguish or being moved by the pain of another means that observers can change their outlooks and conduct.

99. *Young India*, March 1919.

100. Smith claims that when people "sacrifice their own interest to the greater interests of others," it is not because of some "feeble" altruism but because of "conscience, the inhabitant of the breast, the man within, the great judge and arbiter of our conduct" (*Theory of Moral Sentiments* [Oxford: Clarendon Press, 1976], III.iii.4). Smith's agent is expected to use his conscience to discover standards for action that can override instrumental reason: "The man of real constancy and firmness, the wise and just man" commands himself "in the bustle and business of the world . . . in success and in disappointment, in prosperity and in adversity, before friends and before enemies." Detached from his interests, Smith's heroic stoic is honest to and at peace with himself (*Theory of Moral Sentiments*, III.iii.25). For Smith, people who make their own happiness come at the expense of others falsify any proper understanding of the self and, in the process, misunderstand the nature of happiness. Smith hardly wants to embark on a theory that would make people one another's keepers. He is not concerned about how we positively assist strangers but whether our self-interested actions harm others.

101. See *Young India*, August 11, 1920, and December 18, 1924, on courage and action.

102. Gandhi would also object to Smith's celebration of the stoics who rise above the pettiness of their society, seeing themselves as part of a universe whose ultimate purpose they cannot comprehend, much less control. Smith's stoics do not harm others but do not help others either. In contrast to Smithian detachment, Gandhi urges involvement; rather than abstaining from harming others, Gandhi argues for mutual assistance.

103. *Young India*, December 3, 1925.

104. *Harijan*, December 10, 1939. See *Harijan*, July 8, 1933 for Gandhi's discussion of the "struggle" within him when he heard the voice.

105. *Harijan*, March 18, 1933. While hardly liberal, Gandhi's argument parallels the defense of free speech of J. S. Mill who finds that free speech can be abused but this is not a reason to prohibit it. Both Mill and Gandhi hold that the suppression of free expression simultaneously denies people their autonomy and deprives society of potentially helpful discourse.

106. What he says of religion can be applied to an individual's conscience: "I reject any religious doctrine that does not appeal to reason and is in conflict with morality. I tolerate unreasonable religious sentiment when it is not immoral." *All Men Are Brothers*, 75.

107. *Young India*, June 25, 1921.

108. "When people cease to think for themselves and have everything regulated for them, it becomes necessary at times to assert the right of individuals to act in defiance of public opinion or law, which is another name for public opinion. When individuals so act, they claim to have acted in obedience to conscience." *Young India*, August 21, 1921.

109. *Young India*, November 5, 1934.

110. Gandhi sees voluntary suffering as an appeal to the conscience. He expects it to take time and finds the process is uneven; in any case, he believes it forces others to ask questions they had not posed before and open a dialogue.

111. For a discussion of Locke's moral individualism, see Terchek, *Republican Paradoxes*, ch. 4.

112. *Navajivan*, June 27, 1920, in Iyer, *Writings*, 1: 308.

113. See *Navajivan* July 1, 1928, in Iyer, *Writings* 2: 72.

114. "The individual person should have control over the things that are necessary for the sustenance of life. If he cannot have such control, the individual cannot survive. Ultimately, the world is made up only of individuals. If there were no drops there would be no ocean." Letter to Nehru, October 5. 1945, *Collected Works* 81: 320.

115. *Young India*, March 5, 1925.

116. *Hind Swaraj*, ch. 16.

117. "Man is the maker of his own destiny in the sense that he has freedom of choice as to the manner in which he uses that freedom. But he is no controller of results. The moment he thinks he is, he comes to grief." *Harijan*, March 23, 1940.

118. "Man's happiness really lies in contentment. He who is discontented, however much he possesses, becomes a slave to his desires. All the sages have declared from the housetops, that man can be his own worst enemy as well as his best friend. To be free or to be a slave lies in his own hands. And what is true for the individual, is true for the society." *Harijan*, February 1, 1942. Contentment is not altogether possible, not only because modernity and modernization continually churn settled relations but also because people like Gandhi would have us forgo contentment in order to defend autonomy and challenge injustice.

2

RECLAIMING A TRADITION AND MAKING IT YOUR OWN

Gandhi not only reinterpreted and reformed but reconstructed Hinduism on a new foundation. . . . He turned it into a living tradition of critical and unending inquiry.[1]

E dward Said has carefully demonstrated how Europe invented the Orient during the Enlightenment and continued to employ the concept for several centuries: "European culture was able to manage—and even produce—the Orient politically, sociologically, militarily, ideologically, scientifically, and imaginatively during the post-Enlightenment period."[2] For Said, the constructed "Orient" assumes the "status of scientific truth," and Europeans teach India and all Asia and North Africa a (re)constructed tradition about themselves, one that is seen as inferior and has to be left behind if they are to enter the modern age.[3] When most nineteenth-century Orientalists look East, they find squalor, poverty, fatalism, superstition, stasis, flights of transcendence, and hierarchy. For all of its uniqueness, the Orient is seen as exotic, sometimes beguiling, and almost always backwards.

Gandhi contests the assumptions and conclusions of a self-confident Orientalism, particularly its views about the inferiority of the East and the superiority of the modernity of the West. Rejecting readings of Hinduism as inherently fatalistic and passive, he seeks to recover robust conceptions of autonomy and action in his tradition.[4] At the same time, Gandhi and many other Indians are determined to reform parts of their own tradition which, they believe, have become shallow, ritualized, and even corrupt over time. Disputing the Orientalist reading of India that mistakes its problems for its essence, Gandhi finds that its traditional core celebrates unity, action, openness, and courage. Uninterested in a

53

nostalgic retrieval, Gandhi works to invigorate Hinduism to protect these goods.

WHAT TRADITION MEANS TO GANDHI

Gandhi expects any practiced, coherent tradition to give meaning beyond convenience and necessity.[5] This is what he finds in the major religious traditions. He sees them providing individuals with moral materials to frame their choices as they attend to their multiple needs as well as to move beyond them to give themselves a meaning beyond survival. He finds that each tradition speaks to the moral, cooperative nature of men and women and challenges the self-interests that are lodged in every person and any society. In this way, "All the principal religions are equal in the sense that they are all true."[6] Recognizing that different religious traditions have their own distinctive expressions of the good, Gandhi holds that their fundamental teachings share a common origin and finds that all of "the great faiths of the world [are] as so many branches of a tree, each distinct from the other though having the same source."[7] Although each tradition is said to evolve from a common origin, he finds that each speaks in its own vernacular about the shared experiences, moral aspirations, and common problems that reside in their particular community. As such, it becomes a companion and guide. For this reason, Gandhi finds there is no single "best" tradition and rejects the idea that there can be a universal tradition.[8] He wants individuals to work with their own tradition and, when appropriate, challenge what is defective in it.

When Gandhi observes that "To me God is truth and love, God is ethics and morality, God is fearlessness, God is the source of life and light . . . God is conscience," he believes this is at the heart of each religion, and not just Hinduism.[9] He sees the divine assuming innumerable forms and expressed in many different modes. In each expression of the truth, as Gandhi understands matters, individuals learn that goodness is not found in a preoccupation with one's self but in moving beyond and transcending the self.[10] This is what he finds in the *Gita* and what he believes resides in every religion.[11] Each, in its highly distinctive way, confronts the raw ego and provides a moral code that teaches that sensual and material concerns ought not to take precedence over moral and spiritual ones.[12] All the while, Gandhi resists efforts to appropriate dogmatic truth-claims by any tradition, including his own, or to use its understanding of the good to claim a privileged status for itself.[13]

Gandhi's God is not hovering over mortals, ready to judge and punish. His God is a protector of the weak and a teacher about the dignity of persons; his God is revered not by ritual or solitary devotion but through service to the vulnerable.[14] With this in mind, he holds that "all religions of the world describe God pre-eminently as the Friend of the friendless, Help of the helpless, and Protector of the weak."[15]

Although Gandhi prizes tradition, he refuses to make it invincible or infallible. For him, truth not only resides in different traditions; it is also found in the consciences of ordinary men and women who can challenge tradition when it decays. For this reason, Gandhi detects both a tension and a vitalization between tradition and conscience. Tradition provides men and women with moral standards to guide them through life; those same standards also enable individuals to detect decay in the practices of their tradition. Teaching its members moral principles, tradition provides material for its own critique.[16]

TRADITIONS AND THE HOUSEHOLD

The household is the starting place for much political theory for that is where ordinary people live, raise a family, supply themselves with sustenance and security, and teach moral principles as well as standards of citizenship to the next generation.[17] The way the household addresses its multiple needs, particularly the way in which it meets its necessities, strongly influences the kind of life its members lead. Gandhi holds that, ideally, the economic management of the household and moral standards are mutually reinforcing and not disengaged. The members of the household in Gandhi's good society secure their livelihood with dignity and are not required to subordinate their integrity to meet their basic needs. However, he finds that the practices that enable people to meet their multiple needs in a traditional society are fragile. One danger comes when self-interest replaces moral principles. For Gandhi, this threat can emanate from alien sources as well as internal ones, and when the problem is internal it often comes from the household.

Gandhi knows that regardless of setting, ordinary people tend to favor their own household. Sometimes it is to make a comfortable life more comfortable for its members, and sometimes it is addressed to the issues of elementary sufficiency. Gandhi means to challenge the former and attend to the latter. If social institutions make the security and sufficiency of the household problematic, if the norms of efficiency fragment the members of the household from each other and if economic productivity places a premium on discounting many of their obligations, Gandhi fears that many people will choose whatever seems likely to preserve and protect their particular household, even if their conduct undermines their own dignity and ignores their duties to others.

Gandhi recognizes that people can make one set of duties trump their other duties, and this frequently happens regarding the family. He sees many putting their family first and, as a consequence, ignoring their duties to the larger community. When this happens, Gandhi asks householders to sort out the basic from the superfluous needs of the family. Once having satisfied the former, he wants them to attend to the needs of the community:

> Ordinarily the man oscillates between duty to his family and duty to his country. Under ideal conditions these two duties are not incompatible, but in the present situation we often see only conflict between them. That is so because love of family is based on selfishness and the family members are worshippers of selfishness; therefore, as a normal course it may be suggested that one should plunge into the service of the country after providing for the needs of the family in accordance with the poor living conditions in India. No one can serve the nation by leaving the family to fend for itself.[18]

Gandhi finds that no household is complete by itself. Each is part of larger, shared undertakings with other households, and each household depends on other households. If each understands the good only by what serves it, the harmony of local communities is disturbed, and the powerful seek to enhance the well-being of their particular household at the expense of others. Holding that conduct cannot be morally referenced only to itself, Gandhi insists that the good of the household must always remain partial. On his account, conduct needs to be evaluated on the basis of external principles; otherwise, each household privileges its own good regardless of its consequences to others.[19] To combat this partiality,

Gandhi calls on men and women to recognize that they are situated in a cosmos where the good of the parts depends on the good of the whole. To achieve this, Gandhi asks men and women to build a common life that respects the dignity and worth of all.

GANDHI'S HINDUISM

In many ways, Gandhi's Hinduism is a familiar one, relying on many of its central principles, such as the cosmos and *dharma*, and making the spiritual life the best life. One of the most appealing aspects of Hinduism, Gandhi tells us, is that it is open and resilient.[20] However, his Hinduism is not the one conventionally practiced in India during his lifetime.[21] He attacks what he considers to be defective, such as the status of women, untouchability, the role of the Brahmins, and ritualism. However, he does more. He takes some principles of Hinduism that had not been its defining elements, such as nonviolence, and elevates them into positions of central importance. Moreover, he imports ideas, such as conscience and love, from other traditions and makes them an integral part of his Hinduism. With his reformulations, Gandhi offers a new vision of spirituality as action and uses Hinduism as a vehicle for social reform and political mobilization in India.[22]

Gandhi holds that the problem with contemporary Hinduism is that it has departed from its core principles. He finds it has become moribund and weak, maintaining its presence through symbol and ritual, and retains little of the animating force that helps people morally locate themselves. This is troubling to Gandhi because it cannot meet the two related but distinct missions he assigns to Hinduism (and to all traditions). They are to serve as a source of moral judgment and identity and provide the materials to oppose internal pride and external domination. He also expects that where traditions are weak, a preoccupation with the self meets little resistance.

What Gandhi finds in contemporary Hinduism are not scattered deficiencies that must be corrected or a particular practice that must be reformed.[23] Rather, his indictment is sweeping, embracing a multitude of practices and outlooks that he thinks cannot continue if the autonomy of persons is to be protected. For this reason, he holds that "it is the whole of Hinduism that has to be purified and purged,"[24] and he means to make it a tradition that Hindus can live with.

Living traditions are continually revised, and later generations frequently debate which revisions are essentially honest to their foundational principles and which are not. Such internal debates have long described Hinduism. On some readings, the *Upanishads* as well as Buddhism and Jainism enjoin us to see the phenomenal world as unreal and fictitious and hold that renunciation and disengagement lead the way to spiritual reality. In contrast, some find that the *Gita* is an account of an active life which pays particular attention to the ways people conduct themselves in the phenomenal world, particularly the ways they conceptualize themselves as autonomous agents participating in the life of their community. This is Gandhi's Hinduism.[25] Not surprisingly, when he turns to Hindu texts, he reaches for the *Gita*, but it is his *Gita*.[26]

GANDHI'S *GITA*

Ostensibly, the *Gita* is the story of a battle. Arjuna, who has been deprived of his kingdom by his deceptive cousins, leads his army to battle theirs. However, Arjuna recoils at the prospect of fighting and killing his own kinsmen. The divine Krishna, who takes the form of Arjuna's charioteer, shows that duty is primary.[27] After a violent battle, Arjuna, guided by Krishna's teaching, destroys the forces of evil. However, Gandhi's *Gita* is much more. It is also Krishna's teaching regarding the need for human transcendence and detachment, the importance of pursuing the right regardless of consequences, and the necessity for action.

For many, the message of the *Gita* is highly spiritual, inviting a transcendence from the world.[28] A radically different reading is provided by anticolonial terrorists. They read this sacred text literally, that is, as a call to duty through violence. As Parekh summarizes their position, they make violence "morally innocent and a matter of sacred duty."[29] Rather than concluding that the *Gita* invites a withdrawal from the world or makes the violent hero the center of the story, Gandhi finds the *Gita* emphasizes activity, duty, and service in the cosmos, and the violence is allegorical.[30] As he sees it, the subject matter is simply the realization of *Brahman* and the means thereto; the battle is only the occasion for its teaching. One can say, if one likes, that the poet used it on occasion because he did not look upon war as morally wrong. On reading the *Mahabharata*, I formed quite a different impression.

Since the *Gita's* subject is not the description of the battle and justification of violence, it is perfectly wrong to give much importance to these. If, moreover, it is difficult to reconcile a few of the verses with the idea that the *Gita* advocates nonviolence, it is still more difficult to reconcile the teaching of the work as a whole with the advocacy of violence.

. . . The overall teaching of the *Gita* is not violence but nonviolence. . . . Violence is simply not possible unless one is driven by anger, by ignorant love, and by hatred. The *Gita*, on the other hand, wants us to be incapable of anger.[31]

Arjuna acts not for utilitarian reasons but because he believes what he does is right.[32] When Krishna tells Arjuna to "perform all actions for My sake" and to "renounce the fruits of action," Gandhi finds an imperative to act morally regardless of the consequences. In doing so, he expects us to proceed without anger or hatred and to look "on all with love and compassion."[33]

Gandhi claims his interpretation has a special claim because it comes from someone who attempts to put the teaching of the *Gita* into practice in his everyday life.[34] In this sense, his translation and commentaries are not offered as a scholarly exercise for people to pursue at their leisure but, he claims, as a rendering that is honest to the underlying core of the text and is meant for ordinary men and women.[35] What they find in Gandhi's interpretation is that the highest expression of devotion lies in service to the weak and helpless. And they read that the "paramount principles" of the *Gita* are "obligatory duties" and the purest expression of sacrifice "for this country this age is the spinning wheel."[36]

INDIVIDUALS AND THE COSMOS

One of Gandhi's important debts to Hinduism is its cosmological outlook. In the traditional cosmological account, we are interested in the relationships that human beings have with one another and with all of the other parts of the universe. From this perspective, individuals are known not only as distinct persons but also by their relationships to other people, to their natural environment, to time and space, and to the process of order and decay. In the West, theories of ontology and deontology have replaced cosmology as ways of understanding human beings and their relationship with each other and nonhuman subjects. In both ontology, the study of being, and deontology, the study of formal rules to govern behavior, the focus is on the individual. Although attentive to the individual, Gandhi's Hinduism works with the relatedness of persons in the cosmos, not with the isolated self.

The contemporary Indian political theorist V. R. Mehta sees the Hindu concept of cosmology emphasizing regularity, unity, interdependence, freedom, and action. He finds the "creation of the cosmos in Indian mythology" is the result of a conflict between order and disorder. On his account, the cosmos makes the individual and society "safe" from perpetual chaos.[37] However, goodness and virtue are followed by corruption and decay.[38] Rather than reading the cosmos deterministically, Mehta and most other scholars find that Hindu cosmology leaves much to human choice. How conflict is solved depends, in large measure, on how individuals respond, and one of the central tasks Gandhi assigns to the autonomous person is to resist decay and challenge domination wherever it appears. Working with this view of the cosmos, Gandhi finds the good never completely overcomes avarice and ambition which continually threaten cosmic harmony in favor of domination and indulgence.[39] When the cosmic cohesion is broken, then power is abused, moral standards and social practices diverge, and the self becomes isolated and confused.

Gandhi means to challenge a chaotic moral universe as well as question conceptions of order based on stasis, conformity, and fatalism. For him, the parts of the cosmos are always active, and the issue is whether the parts cooperate or one part attempts to control the others. Seeing individuals as autonomous choosers in the cosmos, he finds the ambitious self disturbs the cosmos and needs to be confronted. From his perspective, decay comes not only when some step outside of the cosmic order to serve their personal interests but also when others misconstrue any form of order for justice and relieve themselves of taking responsibility for the injustice they encounter.[40] He takes this to mean not only that injustice must be confronted but so must passivity and fatalism.

DHARMA

To think through how we should act and what we owe others, Gandhi turns to the concept of *dharma*, loosely translated as duty or the "principle of right."[41] In Gandhi's cosmology, everyone has an individual dharma, covering the multiple duties and needs that describe the many interrelated roles of each unique person.[42] Gandhi sees different people having a different dharma which gives meaning, coherence, and intelligibility both to themselves and to society and which they express through action.[43]

Given that each of us has particular duties, talents, and needs, what attitude should we bring to them, and what responsibilities do we carry and to whom?[44] One answer is that our first obligation is always to ourselves and we should do whatever is necessary to improve our own situation. Gandhi wants to promote what he calls "self-help" but he does not conceive of it as narrowly individualistic; it is related, rather, to his views concerning the interdependence of human beings who have their own dharma in the cosmos.[45] Self-help is the first step, not the culmination of Gandhi's dharma. By engaging in self-help, Gandhi believes that individuals address their own basic needs but also contribute to the well-being of their community.

> A farmer who, rejecting friends' help, insists on tilling his own soil, making his own implements, gathering his own harvest, spinning and weaving his own cloth, and building his own house, all by himself, must be either foolish or self-conceited or barbarous. Self-help includes bread-labour and means that every man shall earn his bread by the sweat of his brow. Hence, a man who works in his field for eight hours daily is entitled to help from the weaver, the carpenter, the blacksmith or the mason. It is not only his right, it is his duty to seek the help of these, and they, in their turn, benefit by the agriculturist's labour in the field. . . . we three hundred million members of the Indian body politic, each following the rule of self-help in performing his own function and yet co-operating with one another in all matters of common interest [are mutually helpful and mutually dependent].[46]

Gandhi's conception of dharma is related to his view of moral projects. In his account, our projects are not a series of unrelated choices, roles, or tasks, but come from the way we define ourselves in relation to all of our choices, roles, and duties. We are expected to know our capacities, opportunities, and limitations and define our projects within these considerations. In continually revisiting ordinary people, Gandhi appreciates that each has multiple needs that cannot be satisfied either by making one need absolute, such as an economic one, or by attempting to meet our needs individually. However, Gandhi insists that dharma is not satisfied only by performing the duties that are attached to the specific roles of a person, such as a parent; he makes dharma a duty to serve society as well.[47] Taken together, these duties represent the moral projects of a person.

Such moral projects are threatened, according to Gandhi, by modernizing institutions which he sees fragmenting the personality into several discrete and often incommensurate roles and thereby impede the construction of a coherent project. In the absence of integrating practices, he fears each person is left without a grounding to decide what is morally appropriate. At best, the result is confusion and inconsistency. At worst, it takes the form of a self-centered individualism that is indifferent to costs it assesses on others. For Gandhi, it is possible to perform our duties only if we know what our duties are, and we come to know our duties not in a random way or primarily in response to meeting necessity. Rather, duties are known to us because we see ourselves as part of both our own local cosmos as well as the universal cosmos. This, Gandhi holds, is seriously threatened in the modern world:

> Whereas previously he justified his conduct, he no longer justifies his own or his neighbour's. He wants to set right the wrong, but he does not know that his own practice fails him. The contradiction between his theory and his practice fetters him. His conduct is not justified by logic.[48]

One reason for this confusion, Gandhi believes, stems from the modern emphasis on economic production and consumption which narrows the projects of individuals who are becoming increasingly insular and materialistic. He sees people thrown back on themselves to provide themselves with a livelihood as well as with meaning and purpose in an atomistic society. This leads to a frame of moral reference that is largely if not exclusively interior with little room for a cooperative self. For him, a robust tradition can point the way out of this confusion.

CRITICIZING A TRADITION
(PARTICULARLY ONE'S OWN)

Because of its importance in providing a grounded foundation for choice and action, Gandhi's conception of tradition means that it can never be exempt from moral scrutiny. Gandhi knows as well as any critic of tradition that it can become corrupt, and he acknowledges that simply because something is ancient does not mean that it is beyond criticism or remains necessarily worthwhile.[49] Indeed, he recognizes that tradition can serve as a patina to legitimize conduct that is patently unjust. In offering his critique of Hinduism, Gandhi calls on his own moral sense and reason to guide him. He tells us that he exercises his "judgment about every scripture, including the *Gita*. I cannot let a scriptural text supersede my reason." One reason is that inspired texts "suffer from a process of double distillation. Firstly, they come through a human prophet, and then commentaries of interpreters. Nothing in them comes from God directly."[50] If this is so, then sacred texts lose some of their sanctity.

Not surprisingly, Gandhi reads Hindu scripture selectively, celebrating some texts and criticizing or ignoring others. He condemns some because they are "contrary to universal truths and morals" or are in conflict with reason, such as the child marriages sanctioned in the *smritis*. He also distinguishes between what he takes to be authentic in his own tradition and defective additions to it which, he insists, "must be rejected as interpolations."[51]

On his account, the texts of a tradition must be elastic and open to new readings today, just as they have in the past. "The interpretation of accepted texts has undergone evaluation and is capable of indefinite evolution," according to Gandhi.[52] Commentaries that once made sense but no longer seem compelling need to give way to new ways of understanding. Gandhi emphasizes this in his introduction to his translation of the *Gita* into Gujarati where he observes:

> With every age, the important words will carry new and expanding meanings. But its central teaching will never vary. The seeker is at liberty to extract from this treasure any meaning he likes so as to enable him to enforce in his life the central teaching.[53]

He goes on to argue that no sacred text, including the *Gita*, should be read as "a collection of Do's and Dont's."⁵⁴ For him, the validity of any interpretation must be whether autonomy is strengthened or degraded. With this standard, he continually passes judgment on the central texts of his tradition, sometimes to praise them, sometimes to reformulate them, and sometimes to condemn them. For him,

> The stories told in the *Puranas* are some of the most dangerous, if we do not know their bearing upon the present conditions. The *shastras* would be death traps if we were to regulate our conduct according to every detail in them or according to that of the characters therein.⁵⁵

Given Gandhi's point of moral reference, he finds that a tradition is sound when it celebrates the dignity of all persons and provides the moral materials for the good life and the good community. It does this not by asking people to leave society, but to resist its claims that order and convenience are what count most. For tradition to do the work Gandhi assigns to it, it must confront efforts to swallow the good, whether the threat is internal or external to the tradition.

Gandhi finds that ritualism and dogmatism are ill-equipped to meet this test. This is why he rejects rigid readings of the *smritis* and other texts that provide people with "inflexible codes of conduct." One reason is that universalistic formula, whether modern or ancient, decline to take account of the many differences that mark any society and ignore the diverse but genuine understandings of individuals about the central teachings of their tradition and how to apply it in their own lives. Carrying their own dharma, they, not others, are responsible for their conduct.⁵⁶ For this reason, Gandhi holds that a moral life "cannot be superimposed from without. It is a matter of evolution from within and therefore of individual self-effort."⁵⁷

Gandhi seeks to democraticize tradition in the most basic sense. Its foundational texts are not to be a body of knowledge that can only be understood by a select, initiated few. When interpretation is frozen or restricted to a select minority, the canon can become a resource to protect the advantages and positions of those who claim a privileged knowledge and disenfranchises those who have alternative readings that they seek to incorporate into their own lives. From Gandhi's perspective, formal training cannot substitute for the understanding that individuals have about their tradition and how it should be incorporated into their own lives.

Gandhi's efforts to open texts to diverse understandings and to have them speak in languages that make sense to ordinary men and women is not meant to make texts be anything anyone wants to make of them. For him, the essential core of texts, and by extension, of tradition, is constant; he sees the foundational principles of a vitalized tradition protecting the integrity of individuals, warning about a preoccupation with one's self, and inviting service to the community. To achieve these purposes, Gandhi finds that traditions must shake off the decay that has accrued over time.

CHALLENGING TRADITIONAL ASSIGNMENTS: THE CASE OF WOMEN

Gandhi wants to transport what he takes to be the essence of ancient texts into contemporary society where they can animate social practices and challenge domination. This can be seen in his critique of traditional gender practices. "Of all the evils for which man has made himself responsible," writes Gandhi, "none is so degrading, so shocking or so brutal as his abuse of" women.[58]

Gandhi finds that the contemporary status of women reflects historical, not natural, relationships. Seeing that traditional views of gender relations were made by men and not women, they do not speak to the issue of equality: "The ancient laws were made by seers who were men. The women's experience, therefore, is not represented in them. Strictly speaking, as between man and woman, neither should be regarded as superior or inferior."[59] Gandhi is also disturbed that women have accepted the position assigned to them, "and so woman has developed an inferiority complex. She has believed in the truth of man's interested teaching that she is inferior to him," and this Gandhi means to challenge.[60]

He finds many reasons for the subordinate condition of women, and one stems from the way parents educate their daughters to see any marriage as necessary and tolerable. The traditional practice of dowry, for example, is something Gandhi particularly wants to eliminate because it treats daughters as commodities.[61] On his account, a dowry is "nothing but the sale of girls."[62] Accordingly, parents need to educate their daughters to "refuse to marry a young man who wanted a price for marrying" rather "than be party to the degrading terms. The only honorable terms in marriage are mutual love and mutual consent."[63]

Marriage is a partnership, as Gandhi understands it, not a hierarchical arrangement and one of the things this means to him is that marriage is a relationship between equals, bestowing no sexual rights or claims on men over their wives. For Gandhi, sexual relations must be mutually desired by both parties and when that is not forthcoming, then a "man has no right to touch his wife . . . , and the woman should have the willpower to resist even her own husband."[64]

Gandhi finds that the unequal treatment of women in India has taken many forms and one of the most "brutal" is the custom of child marriage and child widowhood.[65] Child widowhood, in particular, denies girls the freedom to develop and consigns them, as women, to poverty and humiliation. In his account, "Any tradition, however ancient, if inconsistent with morality is fit to be banished from the land." For him, child widowhood and child marriage fall into this category; they are, he writes, "horrible" and "superstitious" and need to be abolished.[66]

The way to change the status of women, he insists, is for women to demand that they be treated as equals and with dignity:

> I passionately desire the utmost freedom for our women. I detest child marriages. I shudder to see a child widow, and shiver with rage when a husband just widowed contracts with brutal indifference another marriage. I deplore the criminal indifference of parents who keep their daughters utterly ignorant and illiterate and bring them up only for the purpose of marrying them off to some young man of means. Notwithstanding all this grief and rage, I realize the difficulty of the problem. Women must have votes and an equal legal status. But the problem does not end there. It only commences at the point where women begin to affect the political deliberations of the nation.[67]

In constructing his ideal conception of persons, Gandhi strives to move beyond gender. As Ashis Nandy argues, Gandhi no more wants women to become men than he wants men to trade places with women.[68] Rather he seeks a synergy that ideally combines what he takes to be the strengths of each gender: "My ideal is this. A man should remain man and yet should become woman; similarly a woman should remain woman and yet become man. This means that man should cultivate the gentleness and the discrimination of woman; and woman should cast off her timidity and become brave and courageous."[69] Whether his view is based on an essentialism regarding gender or whether Gandhi's view reflects the idea that environment and socialization promote different dispositions in men and women, it is clear that he wants a fusion of what he takes to be the most noble parts of each. As he sees it, "Both man and woman can become fearless. Man thinks that he can be fearless, but that is not always true; similarly, woman thinks she is weak and allows herself to be called so; this too is not right."[70]

If the campaign for the dignity and equality for women is to succeed, Gandhi thinks it will be because women are helping women to resist old patterns and develop new strengths, the kind of strategy Gandhi brings to the Indian independence movement.[71] "Only the self can raise the self; the self is the help of the self. Only women can raise women," according to Gandhi who goes on to argue that if a woman "learns *satyagraha*, she can be perfectly independent and self-supporting. She does not have to feel dependent upon anyone."[72]

Gandhi does not call on ancient texts to validate his claims for the autonomous woman. Nor does he reach for modern theories of rights. He proceeds as if autonomy was always a part of Hinduism and argues that if swaraj is to come to all Indians, women must be included. In his efforts to reform and revitalize his tradition by recognizing women as equals, he works with his assumption about a cosmos of interrelated, equal persons who deserve to be autonomous and with his claims that the good society cannot be described by domination and hierarchy.

TRADITION AS A RESOURCE

To challenge domination, inequality, and fatalism, Gandhi finds he does not have to leave his own tradition to locate the moral materials for critique and emancipation. For this reason, he argues that the Hinduism that has been inherited must be superseded by a restored Hinduism that is honest to its core. Moreover, he finds that imperialism and other expressions of domination cannot be best resisted with alien theorizing

but are most effectively challenged with local, traditional ways of thinking that have been reformed and energized.[73]

Gandhi sees two dangers confronting India. One is alien and the
other comes from India itself because of the harm it inflicts on itself. He
wants other Indians to join him in seeing that they are responsible for
much of their misery and humiliation.

> We blame the British for everything; we fell because of their cunning,
> they robbed us of our wealth, and left us beggars, we cannot even
> breathe without their permission. . . .
>
> Though there is much exaggeration in this charge, there is also
> some truth in it. What is the cause of the control the British have
> acquired over us? May it not be our own fault? . . .
>
> The reason (for the present situation) is our inveterate selfishness,
> our inability to make sacrifices for the country, our dishonesty, our
> timidity, our hypocrisy and our ignorance.[74]

India and its people, Gandhi argues, will not become autonomous
simply by winning their political independence from Britain. An autonomous India must ultimately look to itself for its freedom. For him, this
means that ordinary Indians must be empowered by a reformed tradition
to take charge of their own lives and resist both old and new assaults on
their autonomy.[75] With this in mind, he seeks to reformulate Hinduism
to meet the challenge.[76] To do this, he attacks the practices of his tradition without challenging what he takes to be its foundational principles;
at the same time, he borrows concepts from modernity by putting them
into his own idiom without acknowledging his sources.

In his efforts to make tradition into a resource, Gandhi repeatedly
insists that it must be actively incorporated into the everyday lives of
men and women. For him, this means it must be a part of their routines
and work-a-day activities, a topic developed in chapter four. He wants
activity extended to service to the community, both to strengthen what
is worthwhile as well as challenge what is dangerous. Tradition points
the way, according to Gandhi, because it reminds human beings that
their humanity is not found in mastering their biological nature but in
transcending it and reaching out to others, particularly the most vulnerable members of society.

Gandhi finds his tradition not only in texts but also in the countryside. There he sees a remembered time when farmers, artisans, and small merchants were able to work to provide an adequate, if austere, living for themselves. To be sure, he sees the deep scars of untouchability and other expressions of inequality there. But he also imagines that at one time the village is a mini-cosmos where Indians cooperate with one another.[77] Gandhi captures a time before the native textile market was destroyed by imported foreign cloth and other market forces had displaced other traditional labor-intensive occupations. More of Gandhi's folk tradition will be discussed in chapter four; here it is sufficient to notice that he attempts to mold the textual tradition with the folk tradition.

Gandhi means to pay attention to both the textual tradition and the economic and social practices of the folk tradition because he believes neither can survive without the other. This does not mean that new meanings of ancient texts cannot emerge or that new economic and social practices cannot evolve within the folk tradition. What it does mean for Gandhi is that if the textual tradition is bankrupt, it cannot be practiced. Knowing that destitute, humiliated, confused men and women are not apt to transcend their disabilities, he fears that if the folk tradition is shattered, for whatever reason, there is no audience for the textual tradition. And when the latter speaks in the language of privilege and domination, it uses a vernacular that is not convincing to ordinary men and women. Gandhi means to have a reformed textual tradition animate the living practices of the folk tradition.

NOTES

1. Parekh, *Colonialism, Tradition, and Reform*, 95.

2. Said shows that the Orient is a comprehensive term that comfortably merges dozens of ancient and contemporary cultures from the Mediterranean to the Pacific. *Orientalism* (New York: Pantheon Books, 1978), particularly 31–43.

3. Said, *Orientalism*, 2–4. See also Dallmayr, *Beyond Orientalism*.

4. Although he finds defects in his tradition, Gandhi insists that "India is still, somehow or other, sound at the foundation." *Hind Swaraj*, ch. 13.

5. According to Parekh, Gandhi holds that "every tradition was a recourse, a source of valuable insights into the human condition, and part of a common human heritage. Every man was born into and shaped by a specific cultural

tradition which, as it were, constituted his original family." *Colonialism, Tradition, and Reform,* 20.

6. *Harijan,* April 6, 1934.

7. *Harijan,* January 18, 1939. On reading the Sermon on the Mount in the New Testament, Gandhi finds no real difference between it and the *Gita,* and concludes that "both must come from the same source." Chatterjee, *Gandhi's Religious Thought,* 50.

8. Gandhi reports that he does "not share the belief that there can or will be on earth one religion." *All Men are Brothers,* 72–73.

9. *Young India,* March 3, 1925.

10. One of Gandhi's major complaints about modernity is that it is preoccupied with the self and this is what it offers as its standard of judgment.

11. Gandhi asks, "Why blaspheme God by fighting over different media? Koran, Bible, Talmud, Avesta, or Gita? . . . Why make of books and formulas so many fetters to enslave rather than to unify?" G. N. Dhawan, *The Political Philosophy of Gandhi* (Bombay: Popular Book Depot, 1946), 9.

12. See Bondurant, *Conquest,* 152.

13. *Young India,* October 29, 1927.

14. Gandhi reports that he does "not regard God as a person . . . God is an Idea." *Harijan,* March 23, 1940.

15. *Harijan,* February 11, 1933.

16. According to Gandhi, "every living faith must have within itself the power of rejuvenation if it is to live." *Harijan,* September 28, 1935.

17. See Aristotle's discussion of the importance of the household, why it is not sufficient for the good life, and why its members cannot morally flourish if they remain fixed in their household. *Politics* (Chicago: University of Chicago Press, 1984), Bk. 1.

18. *Navajivan,* July 1, 1928, in Iyer, *Writings,* 2: 72.

19. See *Ethical Religion* (Madras: Ganesan, 1922), 34–59. Gandhi makes the same claim about the state and economy: Their conduct cannot simply be evaluated by what is good for them.

20. "I take pride in calling myself a Hindu because I find the term broad enough not merely to tolerate but to assimilate the teachings of prophets from all the four corners of the earth." Statement to the Press, November 4, 1932, in *Collected Works* 51: 145.

21. This creates problems for many orthodox Hindus. Consider Sankaran Nair's reactions to Gandhi's criticisms of Hinduism as then practiced: "There is scarcely any item in Gandhi's programme which is not a complete violation of everything preached by the foremost sons of India till 1929." Nandy observes that "Nair found that Gandhi was not the culmination of the nineteenth-century Indian 'renaissance;' he represented a disturbing, heretical position within Hinduism." Nandy, *Traditions, Tyranny, and Utopias,* 157–58.

22. Parekh finds that Gandhi's "spirituality was . . . intensely worldly." *Colonialism, Tradition, and Reform*, 73.

23. If India is to challenge British "morality," Gandhi insists, the most effective approach is not to boast "of the glorious past" of India but to "express the ancient moral glory in our own lives and let our lives bear witness to our past. . . . If we will but clean our houses, our palaces and temples of the attributes of wealth and show in them the attributes of morality, we can offer battle to any combinations of hostile forces without having to carry the burden of heavy militia." Speech, *The Leader*, December 25, 1916, in Iyer, *Writings*, 1: 361.

24. *Harijan*, August 12, 1933.

25. Raghavan Iyer writes that in the *Vedas*, "It is taken for granted that man is the meeting-point of the gods of the universe or its controlling forces. The world is a world of action, meant for action, and sustained by action. . . . In the *Upanishad* . . . [the] "stress is, however, on contemplation rather than on action. "[In the] *Gita* selfish desire, *kama*, is counted as the enemy of man and the root of all evil" and needs to be actively confronted. *Moral and Political Thought*, 108.

26. Bhikhu Parekh holds that "Gandhi's allegorical interpretation of the *Gita* was untenable" and cites Aurobindo's criticism of Gandhi's readings of the text in support of this position (*Colonialism, Tradition, and Reform*, 166–67). However, allegorical readings of texts are hardly novel or necessarily misleading. See Simon Weil's arresting rereading of Homer's *Iliad* as an antiwar, antiviolence text (*The Iliad* [Wallingford, Pa.: Pendle Hill, 1956]).

27. See Appendix One for selections from the *Gita* dealing with action and duty.

28. For a sample of non-Gandhian commentaries on the *Gita*, see Chatterjee, *Gandhi's Religious Thought*, 38, and A. L. Herman, *A Brief Introduction to Hinduism* (Boulder: Westview Press, 1991), 131–42.

29. Parekh, *Colonialism, Tradition, and Reform*, 153. Gandhi can agree with the terrorists, however, that the *Gita* teaches courage and not cowardice. See *Navajivan*, October 11, 1925, in Iyer, *Writings*, 1: 83.

30. "The Mahabharata and Ramayana . . . are undoubtedly allegories. . . . Each epic describes the eternal duel that goes on between the forces of darkness and of light." *Harijan*, October 3, 1936.

31. "Meaning of the *Gita*," *Navajivan*, October 11, 1925, in Iyer, *Writings*, 1: 81. Gandhi's treatment of the *Gita* also reflects his approach to the *Mahabharata* which, he claims, "is a profoundly religious book, largely allegorical, [and] in no way meant to be a historical record. It is a description of the eternal duel going on within ourselves" (*Young India*, October 1, 1925).

32. *Discourses on the Gita*, 4.

33. *Discourses on the Gita*, 5.

34. "I have endeavoured . . . in the light of my own experiences in trying to live the teaching of Hinduism as interpreted in the *Gita* to give an extended but in no way strained meaning to Hinduism, not as buried in its ample scriptures but as a living faith." *Harijan*, October 3, 1936. On another occasion, he declares that the "*Gita* . . . is my mother." *Harijan*, August 24, 1934.

35. "Only he can interpret the *Gita* correctly who tries to follow its teaching in practice, and the correctness of the interpretation will be in proportion to his success in living according to the teaching" (Letter to Santosh Maharaj, July 2, 1927, in Iyer, *Writings*, 1: 84). He reports that the text he offers stems from his efforts to "enforce the meaning [of the *Gita*] in my own conduct for an unbroken period of forty years." Introduction, Gandhi, *The Gita According to Gandhi*, ed. Mahadev Desai (Ahmedabad: Navajivan Publishing House, 1984), 127.

36. Letter to Santosh Maharaj, July 2, 1927, in Iyer, *Writings*, 1: 88.

37. Mehta, *Foundations*, 14. Mehta holds that the cosmic order arises out of very different but not oppositional phenomena "in which consciousness and matter, form and emptiness are blended together."

38. See Mehta, *Foundations*, 19.

39. In important ways, this reflects the republican position regarding decay and corruption. For writers like Aristotle, Machiavelli, and Rousseau, the good republic does not sustain itself out of its own goodness but requires the continued dedication and participation of its citizens. In their accounts, citizens are continually tempted to be concerned about themselves and their property and leave politics to others. When this happens, a civic void opens that is filled by the politically ambitious who grasp power for their own benefit, not the good of the whole. To forestall this possibility, republican writers insist that citizens continually renew their civic commitments through action.

40. See "Meaning of the *Gita*," *Navajivan*, October 11, 1925, in Iyer, *Writings*, 1: 82–83.

41. The following sampling from ancient texts indicates the status of dharma in Hindu thought:

"Dharma is the foundation of the whole universe. . . . By means of dharma one drives away evil. Upon dharma everything is founded. Therefore, dharma is called the highest good" (*Taittiriya Aranyaka* 10.79).

"For the sake of the promotion of strength and efficacy among beings, the declaration of dharma is made. Whatever is attended with nonviolence, that is dharma. Such is the fixed opinion" (*Mahabharata* 12.110.10).

"Better one's own dharma, though done imperfectly, than another's well performed. . . . To adopt the dharma of another is perilous" (*Bhagavad Gita* 3.35).

"Dharma, when violated, verily destroys; dharma, when preserved, preserves" (*Manu Smrti* 8.15).

These selections are taken from Ainslie Embree, *Sources of Indian Tradition* (New York: Columbia University Press, 1988), 217–18.

42. For a critical view of Gandhi's conception of dharma, see Parekh, *Gandhi's Political Philosophy*, 210.

43. See Iyer, *Thought*, 67–68.

44. Gandhi holds that "talents of all kinds are a trust and must be utilized for the benefit of society. The individual has no right to live unto himself. Indeed, it is impossible to live unto oneself. We fully live unto ourselves when we live unto society." "Ashram Observances in Action," in Iyer, *Writings*, 2: 600.

45. See *Bread Labour* (Ahmedabad: Navajivan Publishing House, 1960).

46. *Young India*, May 13, 1926. In our attitude to work, we can also emphasize, as Calvin does, the importance of the "calling" of each individual. Carpenters, on this account, do their best because the work of being a carpenter is worthwhile in itself and carpenters do their duty by performing their calling. While Gandhi can accept the Calvinist position that people should strive to be the best in their occupation, he would also find this position limited. On the one hand, it concentrates on the activity itself and not on its effects on others; on the other hand, it says little about the many aspects of a person's life outside work.

47. "Satyagraha—Not Passive Resistance," April 1917, in Iyer, *Writings*, 1: 44–50.

48. *Harijan*, June 1936.

49. *Young India*, January 8, 1925.

50. *Harijan*, December 5, 1936.

51. *Harijan*, November 16, 1935.

52. *Harijan*, November 16, 1935. Gandhi appreciates that traditional practices change. The key for him is that the core is maintained. He notices that a woman once could have "five husbands at one time and yet has been called 'chaste.' This is because in that age, just as a man could marry several wives, a woman (in certain regions) could marry several husbands. The code of marriage changes with time and place." "Talks to Ashram Women," 1926, in Iyer, *Writings*, 3: 392.

53. *Gita According to Gandhi*, 134.

54. *Gita According to Gandhi*, 134.

55. Gandhi, *Hindu Dharma*, 23.

56. "The Vedic ritual lays down countless ceremonies and rites with a view to attaining merit and heaven." However, these rituals "are worthless" because they are detached "from the essence of the Vedas." *Gita According to Gandhi*, 159.

57. *Young India*, November 25, 1926.

58. *Young India*, September 15, 1921.

59. "Talks to Ashram Women," 1926, in Iyer, *Writings*, 3: 394.

60. *Harijan*, February 24, 1940.

61. The dowry "system has to go. Marriage must cease to be a matter of arrangements made by parents for money. The system is intimately connected with caste. So long as the choice is restricted to a few hundred young men or young women of a particular caste, the system will persist no matter what is said against it. The girls or boys or their parents will have to break the bonds of caste if the evil is to be eradicated. All this means the education of a character that will revolutionize the mentality of the youth of the nation." *Harijan*, May 23, 1936.

62. *Harijan*, March 16, 1947.

63. *Young India,* December 17, 1928. As he sees matters, "Marriage is a natural thing in life, and to consider it derogatory in any sense is wholly wrong" *Harijan*, March 22, 1942.

64. *Harijan*, May 5, 1946.

65. The complete quotation is: "To force widowhood upon little girls is a brutal crime. . . . If our conscience was truly awakened there would be no marriage before 15, let alone widowhood. . . . If we would save Hinduism, we must rid ourself of this poison of enforced widowhood." *Young India*, August 5, 1926.

66. *Young India*, September 22, 1927. Earlier, he writes that enforced "widowhood imposed by religion or custom is an unbearable yoke and defiles the home . . . and degrades religion." *Young India*, August 5, 1926.

67. *Young India*, July 21, 1921.

68. Ashis Nandy, "Woman versus Womanliness," in *At the Edge of Psychology: Essays in Politics and Culture* (New Delhi: Oxford University Press, 1980), 38–39.

69. "Talks to Ashram Women," 1926, in Iyer, *Writings*, 3: 391.

70. "Talks to Ashram Women," 1926, in Iyer, *Writings*, 3: 391.

71. "Women workers should enroll women as voters, impart to them practical education, teach them to think independently, release them from the chains of caste that bind them so as to bring about the change in them which will complement efforts to realize woman's strength." *Harijan*, April 21, 1946.

72. "Talks to Ashram Women," 1926, in Iyer, *Writings*, 3: 394. A year earlier, he writes, "When woman, freed from man's snares, rises to the full height and rebels against man's legislation and institutions designed by him, her rebellion, no doubt nonviolent, will be none the less effective." *Young India*, April 16, 1925.

73. Colonialism is also heavily implicated in the breakdown of traditional culture in Gandhi's account. For him, colonialism in India is not merely exploitative, it is justificatory, presenting itself as a superior moral enterprise which embodies the highest stage of civilization. (See Nandy, *Traditions, Tyranny and Utopias*, 1987.) Its politics, science, morality, and technology are celebrated as the culmination of the historic process, and its industrial achievements are seen as the concrete reflection of its superiority. That the British feel themselves supe-

rior to the Indians is not altogether surprising. But what especially disturbs Gandhi is that many Indians should accept the British diagnosis of Indian society and adopt the implicit British prognosis that India will remain inferior until Indians leave their own tradition and become like the British.

74. *Navajivan*, June 27, 1920, in Iyer, *Writings*, 1: 307.

75. Nandy finds that Gandhi embodied "a critique of traditions coupled to a critique of modernity." *Traditions, Tyranny, and Utopias*, 157.

76. "Gandhi's Hinduism differed from that of some of his predecessors for the very reason [his critics] disapprove: it reaffirmed the non-canonical and the folk, on the assumption that, with such a base, Indians would cope better with modernity." Nandy, *Traditions, Tyranny, and Utopias*, 156.

77. Ashis Nandy argues that "Gandhi's was not a systematic theory outlining an alternative, non-modern, non-Western society. His was a vision which triggered imageries of another class of society, latent in the minds of men living in, or with, modernity." See Nandy, *Traditions, Tyranny and Utopias*, 129.

3

GANDHI'S CRITIQUE OF
MODERNITY

> Modern men were not thrown back upon this world but upon
> themselves. One of the most persistent trends in modern philosophy
> . . . has been an exclusive concern with the self, as distinguished
> from the soul or person or man in general. . . . World alienation has
> been the hallmark of the modern age.[1]

G andhi is one of the most resolute critics of modernity in the twentieth century. He sees modernity, unless unchecked, sweeping away everything that stands in its way as it tries to take "charge of the world."[2] Taking charge of the world implies that we can know how to organize the world (through science and rational, neutral theorizing) and how to implement our plans (through research, technology, and instrumental reasoning). At the heart of modernity is a questioning of and dissatisfaction with the present and a faith that reason and the changes it fosters will lead to a progressively better future.[3] In mounting his challenge, Gandhi confronts the foundational principles of the modern world and, in their place, he offers an idealized conception of traditional life in rural India, which he sees providing an alternative to the complexity, materialism, and poverty he detects in modern society.

The usual reading of Gandhi presents him as relentlessly antimodernist: Ramashray Roy, for example, argues that "Gandhi's critique of modern civilization is total."[4] I show why this is only partially true. Much that follows in this chapter will build on Gandhi's skepticism, and at times even disdain, of modernity. However, this is not the last word about his critique of modernity. Not only does he write about the ways it can be part of the good society, but his theory is also closely tied to such modern concepts as autonomy and equality.[5]

However much Gandhi builds on important modern conceptions such as secular equality and universal rights, his encounters with modernity do not prompt him to merge it with tradition. Unlike some of the leading Indian thinkers of the time, he does not want to synthesize modernity and Hinduism or to self-consciously borrow aspects of modernity. His reconceptualization of autonomy and equality, allied as they are with community, duty, and cohesion, are oppositional to modern ones, and he seeks to buttress these goods by mounting a critique of modernity and modernization that is simultaneously conservative and radical. He wants a reformed tradition to stand, erectly and resolutely, to confront modernity. Only in this way, he reasons, can the dangerous elements of modernity be exposed and the modern project be made to explain itself. In advancing his position, Gandhi seeks to complicate modernity and rob it of its certainty.

What follows is not a literal reading of Gandhi's attack on modernity and his defense of rural India which, I believe, misses his purpose. He knows modernity and modernization are here to stay, and he wants to question their confident claims to truth. For him, the pressing challenge is to disturb what is settled in the modern project in order to keep it from smothering the kinds of standards and practices he considers essential to autonomy. In this way, he hopes to make room for alternative logics that he thinks speak to the dignity and equality of persons in ways that modernity, by itself, cannot.[6] Gandhi's alternatives come from traditions but, unlike most conservatives and communitarians, he is not content to leave traditions where he finds them, including his own. The primary focus of this chapter is Gandhi's critique of modernity as a claim to progress and its reliance on reason and science. The following chapter takes up Gandhi's views of economic modernization.[7]

PROBLEMATIZING MODERNITY AND MODERNIZATION

In mounting his critique, Gandhi launches a broad indictment on modernity and modernization to expose them as constructions that come with heavy and often hidden costs. Uninterested in debating the intellectual roots of modernity, he concentrates on its character and effects. For him, modernity is powerfully seductive, and part of its attractiveness stems from its proclivity to speak to what Gandhi considers a natural but partial aspect of the human condition.[8] In appealing to our basic needs as well as newly acquired ones, modernity focuses on the immediate and the observable, matters that Gandhi thinks are necessary but hardly the highest aspects of our lives. He sees modernity addressing a person's interests or wealth (*artha*) and desires (*kama*),[9] but ignoring questions about a person's responsibilities in the wider world (dharma). In his view, modernity displaces other modes of thinking and moral points of reference, such as those found in religion, tradition, and the folkways of rural societies.[10] For him, these alternative modes of knowledge are not merely one option among many ways of knowing; he sees them addressing persistent moral issues about the nature of human beings in ways he thinks modernity cannot. This is so, Gandhi believes, because modernity has only partial ways of organizing knowledge and guiding practice; at best, it offers slices of knowledge but cannot collect its findings into a coherent whole. Moreover, he holds that modernity, fixed on present performance, is unwilling to learn from the past and unconcerned about the fate of real human beings in the future. Working with these claims, Gandhi finds that modernity does not have the resources to correct its own defects.

One problem Gandhi finds with modernity is that its standards are internal and, if it meets the standards it has set for itself, it declares itself a success. This Gandhi vehemently rejects. Goals and practices must be judged by more rigorous standards than provided by artha and kama or production and consumption. For Gandhi, a person's own tradition as mediated by a person's conscience provides men and women with grounded, external standards to judge. Holding that modernity has only self-referential performance standards to see how well it is doing, Gandhi finds that it is not alert to the costs it is assessing on other goods.

With many other critics, he questions the modern belief that rationality provides the only material we need to determine the truth.[11] For Gandhi, the issue is not that rationality has nothing to offer; he rejects traditional practices and ideas that he sees as "irrational," such as child marriages or untouchability. For him, however, reason can overstep what he takes to be its appropriate boundaries; it cannot always be the sole arbiter to truth claims.[12]

Rationalism is a hideous monster when it claims for itself omnipotence. Attribution of omnipotence to reason is as bad a piece of idolatry as is worship of stock and stone believing it to be God. I plead not for the suppression of reason, but [an appreciation of its inherent limits].[13]

In Gandhi's account, there are some things we know apart from reason. Our love, trust, forgiveness, and generosity do not flow primarily from reason. Indeed, for some rationalists these feelings may be misplaced; but not for Gandhi. He sees these dispositions and the actions that flow from them embodying the best in human beings. He also knows that the opposite of these dispositions is not always reason. When love or trust is involved, the choice is not invariably between them and reason but between love and hate or trust and suspicion. To assume that reason should always be the arbiter is to misunderstand both its strengths and limitations. Reason can speak to an impulse to love, for example, but after a while reason is exhausted and has nothing more to say. We love or we do not. Gandhi wants to untie love, trust, and forgiveness from calculation and join them to the developmental capacities of everyone.

As rationality is the hallmark of modernity, so increased productivity and technological innovations are the emblems of modernization.[14] New and ever-evolving methods of production, transportation, and communication bring more new goods to more people and promise even more in the future. But Gandhi finds that many of the apparent successes of modernity are not real successes at all because many of their purported benefits come at terrible costs. He sees the successes transforming society from a place of coherence and community to one that is becoming increasingly unintelligible and impersonal and where identities are becoming disjointed as time and space become fragmented. He argues that industrialization, the division of labor, and technological innovation contribute to severe unemployment and poverty, depriving people of their ability to meet their basic needs. Deeply troubled by what he takes to be the destruction of shared institutional practices which enable individuals to challenge necessity collectively, he sees people increasingly forced to address their basic needs on their own in the modern world.[15] For this reason, Gandhi concludes that although he knows that some aspects of modernity "are good, . . . I have examined its tendency in the scale of ethics" and finds, in making the material self the basis of judging good and evil, "the spirit of it is evil."[16] These concerns reflect his premise that modernity cannot harmoniously coexist with tradition and, unless there is a constant struggle on the part of tradition to defend its core principles and practices, modernity will win the day. Seeing modernity and modernization penetrating into every facet of life, he means to make his critique comprehensive.

THE DECLINE OF TRADITION:
SOME WESTERN CRITIQUES

Gandhi's analysis of modernity comes from a person who is part of an ancient, practiced tradition as well as of a colony where alien principles and practices are presented as superior to indigenous ones. In attacking British colonialism, Gandhi insists that political independence is an essential but only partial requirement for an India where everyone is autonomous. What is needed, according to Gandhi, is to challenge modernity with its emphasis on materialism and its destruction of community and tradition. This kind of argument, once robust in the West, has been overshadowed by the triumph of modernity in its birthplace, so I turn briefly to some of these early suspicions to show how Gandhi's voice blends into a broad critique of modernity as well as to demonstrate some of what is distinctive in his critical response.[17]

The Westerners with whom Gandhi is usually compared on this point are John Ruskin and Leo Tolstoy, and the reason is that Gandhi openly acknowledges that he has learned much from them.[18] Each celebrates an idealized rural economy, simple social relations, and manual labor, issues that are central to Gandhi's outlook. Here I consider a different group of Western writers who share his impulse to problematize modernity. For each of these critics, there is the fear that a narrow materialism and bloated individualism are increasingly marking the modern age.

In many ways, Gandhi's attack on modernization parallels Rousseau's reading of civilization in *The Discourses on the Origins of Inequality.*[19] Although their respective criticisms rest on different theoretical groundings, they see modernization exacting heavy costs, and in very different ways they offer alternatives to safeguard the autonomy of everyone. Rousseau begins his narrative in a state of nature where everyone is free and equal. When we leave its simplicity and innocence and march down the road of complexity, dependence, and acquisitiveness, Rousseau detects individuals losing their equality and freedom. For him, they travel this road because they deceive themselves about what is important and believe they can remain free in spite of growing inequalities and dependencies. Rousseau puts the matter starkly when he writes that he can show a people how they can become wealthy, educated, militarily strong, artistically accomplished, and scientifically advanced *or* he can tell them how to be free. But, he insists, he cannot tell them how to have both.[20] In many ways, this is Gandhi's message to India, and he, with Rousseau, wants people to think the prize worth having is freedom.

For Rousseau, we are implicated in our own misery and inequality because we do not see the costs of the new order. We cannot imagine doing without the products it offers because we think they will make us happy but, finding that they do not satisfy, we continually seek something new that promises to appease our desires. In his account, civilization is constantly constructing artificial needs and artificial divisions among individuals. In the process, it slowly but inexorably repeals the equality, freedom, and innocence Rousseau imagines in the early state of nature. The unceasing invention of new tools, the discovery of new modes of making a living, and the appearance of great wealth combine to produce subordination and dependency. For Rousseau, the misery, alienation, and inequality generated by civilization can only be overcome with the small, simple, participatory community he offers in the *Social Contract*.[21]

A century later, another critique of modernity is offered by Ferdinand Toinnes who juxtaposes culture and society, tradition and rationality, community and market as incommensurable pairs. Like Gandhi, he fears that the foundations of traditional communities are seriously threatened by the impersonality, rationalism, and materialism characteristic of modernity; people no longer lead lives that are stable and coherent. Toinnes argues that we have traded in our ability to conduct honest relations with one another in a robust community for a calculating, instrumental society where attention to personal advantage is the pervasive standard of the day. The affliction he finds in the modern age comes with individuals no longer concerned about their own moral character or that of others but rather with their economic worth.[22]

Max Weber's critique has a different emphasis, examining the rationalization of modern capitalism and the decline of traditional "worldviews." He discovers a relentless process of disenchantment in a world growing formalistic and legalistic. As Weber sees it, the "intellectualization" of the modern world "means that principally there are no incalculable forces that come into play, but rather that one can, in principle, master all things by calculation. This means that the world is disenchanted."[23] For him, technical and scientific reasoning has swept aside old certainties, and individuals now have to determine for themselves "which of the warring gods we should serve." Bereft of tradition and religion, individuals are now thrown on themselves to make choices, which, according to Weber, is "the fate of an epoch which has eaten of the tree of knowledge."[24]

With the magical and spiritual having fled the modern world, Weber finds that some reach to science to fill the void, but for many it provides no ready direction. The latter group craves "not only religious experience, but experience as such." The problem, Weber despairs, is that this takes people to "the spheres of the irrational, the only spheres that intellectualism has not yet touched." Such a move to emancipation, however, "may well bring about the very opposite of what" is desired, namely a dangerous fanaticism.[25]

It is in Nietzsche's critique that we encounter the most daring and sweeping indictment of modernity. He sees the world at a crossroads with the death of God that comes with modernity. Once the touchstone for identity and transcendence, God had provided humanity with standards of good and evil. But in the modern era, God starves to death, neglected by mortals too busy with the affairs of the material world to nourish the spiritual. Lacking any reason to move beyond their own security and pleasure, human beings are now unable to even think about transcendence, much less create a meaning for themselves beyond the mundane.

Nietzsche sees individuals in the modern age packed into a mass society marked by conformity and materialism. There, individuals are governed by a proceduralism that celebrates instrumental reason and science.[26] After the death of God, Nietzsche finds that science provides information but no meaning. The state assumes the moral role that God once occupied. This "new idol" becomes the universal law-giver for society and promises security and contentment to small men in return for their obedience. And Nietzsche sees the market busy with activities that replace the imaginative and spiritual in a search for material comfort.

In modern, mass society, he finds individuals are unable to muster the traditional virtues now scattered among the rubble or to know how to create new meaning for themselves. As a consequence, they invite an unthinking nihilism into their lives. For Nietzsche, the time of the last man—the person preoccupied with security, order and pleasure—is impending, and human dignity is in danger of expiring in a world of consumption and nihilism.[27]

Alexis de Tocqueville's account of the decline of tradition and its consequences is filled with irony and paradox.[28] He sees tradition decaying before the pervasive force of equality, by which he means the idea that each individual wants to be the arbiter of what is good and true. Not only does the divine right of kings fall before this form of equality, so do once robust traditions. Tocqueville fears this means that individuals in the modern world are left more and more to themselves to find meaning. In his account, identity in the most modern political society, the United States, is expressed with an unbounded individualism which uniformly defines its own success by reference to materialism. In a world growing more conformist, Tocqueville insists the challenge of the modern era is how to protect autonomy.

Tocqueville understands the relationship between autonomy and modernity in very different ways than the one usually posited in Anglo–American constructions which emphasize liberty as the absence of coercion and modernity as liberating. For him, as well as Gandhi, freedom of action presupposes the ability of people to think about who they are as moral agents and to judge the world around them. Both Tocqueville and Gandhi fear that in the modern world, there is the oppressive danger that individuals blindly follow the norms of production and consumption and are left without an independent standard to judge. For this reason, Gandhi can readily agree with Western critics such as Tocqueville that when people conform to materialistic norms, their lives lack depth, reveal a crude presentism, and make little room for an extended social self.

In a sense, the Gandhian critique of modern society is part of a continuing intellectual and moral exercise in both the East and the West, but there is something highly distinctive about his work. He clearly parts company with Rousseau whose noble savage stands alone rather than in a cosmos and whose heavy reliance on the general will to order social relationships challenges Gandhi's argument that decentralization and diversity serve to guarantee autonomy. Unlike Weber's efforts to tame the excesses of the rationalistic, bureaucratic state with new forms of ethical leadership or Nietzsche's doctrine of the overman who creates his own values and meaning amidst the ruins of tradition, Gandhi tries to vitalize tradition to protect autonomy. However, he is not another Toinnes who wants to retire into insular enclaves of tradition shielded from modernization. For Gandhi, withdrawal signals the success of modernity because, as he understands it, tradition is not a lonely exercise but must be practiced with other members of the community if it is to maintain its vitality.

Gandhi's own view of traditional culture also departs from most conservative critiques, such as those offered by Edmund Burke and Thomas Carlyle, who want to reclaim the past without changing it much. To rely on a tradition to guide practice means to Gandhi that tradition must eliminate those corrupting practices that have intruded over time and debased its core moral vision concerning the dignity and worth of all persons. In this way, he credits traditionalism with a power and vitality that Tocqueville thinks has been exhausted in the modern world. For Tocqueville, there is an inevitability about the march of modernity, tradition cannot recover its earlier strength, and the best that can be expected is an accommodation between a materialistic individualism and the autonomous citizen.

What is unique in Gandhi among the critics I have discussed is his conviction that it is still possible to work within his own tradition to assure the dignity of individuals. He confronts modernity and modernization not only by challenging their basic assumptions and denying their stories of success and superiority but also by celebrating the traditions that modernity considers inferior and wants to discard. His problematized reading of modernity and modernization is meant to open up a debate that many, particularly in the West, think has been closed; in this way, he makes tradition a radical force to critique and interrogate both modernity and itself.

THE NEW HISTORY

Gandhi reflects much Hindu thinking that emphasizes that the past is embodied in tradition rather than history.[29] For Gandhi, it is possible to transport the past into present-day activities with tradition; with history, however, the past remains past. Its distant subject matter provides objects to be studied but does not have much to say about contemporary action. Working with these assumptions, Gandhi seeks to make tradition a guide for daily life, something he does not think possible with the chronologies and catalogues of great events that dominate history.[30] For him, the subject matter of history is about the way the cosmic order has been disturbed and how the ordinary, peaceable relations among individuals dissolve. On his account:

> History as we know it is a record of the wars of the world, and so there is a proverb among Englishmen that a nation which has no history, that is has no war, is a happy nation. . . . [If wars] were all that happened in the world, it would have been ended long ago.[31]

Gandhi complains that history, as the chronicle of violence, ignores the "natural activities" of individuals.[32] It "does not record the day to day incidents of love and service."[33] But ordinary human beings in their ordinary activities are important to Gandhi, and he means to show how tradition enables them to understand how to live in dignity, something he finds missing in modern history. The history written in the modern era is a metanarrative about progress and carries the ring of objectivity and the aura of authenticity.[34] The heroes, their battles, and their conquests recorded in history, after all, actually happened, and their stories are organized around "great" events. For this reason, nineteenth-century historians typically record the deeds of inventors, explorers, and heroes who discover meaning and places where there had only been darkness or ignorance previously or who conquer and enlighten the primitive and backward. As a metanarrative, modern history tells readers that what is recorded is truly important and what is discarded is simply irrelevant or unnecessary to the grand account of progress.[35]

Whatever its effects in shaping understanding in the West, history as metanarrative comes into a radical conflict with a cosmological outlook in places such as India. The issue is not primarily that Western historians emphasize different places and actors than their Indian counterparts and deny validity to mythic, fabled, or spiritual figures or events that occur outside conventional time and space. Of greater significance is the way history as the metanarrative of progress provides an antithetical (and not merely different) alternative to traditional ways of understanding the world, the people in it, and oneself.[36] In modern versions of history, the ordinary reader stands apart from the great events and great men who are admired but unreachable; the modern account makes readers into spectators of people unlike themselves and of awe-inspiring events they can never repeat. When they look back in time, they see a story of change which is converted into the story of progress, and they learn how much better off they are than preceding generations who are trapped in their traditions and blind to their own ignorance. Enamored of progress, this metanarrative does not bother to assess the costs of change or consider what is being discarded, confusing greater control over nature with control over oneself and mistaking new powers over nature for wisdom. For Gandhi, replacing tradition with history means people no longer have standards they can incorporate into their own lives. What they are given in the metanarrative of progress is the claim that the present is better than the past and the future will be better still.

Fearing that many Indians are finding the metanarrative attractive, Gandhi means to challenge its validity as well as reveal its remainders. On Gandhi's reading, traditional Hinduism places activity over passivity, proclaims the importance of the ordinary, and is concerned with how people lead a coherent, autonomous life nonviolently.[37] More than that, Gandhi wants to enable ordinary people to be heroes in their lives as they contend against the forces of domination as well as with their own pride.

For all of his complaints about history, Gandhi offers his own brief sketch of human history in which progress occupies an important role. He sees the human race evolving from savagery, barbarism, and violence to cooperation, interdependence, and nonviolence as practiced in local settings. "Our remote ancestors were cannibals," he writes, and were replaced by hunters, then farmers, and finally villagers. Then, they became members "of a community and a nation. All these are signs of progressive *ahimsa*." However, Gandhi's historical sketch is not a narrative about an unbroken path of improvement. In the same article, he argues that "nothing in this world is static, everything is kinetic."[38] As he sees matters, the conflict between good and evil never ends because pride is always ready to express itself somewhere. Armed with these propositions, Gandhi sees a "progressive" pattern that cannot escape periodic obstacles but can overcome each expression of pride through struggle.

In this way, Gandhi's "real" history is meant to be repetitious and restorative, rotating around cooperation and decay in local settings.

Is not Gandhi offering his own metanarrative when he reaches back to the ancient texts such as the *Gita*? In one way, the answer is yes. He converts Hinduism into a countermetanarrative to offer its explanations of community and change, its efforts at inclusion and nonviolence, its appreciation of diversity rather than uniformity, and its concern with both the spiritual and the contingent.[39] What is particularly striking in Gandhi's countermetanarrative when contrasted with the modern metanarrative is his reliance on an integrating cosmology designed to celebrate and protect the integrity and interrelatedness of the parts and the whole. Equally arresting is his insistent position that Hinduism cannot be converted into a convincing countermetanarrative unless it reforms and democratizes itself by ridding itself of its own accumulated rigidities and hierarchies.

MODERNITY AND THE DEATH OF THE COSMOS

Whatever its story, modern history claims to be objective and neutral, penetrating below and beyond the world of appearance and accident to unearth reality. Its claims to truth, objectivity, and neutrality are what Gandhi most wants to challenge and part of his project is to call into question the entire modern project. He continues this interrogation when he takes up the issue of modern science.[40]

Some of Gandhi's most discordant, some would say most outlandish, comments concern his understanding and criticism of modern science and technology.[41] Particularly in his early works, he warns Indians about accepting modern technology and, like some other earlier critics, deprecates what many take to be its crowning achievements, such as those found in medicine. Later I show how Gandhi attempts to make room for modern technologies.[42] Here, I want to establish that he finds something inherently disturbing about modern science and wants to struggle with what he takes to be its dangerous side. In confronting modern science as he does, Gandhi seeks to join it with ethics, asking how it affects the capacity of individuals to be self-governing in much the same way he links politics, economics, and social practices to ethics.

He is dismayed at the new and horrifying forms of death and destruction that come with modern science, but that is the not the primary reason he attacks it.[43] For him, its greatest danger comes from its mode of thinking: sweeping aside alternative ways of understanding the cosmos, morality, and oneself.[44] An example of his disdain for modern science can be seen in his blistering critique of modern medicine in *Hind Swaraj*.[45] He finds that the promise of prolonging life and curing disease encourages people to believe that biological life is itself the highest good. Equipped with this understanding, Gandhi argues, people today are disinclined to ask questions about what constitutes the best moral life. Moreover, he sees them increasingly failing to take responsibility for what they do to themselves when they believe that they can pay a physician and be cured.[46] In addition, he finds that modern patients hand themselves over to their physicians and transfer control over their own bodies to others. In his critique, Gandhi anticipates some contemporary critics who find that modern medical discourse is presented as objective and unchallengeable (by the lay public) and that this same discourse is a construction that often masks political outlooks. Several writers on women's health issues, for example, find that various diagnoses reproduce and reinforce conventional stereotypes of gender and fail to address many health issues confronting women.[47]

But more is involved here. To understand life and the living, modern science turns to death. In *The Birth of the Clinic*, Michel Foucault argues that modern medicine looks at death in a new way. Wanting to prolong life and cure the sick body so a healthy life can be lived, modern medicine is, on Foucault's account, highly dependent on autopsies performed immediately after death. The reason is that such medical investigations can tell us more about pathologies and how to respond to them than if only the living are studied. However, Foucault argues, this comes at a cost. No longer do we carry the view that "the knowledge of life was based on the essence of the living." Now, the "knowledge of life finds its origin in the destruction of life."[48] It is this movement away from life, how it is lived, and what makes for a good life (and not merely a healthy life) that disturbs Gandhi.[49]

His criticism of modern science is political and moral and, in this way, parallels that of Hannah Arendt's.[50] Like Arendt's, his argument with modernity and modern science must be seen as a central feature of his work. Each means to critique modern science with criteria outside of boundaries established by scientists for scientists and, therefore, thought inappropriate to the task. Both Gandhi and Arendt find that the discoveries of modern science carry no inherent or compelling instructions or limits on their use, but how they are applied is of the greatest consequence.[51] This is particularly so when science stands above judgment. For his part, Gandhi finds that "we cannot live without science, if we keep it in its right place," and for this to happen, science must be judged by standards that are often independent of science.[52]

Several features of modern science are particularly troubling to Gandhi and Arendt. In the first place, it has no pretensions toward understanding the world as a whole; it carves out parts of the world for investigation.[53] Its great discoveries occur within distinctive fields, such as microbiology, nuclear physics, or quantum mechanics, with new findings expanding or replacing prior understanding of particular phenomena. In the process, a once-integrated whole collapses. Second, modern science is dependent on a method or process that discards the particular and contingent in favor of general rules and explanations. Third, it is claimed that modern science is ethically neutral.[54]

The division of the world into discrete fields of inquiry has produced incredibly impressive but unrelated bodies of knowledge in the biological and physical sciences. Scientists know more about their specialties than ever before, but, increasingly, scientists in one field have little to say to those in other fields. With no master science to hold discrete and often unrelated fragments of knowledge together, and with each of the specialties undermining traditional conceptions of a unified whole, modern science inevitably leads to the fragmentation of the cosmos.[55] In doing so, new remainders are created. No longer do people understand how they are connected to one another (if at all), and little room is left for science to contribute to a discussion of what it means to lead a purposeful life.[56] For Gandhi, humanity is about choosing, whereas science is about a law-like regularity.

Gandhi sees the universalizing impulse of modernity as inhospitable to plurality.[57] In its search for general rules, modern reason seeks to identify relevant variables and discard superfluous ones that carry no explanatory weight. What remains outside of the realm of the verifiable is unimportant to the enterprise that seeks to generate theory that can be replicated with the same result by distant, neutral strangers. Gandhi fears that such an outlook decenters not only traditional morality but also common sense and reason, and ultimately the autonomous self, which becomes a remainder. For her part, Arendt argues that science has taught us not to trust our sense and reason.[58] She is particularly troubled with the claim that the "faculty of reasoning can only happen to be the same in everybody."[59]

For Gandhi, modern science is wholly inadequate to serve as the epistemological arbiter of how the discrete parts should be joined together. In his view, plurality simultaneously requires distinctiveness and unity, individual integrity, and cooperation. He is concerned that the universalizing impulse of modernity threatens diversity as well as enervates the quest for moral judgment, and it does this with its emphasis on procedures that require detachment and indifference.[60] Such modern claims represent the antithesis of everything Gandhi desires. Morality, in his account, is no more revealed through the scientific method than through a blind faith in a sacred text.[61]

Moral truth, he argues, is not discovered by disengagement or neutrality but comes through an active involvement in the world, and he wants to apply the same ethical standards to the institutionalized power of modern science that he assigns to his own tradition.[62] For him, any claim to the truth must show that its application contributes to the harmony of the cosmos and individual autonomy and not to the loss of control of the things that should be most important to people.[63] As he sees it, "science is essentially one of those things in which theory alone is of no value whatsoever." What counts, he claims, are the uses to which science is applied.[64]

Gandhi rejects the premise that science and ethics are separate; that ethics only has something to say when something goes wrong.[65] He fears that such reasoning assigns science the superior position, relegates ethics to a subordinate realm, and absolves people of responsibility. For Gandhi, the primary issue is not how we "take charge of the world" but how we live with nature and take control of ourselves.[66] In challenging the modern aspiration to conquer nature, Gandhi does not claim that every discovery of the modern era falls somewhere between the valueless and the corrupt. On the contrary, he acknowledges that certain scientific and technological discoveries should be incorporated into Indian society, but only on the proviso that human beings control the process rather than are controlled by it. Confronting modern science this way, he again shows he is more concerned with its applications than with modern science itself.[67]

In raising the objections he does, Gandhi seeks to challenge modernity, and he does this by summoning allies that have been thought to have grown weary and paltry. Knowing that modern science will not disappear, he wants to convince people they must judge the entire modern project by its consequences to the autonomy of persons. He wants people to appropriate what is valuable in modernity, not in a random but in a deliberative way, knowing their purposes in borrowing what they do.[68] He knows full well there is no turning back to an earlier time when science did not occupy the place it does today. But he refuses to allow science to proceed without requiring its advocates to explain themselves.

THE ADAPTABILITY OF TRADITIONS

Is it possible to adapt traditional standards with modernity? There are two different answers in modern Western theory: one holds that adaptability is impossible, and the other finds that what is valuable in the past can be accommodated to modernity. The former holds that the march of progress requires the rational conquest of the blind faith it finds embedded in tradition. From this perspective, the penchant of traditionalism for stability, continuity, and unity is antithetical to the modern temper, with its celebration of change, its skepticism of the ancient, and its heavy emphasis on rationality.[69]

These critics see tradition as an enemy of freedom and reason because it is understood as directing choice and relieving a person of moral responsibility. On this account, tradition plays a deterministic and restrictive role in thought and action. Hobbes's attack on tradition is not the first but represents one of the most powerful. For him, the dead hand of the past serves as an obstacle to rationality, and only when emancipated from the shackles of tradition, can the thoughts serve as "spies and scouts," free to roam in service of an independent self.

An alternative reading of tradition is supplied by Locke who argues that secular reason and Christianity are compatible with one another and reinforce each other.[70] For him, unguided reason is insufficient for a moral life and is unable to show people that they need, in his language, "to deny themselves." To supplement reason, Locke offers religion and ethics to provide reliable guides. By extension, he and many others think that what is discarded is not intrinsically valuable. Locke's difficulty, however, lies in the fragility of moral standards in a world fraught with intense social and economic change. His solutions are simply unable to combat, much less resist, modern institutional incentives that reward people for not denying themselves. Locke's strong defense of religious and ethical standards is sincere, but his solution is frail and inadequate in a changing world.[71] This is the legacy Gandhi sees modernity bestowing on India. Good intentions to maintain a vitalized, coherent, practiced tradition are bound to fail unless Indians are willing to challenge modernity and defend their tradition.

For Gandhi, modernity and modernization are unlike any of the earlier challenges to traditional Hinduism.[72] Previous ones, such as Buddhism and Islam, are about which kind of spirituality should prevail, not whether any should. Those who leave Hinduism for one of its alternatives do not reconstitute many of their outlooks and routines and the ways they meet necessity. And Hindus who remain with their tradition are not radically reconstituted when many of their neighbors convert. With modernity, however, we are introduced to radically new practices and self-understandings that at best marginalize traditional forms of knowledge, action, and identity. This is what makes modernity so discordant to Gandhi who finds that earlier patterns of adaptability and resilience no longer apply.[73] Because the prospect for an accommodation between traditionalism and modernity is elusive for Gandhi, he insists that the need for struggle intensifies in the modern world. The genie of modernity is out of the bottle and there is no way to return to settled traditions as premodern generations had done. For this reason, Gandhi expects people to be self-conscious about the world in ways that were unnecessary before.

Why should we expect that modernity and modernization will replace tradition rather than have it go the other way? Gandhi's answer is tied to necessity. What makes ordinary people ordinary is that they cannot escape necessity; they are not like Socrates' philosopher-kings who leave behind their possessions and families in their quest for wisdom. Ordinary people are concerned about their well-being, and Gandhi sees nothing strange or wrong about this; for him, the issue is how people frame and act on their concerns. As he sees matters, modernity and modernization have invaded the economy and set new terms for meeting necessity.

As much as he wants a cosmic harmony to remain a beacon to help people respond to modernity, he knows that a return to a stable, harmonious society is elusive and the quest to find one is dangerous and disguises the real problem. For Gandhi, tradition and modernity cannot harmoniously adjust and adapt to each other and the task is to promote a self-conscious tension between them. This is why he wants to approach modernity not with an eye to synthesis or accommodation but struggle. The alternative, he fears, is a fatalism that feeds the worst features of a self-indulgent modernity and a complacent tradition.

INTERROGATING MODERNITY

The contest Gandhi draws between tradition and modernity is about autonomy. The weakening of moral standards, the impersonality of the city, the emphasis on productivity, the acceptance of unemployment and underemployment, and the explosion of consumerism are understood by Gandhi as dangerous intrusions.[74] The very magnitude of the changes he witnesses poses a greater threat to his ideal of Indian civilization than colonialism by itself.[75] Gandhi sees modernity presenting itself as the highest form of historical development, meeting many of the short-term material needs it has created and delegitimizing alternative conceptions of the good. For him, modernity is not benign, leaving work, family, and social relations intact and standards of self-worth untouched. The profound moral transformation he attributes to modernity and modernization stems from its destruction of traditional standards, institutions, and practices. Gandhi's critique is not that modernity transforms people who are innately good into individuals who are thoroughly corrupt. For him, the great danger is that people are becoming morally numb. Transfixed on production and consumption as self-justifying goals and on new ways of meeting necessity, he fears that people do not understand that they are being morally redefined.

I have framed Gandhi's critique of modernity and modernization around his defense and celebration of autonomy. By contrasting the transcendent qualities that Gandhi locates in a tradition with the efficiencies and materialism he sees residing in modernity, I have juxtaposed two very different ways of self-understanding and action. For Gandhi, the issue centers on how traditional institutional frameworks can overcome their own deficiencies in order to confront the disabling aspects he sees in modernity and modernization. The issue becomes, then, not about which framework should triumph but how the excesses of each can be resisted.[76]

Gandhi is not content to embrace his own tradition without testing it and he continually challenges some of its most common practices (untouchability and fatalism) and basic assumptions (the violent hero). He repeatedly argues that each generation must understand how the foundational principles of its tradition should be applied in ways that recognize the interdependence and dignity of everyone. To do this, Gandhi wants each generation to confront the remnants of its own tradition that it finds unjust. Recognizing that modernity and modernization have the resources to detect many traditional deficiencies, he insists they do not have the capacity to provide a coherent alternative. He fears that even the most generous impulses in modern society are bound to fail; efforts to save autonomy by redefining it—by forcing it to adjust and adapt, accepting the commercial standards of the day—leave autonomy fractured and agents incoherent and vulnerable. For Gandhi, these countless adjustments bring the most fundamental (and fearful) transformations imaginable: people no longer govern themselves but are directed and defined by the impersonal institutions of modernity and, worst of all, many do not care.

HOW MODERN IS GANDHI?

That Gandhi is a defender and champion of a reformed, traditional Hinduism is clear. And it is obvious that he offers a wide-ranging indictment of modern rationality, science, and technology. For some, these positions show Gandhi to be inflexible and blind to the positive aspects of modernity. For others, Gandhi borrows more from modernity than is usually acknowledged.[77]

To advance this latter argument, it is helpful to consider historical Hinduism. As has already been argued, there is no recognized orthodoxy or text that adequately captures Hinduism but, as Bhikhu Parekh argues in his political analysis of Hinduism, there are some important teachings and practices that cut across caste, region, and time.[78] One is dharma (or duty), which is woven in and out of the major Hindu texts. As people perform their dharma, society is said to be a unified, organic whole. However, dharma is assigned not so much to individuals, as Parekh sees it, but to social categories, that is to castes. The members of each caste have their assigned responsibilities, and Parekh finds "detailed rules governing almost every aspect of human conduct" and that infractions are severely punished, particularly for the lower castes.[79] Moreover, he holds that "almost the entire Hindu tradition of political thought was based on the unquestioned assumption of a close alliance between the two highest castes."[80] The historical Hinduism that Parekh unfolds is the one that Gandhi wants to reform. It is "basically inegalitarian;" its pluralism covers groups, not individuals; and it "is largely uncritical and apologetic of the established order."[81]

The views of Gandhi about equality and autonomy may have metaphysical counterparts in ancient Hinduism, but the concepts lack clarity, specificity, and power in these texts. As used by Gandhi, equality and liberty take on much of the character they do in modern claims about legal, political, and social equality and autonomy.[82] That Gandhi and others refuse to buy all of the goods offered by modernity and modernization and are critical of many of them does not mean that he sees nothing important in his enforced encounters with British colonialism. On the one hand, he detects a failure of colonialism to treat Indians with the same standards of equality and dignity that the modern project claims are due everyone. On the other hand, he simultaneously sees a disparity in his own society between its social practices and what he comes to believe is due to all Indians.

In advancing claims for equality and autonomy for all Indians, Gandhi uses his own idioms, not Western ones, relocating and redefining modern concepts beyond formal equality and rights. He also gives a larger space to civil society than found in most Western theories; questions the acquisitive, materialistic impulses common in many versions of modernity; and gives equality and autonomy a transcendent, spiritual quality. In his unique way, he grafts fragments of modernity to his own tradition as he radically redefines autonomy and expands expectations for individual dharma, laying the basis for his theory of nonviolent civil disobedience.

The modern society that Gandhi surveys has become a place where efficiencies overwhelm individuals, the household is under siege, artificialities abound, nothing is fixed, and social practices and moral principles are increasingly uncomplimentary and often contradictory. In such a world, he finds people are lost, and he wants to provide them with materials that serve as a guide. In this way, he seeks to empower individuals to guard their own autonomy in the confusion and dangers he detects in the modern world.

That Gandhi borrows much from modernity for his project cannot disguise his continued dependency on tradition and his skepticism of modernity. His debts to modernity never cancel his serious doubts about many of its central assumptions, particularly its faith in progress and reason; its reliance on universalism, neutrality, and proceduralism; its aspiration to control nature; its tolerance of violence; and its ready acceptance of change and fragmentation. Indeed, Gandhi appeals to many because he borrows important principles from modernity without letting modernity set the terms of his discourse. He thinks that by struggling with modernity, he can chasten it. Gandhi's struggle seeks to force it to explain itself—to recognize that its answers must not only satisfy the criteria it has established for itself but must speak to other logics as well.

NOTES

1. Arendt, *The Human Condition*, 254.

2. Gandhi could readily agree with William Connolly's observations that modernity refers to a disposition about "taking charge of the world" and that with "modernity, modernization is always under way" (*Political Theory and Modernity* [Oxford: Basil Blackwell, 1988], 2–3).

3. The claim inherent in modernity is not that each and every change is progressive and therefore beneficial, only that the pattern of change over time carries these properties.

4. *Self and Society* (New Delhi: Sage, 1985), 38.

5. See Anthony Parel, "Introduction," in *Hind Swaraj*, ed. Anthony Parel (Cambridge: Cambridge University Press, 1997), xvi.

6. See Pantham, "Gandhi's Intervention in Modern Moral-Political Discourse," 58.

7. Concepts such as modernity and modernization are not only complex; they are often given such different interpretations that it is difficult to know what is at stake. I consider modernity to take reason to be the basis of knowledge over other alternatives, such as tradition. With modernity, the rational self becomes the arbiter of good and evil and rationality identifies what is true and

false. Over time, the Enlightenment concept of reason as a detachment from contingency gave way to instrumental reason or the reason of problem-solving. Modernity, then, can be considered a way of thinking just as religion or tradition provides us with its own ways of conceptualizing the person, what is due to a person, and what the person owes others.

I take modernization to be the institutionalization of modernity. Economically, modernization is characterized by industrialization, the division of labor, and technological innovation. Politically, it tends toward centralization, bureaucracy, and the rise of the nation-state. Socially, modernization promotes mobility and change and is characterized by urbanization, extensive communication and transportation, and the replacement of the extended family with the nuclear one.

8. For this reason, he concludes that modern civilization is "a civilization only in name." *Hind Swaraj*, ch. 5.

9. For Gandhi, "The distinguishing characteristic of modern civilization is an infinite multiplicity of human wants" (*Young India*, June 2, 1927). According to Gandhi, "The mind is a restless bird; the more it gets the more it wants and still remains unsatisfied. The more we indulge our passions the more unbridled they become" (*Hind Swaraj*, ch. 13).

10. See Nandy, *Traditions, Tyranny, and Utopia.*

11. Gandhi does not deny the importance of reason in understanding oneself and the broader world. However, he holds it is only one way of organizing ideas and, in some cases, not the most important one. For him, Hindu cosmology provides an account of the organization of the world, its fixity and fluidity, and the relationship of human beings to the cosmos as well as each other. For Gandhi, this provides a grounding for reason but is not something that unaided reason can discover by itself. For a discussion of the role of reason in Hindu philosophy, see Mehta, *Foundations of Indian Political Thought*, ch. 2. Also see Dalton, *Indian Idea of Freedom.*

12. He repeatedly insists that morality must meet some minimal rational standards. See Thomas Pantham, "On Modernity, Rationality, and Morality: Habermas, and Gandhi," *Indian Journal of Social Science* 2 (1988): 187–208; and Parekh, *Gandhi's Political Philosophy*, 74.

13. *Young India*, June 27, 1939.

14. For helpful discussions of Gandhi's view of economic modernization, see Nandy, *Traditions, Tyranny, and Utopia*; Parekh, *Colonialism, Tradition and Reform*; and Pantham, "Gandhi, Nehru, and Modernity," 98–121. I take up Gandhi's critique of modernization in the next chapter.

15. Because of the magnitude of the problem, Gandhi is impatient with those who want to reconfigure or remodel modernization and modernity, often along state-socialist lines. For Gandhi, state-socialism hardly solves the problem; indeed he sees it introducing its own unique set of difficulties. For representative

criticisms of state-socialism by Gandhi, see *Young India*, December 11, 1924; *Young India*, November 15, 1928; *Young India*, March 26, 1931; and *Harijan*, September 28, 1934. For Gandhi's own view of nonstate-socialism, see *Socialism of My Conception*.

16. *Indian Opinion*, May 21, 1920, in Iyer, *Writings*, 1: 298.

17. According to Ashis Nandy, "Gandhi was not *one* single critic of the modern West; he represented a whole class of critics of modern civilization. And like many others in the class he can be interpreted or reinterpreted in more than one way. To deduce one final supervening Gandhi from his life and work would be both anti-Gandhian and self-defeating." *Traditions, Tyranny, and Utopia*, 129.

18. See Martin Green, *Tolstoy and Gandhi* (New York: Basic Books, 1983). Also see Brown, *Gandhi: Prisoner of Hope*; Chatterjee, *Gandhi's Religious Thought*; Iyer, *Moral and Political Thought*; and Bondurant, *Conquest*. For books by Ruskin and Tolstoy read by Gandhi, see Pandiri, *A Comprehensive, Annotated Bibliography*, 1: 298–99, 304–6.

19. Jean-Jacques Rousseau, *The Social Contract and Discourses* (London: Dent, 1983), 27–114.

20. See J. J. Rousseau, *Government of Poland* (Indianapolis: Library of Liberal Arts, 1972).

21. Rousseau's discussion of the disappearance of innocence parallels much of Gandhi's observation that modern civilization brings its own forms of degradation and enslavement: "Formerly, men worked in the open air only as much as they liked. Now thousands of workmen meet together and for the sake of maintenance work in factories or mines. Their condition is worse than that of beasts. . . . Formerly, men were made slaves under physical compulsion. Now they are enslaved by temptation of money and of the luxuries that money can buy." *Hind Swaraj*, ch. 6.

22. Toinnes, *Community and Society* (East Lansing: Michigan State University Press, 1957).

23. "Science as a Vocation," in *From Max Weber*, ed. H. H. Gerth and C. Wright Mills (New York: Oxford University Press, 1958), 138.

24. "Science as a Vocation," 152–53.

25. "Science as a Vocation," 143.

26. For Nietzsche science leads to "a certain impoverishment of life." As he sees it, "Since Copernicus, man seems to have got himself on an inclined plane—now he is slipping faster and faster away from the center into—what? into nothingness," into a "*penetrating* sense of nothingness?" *Genealogy of Morals*, trans. Walter Kaufmann and R. I. Hollingdale (New York: Vintage, 1989), sec. 25.

27. *Thus Spoke Zarathustra*, in *The Portable Nietzsche*, ed. Walter Kaufmann (New York: Viking, 1954), part one.

28. Alexis de Tocqueville, *Democracy in America,* ed. J. P. Mayer (New York: Harper & Row, 1966).

29. See Organ, *Hinduism,* 4–7. Also see Chatterjee, *Gandhi's Religious Thought,* 6.

30. *Indian Opinion,* May 21, 1910, in Iyer, *Writings,* 1: 298.

31. *Hind Swaraj,* ch. 17. Almost thirty years later, he finds that "history is a chronicle of kings and their wars. The future history will be a history of man" (*Harijan,* August 11, 1940).

32. The full quote is: "History is for the most part a record of armed activities. Natural activities find very little mention in it." About September 2, 1917, in Iyer, *Writings,* 3: 47.

33. "Talks to Ashram Women," 1926, in Iyer, *Writings,* 3: 404.

34. Michel Foucault sees history as "the great obsession of the nineteenth century" ("Of Other Spaces," *Diacritics,* Spring 1986: 22–27, translated from the French by Jay Miskiewic). Also see Said, *Orientalism.*

35. Gandhi also has difficulty with Marxist interpretations of history. Marxists "have concentrated their study on the depths of degradation to which human nature can descend. What use have they for the study of the heights to which human nature could rise?" Cited in Iyer, *Moral and Political Thought,* 102.

36. See *The Leader,* December 25, 1916, in Iyer, *Writings,* 1: 359.

37. For a different reading of Gandhi's approach to history than the one taken here, see Iyer, *Thought,* 101–6; see also Parekh, *Colonialism,* 161–65.

38. *Harijan,* August 11, 1940, in Iyer, *Writings,* 2: 250.

39. He recognizes the flaws in "historical Hinduism with its untouchability [and] superstitious worship." *Harijan,* December 8, 1946, in Iyer, *Writings,* 2: 262.

40. Gandhi can agree with Sheldon Wolin's observation that "The supposition that underlays the variations on the theme of modernity was that modern science and advanced technology represented what is quintessentially and uniquely modern, the discovery of how progress and growth could be rendered perpetual, produced and reproduced at will." *The Presence of the Past* (Baltimore: The Johns Hopkins University Press, 1989), 69.

41. See *Hind Swaraj* for one of his sustained attacks on modern technology. Although he denies he is "an opponent, a foe, of science," he interprets it so broadly that it seldom carries the usual attributes conventionally accorded to science. See Speech, 1925, in Iyer, *Writings,* 1: 310. When he offers an example of good science at work, it is usually about efforts to improve the spinning wheel. See *The Hindu,* March 19, 1925, in Iyer, *Writings,* 1: 314.

42. Thomas Pantham makes it abundantly clear that Gandhi alters his views about science and technology after 1920. His initial, blanket resistance gives way to a general if halting acceptance of science ("Gandhi, Nehru, and Modernity"). However, he wants to accept science on his, not science's, terms.

43. See *Indian Opinion*, April 2, 1910, in Iyer, *Writings*, 1: 340–42.

44. Nandy holds that "Gandhi rejected the modern West primarily because of its secular scientific worldview." *Traditions, Tyranny, and Utopia*, 129.

45. *Hind Swaraj*, ch. 12.

46. "I overeat. I have indigestion. I go to a doctor, he gives me medicine, I am cured. I overeat again, I take his pills again. Had I not taken the pills in the first instance, I would have suffered the punishment deserved by me and I would not have overeaten again. The doctor intervened and helped me to indulge myself. My body thereby certainly felt more at ease; but my mind became weakened" (*Hind Swaraj*, ch. 12). In this regard, he parallels Rousseau's earlier indictment of modern medicine (see *Discourses on the Origins of Inequality*, part one in *Social Contract and Discourses*).

47. For example, criticism is made of the blanket diagnosis of hysteria in the nineteenth century and of post-menstrual syndrome in the late twentieth century to address the medical problems of women. For a representative sampling of critiques of medical science as constructions, see Alice Dan, *Reframing Women's Health: Multidiciplinary Research and Practice* (Thousand Oaks: Sage, 1994); Catherine Kohler Riessman, "Women and Medicalization: A New Perspective," *Social Policy* 14 (summer, 1983): 3–18; and Sandra Harding, *Racial Economy of Science* (Bloomington: Indiana University Press, 1993).

48. *The Birth of the Clinic* (New York: Pantheon, 1973), 145. "In anatomical perception, death was the point of view from the height of which disease opened up onto truth: the life/disease/death trinity was articulated in a triangle whose summit culminated in death" (158).

49. Throughout his life, Gandhi insists that people have an obligation to be attentive to their own health. See his *The Health Guide* (Trumansburg, N.Y.: Crossing Press, 1978) and *Diet and Diet Reform* (Ahmedabad: Navajivan Publishing House, 1949).

50. See particularly Arendt, *The Human Condition* and *Between Past and Future* (New York: Viking, 1961). Also see Margaret Canovan, *Hannah Arendt* (Cambridge: Cambridge University Press, 1992).

51. This can be seen in his observation that "no harm may result from chemistry itself but its misuse will certainly do harm. It is being misused much" today. Letter to Parasram, April 10, 1932, in Iyer, *Writings*, 2: 79.

52. *The Hindu*, March 19, 1925, in Iyer, *Writings*, 1: 310.

53. "The higher morality must be comprehensive; it must embrace all men. Considering our relation to mankind, every man has a claim over us, as it is our duty always to serve him." *Ethical Religion*, 17, in Iyer, *Writings*, 2: 66.

54. Gandhi sees people numbed into accepting catastrophic consequences generated by modern science: "The ceaseless rush in which we are living does not leave any time for contemplating the full results of" the new technologies.

After some brief period of concern following a disaster resulting from a new technology, "the dead will be soon forgotten, and in a very short time," people will resume their "usual gaiety as if nothing whatsoever had happened." *Indian Opinion*, August 20, 1903, in Iyer, *Writings*, 1: 291.

55. Once the cosmos is fragmented, it is no longer possible to heed Gandhi's admonition that it is necessary to "understand Nature's purposes and ponder over them" (*Indian Opinion*, February 5, 1910, in Iyer, *Writings*, 1: 335). Later, he observes that "it is our task to analyze and explore the body, the brain and the mind of man separately; but if we stop there, we derive no benefit despite our scientific knowledge." *Ethical Religion*, ch. 1, in Iyer, *Writings*, 2: 52.

56. Gandhi holds that "morals, ethics and religion are convertible terms. A moral life without reference to religion is like a house built upon sand. And religion divorced from morality is like 'sounding brass' good only for making a noise and breaking heads" (*Harijan*, September 3, 1936). What Gandhi says about "morals, ethics, and religion" also applies, for him, to science.

57. As I argued above, Gandhi is apprehensive about rules and procedures that universalize and wants to protect what is local and individual. In this respect, his concerns parallel Foucault's "genealogical project" which looks to "local, discontinuous, disqualified, illegitimate knowledges against the claims of a unitary body of theory which would filter, hierarchize, and order them in the name of some true knowledge and some arbitrary idea of what constitutes science and its objects . . . . [Genealogies] are concerned . . . with the insurrection of knowledges that are opposed primarily not to the contents, methods, or concepts of a science, but to the effects of the centralizing powers which are linked to the institution and functioning of an organized scientific discourse within a society such as ours" (*Power and Knowledge*, ed. Colin Gordon [New York: Pantheon, 1980], 83–84).

58. Arendt, *Human Condition*, 277.

59. Arendt, *Human Condition*, 283.

60. In this connection, Arendt observes, "The shift from the 'why' and 'what' to the 'how' implies that the actual objects of knowledge. . . must be processes, and that the object of science therefore is no longer nature or the universe" (*Human Condition*, 296). In her reading, everything now becomes a matter of "process" (*Human Condition*, 301).

61. Chatterjee argues, "To Gandhi, then, truth did not lie in history, nor did science have any privileged access to it. Truth was moral: unified, unchanging, and transcendental. It was not an object of critical inquiry or philosophical speculation. It could only be found in the experience of one's life, by the unflinching practice of moral living. It could never be correctly expressed within the terms of rational theoretical discourse; its only true expression was lyrical and poetic" (*Nationalist Thought*, 97). This captures an important aspect of Gandhi's concept

but it is also necessary to notice that Gandhi's truth is expressed in action. The action can be routine, as in the case of his idealized villagers who meet necessity for themselves and their family and attend to their many responsibilities. Or the action can be heroic, as in the case of the *satyagrahi* resisting injustice.

62. Early in his career, Gandhi argues that "the boast about the wonderful discoveries and the marvelous discoveries of science, good as they undoubtedly are in themselves, is, after all, an empty boast. They offer nothing substantial to the struggle of humanity" (*Indian Opinion*, August 20, 1903, in Iyer, *Writings*, 1: 291). For Gandhi, that struggle is essentially moral.

63. From a Gandhian perspective, the vast environmental harm that has oc‐ curred from a blind application of modern technology stands as ample evidence that the uses of science must be continually interrogated.

64. This quotation is drawn from a speech Gandhi originally gives to students. He tells his audience that they have a responsibility to translate their knowledge into practical policies that benefit ordinary people ("Science and Civilization," *The Hindu*, March 19, 1925, in Iyer, *Writings*, 1: 313–14).

65. See Chatterjee, *Nationalist Thought*, 100; and Nandy, *Traditions, Tyranny, and Utopias*, 129.

66. See *Harijan*, June 22, 1935, in Iyer, *Writings*, 3: 525.

67. Although not opposed to all science, Gandhi admits that "it is perfectly true . . . that I am not an admirer of science unmixed with something that I am about to say to you. I think that we cannot live without science, if we keep it in the right place. But I have learnt so much during my wandering in the world about the misuse of science that I have often remarked... as would lead people to consider that I was really a foe of science. In my humble opinion, there are limitations even to scientific search and the limitations are the limitations that humanity imposes upon us." Speech to students, March 13, 1925, in Iyer, *Writings*, 1: 310.

68. In this connection, he observes, "There is nothing to prevent me from profiting by the light that may come out of the West. Only I must take care that I am not overpowered by the glamour of the West. I must not mistake the glamour for true light." *Harijan*, January 13, 1940.

69. See Bernard Yack, *Longing for Total Revolution* (Princeton: Princeton Uni‐ versity Press, 1986), 6, 20.

70. See John Dunn, *The Political Thought of John Locke* (New York: Cambridge University Press, 1969).

71. Terchek, *Republican Paradoxes*, ch. 4.

72. For Gandhi, there are limits to the elasticity of a tradition, just as there are limits to the elasticity of individuals (*Harijan*, June 1942); beyond certain limits, adjustment is not possible if a tradition or person is to maintain its own internal integrity.

73. Efforts such as those proposed by Aurobindo and several other nineteenth- and early twentieth-century Indian writers to synthesize Indian thought with modernity and modernization are, for Gandhi, not only futile, they are dangerous.

74. "All the sages have declared from the housetops, that man can be his own worst enemy as well as his best friend. To be free or to be a slave lies in his own hands. And what is true for the individual, is true for the society" (*Harijan*, February 1, 1942). Contentment may no longer be possible, not only because modernity and modernization continually churn settled relations but also because people like Gandhi would have us forgo contentment in order to defend autonomy and challenge injustice.

75. See *Young India*, October 7, 1931. Parel argues that Gandhi believes that " 'modern civilization' posed a greater threat to [India] than did colonialism" (Parel, "Introduction," *Hind Swaraj*, xv).

76. For a contrary view, see Pantham who argues that "the distinctive contribution of Gandhi's intervention in the political thought and praxis of our times was to release both Indian tradition and Western modernity from the regressive pact between the substantive orthodoxy of traditionalism and the divisive or exploitative rationalism of modernism. His project or programme is one of overcoming modernism without regressing to traditionalism. In his approach, there is a merging of the reconstruction of Indian tradition and the reconstruction of Western modernity" ("Gandhi, Nehru, and Modernity," 108–9). I am not convinced that Gandhi seeks or achieves "a merging" of the two, reconstructed or not. On my reading, he uses tradition to interrogate and challenge modernity and modernization. However, Pantham is correct to emphasize that Gandhi is uninterested in remaking modern India into some reformed, idealized version of a distant past nestled in its countless villages.

77. Pantham finds that "the Gandhian critique of modernity is informed by, and generative of, a trans-liberal, decolonizing, or post-colonizing political morality in which there is a merger between some aspects of the modern, deontological, universal morality of right-justice and some aspects of an hermeneutical-ontological or contextual/historical ethics of love and caring responsibility" ("Gandhi's Intervention in Modern Moral-Political Discourse," 58).

78. Bhikhu Parekh, "Some Reflections on the Hindu Tradition of Political Thought," in *Political Thought in Modern India*, ed. Thomas Pantham and Kenneth Deutsch (New Delhi: Sage, 1986), 17–31.

79. Parekh, "Some Reflections," 20.

80. Parekh, "Some Reflections," 23.

81. Parekh, "Some Reflections," 27–29.

82. Many critics of Western modernity nevertheless find that its crowning

achievement is something like rights and equality. Alain Touraine, for one, argues that "the consciousness of the subject [or autonomous agent] and human rights have a history, and it is the history of modernity." *What is Democracy?* (Boulder: Westview Press, 1997), 118.

4

DEFENDING CIVIL SOCIETY BY QUESTIONING MODERNIZATION

The chief characteristic of [the modern] malaise is the obsolescence of man himself. In fact, it is worse than obsolescence. In the years and decades to come, man will be looked upon as something undesirable, as a burden on both society and nature, straining the management capacities of the former and the life-sustaining resources of the latter.[1]

This chapter seeks to make sense of Gandhi's economic theories, including his persistent skepticism of modern technology.[2] Although his views of nonviolence are well known and have excited considerable controversy, Gandhi's economic theories have often been discounted in India and elsewhere. The reason for the low status of his economic theories is clear enough. His vision of a reconstructed and responsive economy is found in rural India, far away from modern technologies and capital-intensive industries. For many, the problem with Gandhian economics is that it is rooted in a nonrecoverable (and often unwelcome) past.

For his part, Gandhi brings the same skepticism he has about modernity to economic modernization and refuses to let it have its own way. He sees the new economy undermining traditional standards and practices, transforming social relations based on cooperation to ones tied to individual competition, and assigning worth to persons because of their place in the economic process. When he looks at the modern economy, he sees expanding inequalities, growing unemployment, an increasing tolerance for violence, and diminished personal autonomy. As an alternative, he offers a morality tale where there is full employment and where people are said to control the productive process rather than being controlled by it. In his idealized reading of a rural economy, Gandhi draws lessons about what he takes to be valuable and necessary in judging any economy. Here, we find he draws a close connection between the availability and character of work and the ability of people to control the productive process.

Put this way, the Gandhian view of economics is visionary, and even though many can accept much of his critique of modernization, they find that in his embrace of a rural economy and his opposition to industrialization, he misreads the nature of the modern economy and, therefore, is unable to respond to its defects adequately. Partha Chatterjee, for one, finds that Gandhi fails to take account of the unavoidable, persistent reality of the modern world and that Gandhi's efforts to transport India back to a traditional economy ignore the hard problems that Gandhi says he wants to address. For Chatterjee, Gandhi is a precapitalist thinker who brings "a false resolution to the contradictions of modern reason and capitalism." For this reason, Chatterjee sees Gandhi seeking "conflict accommodation" rather than addressing the core difficulties of the modern market economy.[3] Gandhi cannot accept Chatterjee's invitation to replace capitalism with a modern alternative for two reasons. For one, Gandhi argues that the modernized economy, not just capitalism, is the danger and, second, he finds that any solution is open to corruption and decay, necessitating continued struggle against any ruling paradigm. In our time, Gandhi finds the chief economic struggle must be with any form of economic modernization.

Another objection to Gandhi's economics that needs to be taken seriously is that his return to a rural economy seems to leave many people impoverished. This Gandhi strenuously denies. He sees the constant innovation of the modernizing economy eliminating traditional occupations on a massive scale, tolerating its costs as regrettable but necessary steps to economic progress.[4] He sees millions of workers replaced by new technologies and treated as expendable "things" in the march to modernization and not as persons. For him, any new technology must be primarily judged by its effects on the present generation, particularly its most vulnerable members, and not by some future good.[5] In place of the new economy, Gandhi promises one that provides an austere livelihood to everyone. As he sees matters, the modernized economy will offer much more to some people at the very time it deprives others of everything. In developing his alternatives, Gandhi wants to distinguish an austere life that has conquered necessity from an impoverished life, and he promises India the former.

Gandhi's critique of modernization reveals valuable contributions to both political theory and the literature of economic modernization. Before it is common, he raises serious questions about capital-intensive development and shows that economic growth, productivity, and efficiency often exact high and debilitating costs on other social goods. Gandhi also reminds us that people have multiple needs that are affected by the economy, not just economic ones. Gandhi also asks whether institutional practices enable people to address necessity in ways that enhance or degrade persons.

MODERNIZATION AND AUTONOMY

To understand Gandhi's critique of modernization, it is helpful to return to the way he links institutions and autonomy. Institutionally, modernization introduces radically new opportunities, incentives, and costs, making some actions expensive and others relatively welcome. It sponsors structural changes at many levels, and as a rule of thumb, we can say that extensive, intensive modernization means massive institutional transformation. For his part, Gandhi holds that the modernized economy transforms ordinary social practices, changes conceptions of needs, and destabilizes traditions. Moreover, he understands that the sense of duties individuals once carried for one another are declining in the new economy.

Modernization poses a special danger, according to Gandhi, because of what he takes to be its surface attractiveness: after all, it promises (and often delivers) increased standards of living, better medical care, and educational attainment. Gandhi finds these are expensive goods which significantly introduce new meanings of the self as well as new patterns of social relations. He sees people depending less on their community and more on themselves to meet their necessities, thereby fostering a world that is fractured and disconnected. The irony of the new freedom from traditional practices promised by modernity is that people now rely on unseen and unknown actors in more and more ways. Individuals are now enmeshed in a series of interlocking dependencies as consumers and producers who, as strangers, do not care much for one another. This is not the kind of interdependence Gandhi wants; he seeks a society of mutuality among people who know and care about each other and who recognize the many debts they owe one another.[6] However, he fears that the localized communities that support cooperation are irrelevant to the modernizing project and are, like useless relics of the past, ready to be discarded.

Some of the costs of modern organizations have been carefully spelled out in Max Weber's discussion of bureaucratic society where people lose their status as moral agents and are primarily judged by their contributions to an institutional project, particularly to the productivity or efficiency of the enterprise. Weber fears that the modern economic order

> is now bound to the technical and economic conditions of machine production which today determine the lives of all the individuals who are born into this mechanism, not only those directly concerned with economic acquisition, with irresistible force. Perhaps it will so determine them until the last ton of coal is burnt. In [the] view [of some], the care for external goods should only lie on the shoulders of the "saint like a light cloak, which can be thrown aside at any moment." But fate decreed that the cloak should become an iron cage.[7]

Weber finds that the freedom from tradition promised by the modernized economy turns hollow as it replaces old forms of dominance and drudgery with new ones. The new order requires its own forms of discipline, predictability, and routinization, and Weber sees this producing bureaucrats, "men who need order and nothing but order." The great danger is that "the world could one day be filled with nothing but those little cogs, little men clinging to little jobs and striving towards bigger ones." For Weber, "the central question is . . . what we can oppose to this machinery, in order to keep a portion of humanity free from this parcelling out of the soul, from this total dominance of the bureaucratic ideal of life."[8] Gandhi takes it as one of his principle tasks to resist such an "iron cage" and encourages the struggle that Weber later takes to be essential for freedom. But Gandhi goes further than Weber and seeks autonomy, not for "a portion of humanity" but for humanity at large.

The critique of modernization I offer intentionally emphasizes its dour side and applies to both market and socialist economies. My discussion ignores many of the positive features we conventionally attribute to modernization. The reason for both my emphasis and omission lies in the thrust of the remainder of this chapter: namely, Gandhi's insistence that modernization contributes significantly to our present discontents. The problems cannot be overcome, on his account, with more goods or even a more equitable distribution of goods, no matter how desirable the latter goal may be for him. As in his other critiques, Gandhi wants to provide an alternative logic to the reigning paradigm and argues that economics, like any social practice, ought to be judged not only on its own terms but also by ethical standards.

I am less interested in Gandhi's specific policy proposals to confront modernization and want to do more than to tease from Gandhi his assessment of the costs of modernization. In what follows, I consider his views about the fragile nature of moral autonomy and equality and why he believes they must be the central criteria in judging institutions. I use these criteria to return to Gandhi's desire to take people off lifeboats and locate them in a secure institutional setting where dignity and responsibility are not goods that are elusive because they are so expensive.

To achieve his goal, Gandhi insists the good economy must assure that the basic necessities of everyone are met; anything more than the basic necessities "must come after the essential needs of the poor are satisfied. First things must come first."[9] The reason is that they are not only required for biological survival but are also essential to a person's moral development. When some are left without the basic necessities, they do not so much become unethical but numb, preoccupied with their own survival.[10] This can be seen in Gandhi's argument that

> A starving man thinks first of satisfying his hunger before anything else. He will sell his liberty and all for the sake of getting a morsel of food. Such is the position of millions of the people of India. For them, liberty, God and all such words are merely letters put together without the slightest meaning. If we want to give these people a sense of freedom, we shall have to provide them with work which they can easily do in their desolate homes and which would give them at least the barest living. This can only be done by the spinning wheel. And when they have become self-reliant and are able to support themselves, we are in a position to talk to them about freedom, about Congress, etc.

Those, therefore, who bring them work and the means of getting a loaf of bread will be their deliverers and will be also the people who will make them hunger for liberty.[11]

To be in charge of our life means, first and foremost to Gandhi, that people are able to subdue necessity and meet their basic needs. Once this happens, he holds that people will crave their autonomy; they will want to be in charge of their lives and give themselves a moral character through their free choices in an interdependent cosmos.

READING GANDHI'S ECONOMIC THEORIES

In exploring Gandhi's political economy, it is helpful to remember that he wants to address the ordinary people of India. To do so, he writes in an idiom that his audience readily understands.[12] The language, metaphors, and symbols he uses are not always ours, and if we read Gandhi literally, we run the danger of sometimes reading him incompletely. It is necessary to ask what he wants: that is, what purposes are his specific texts designed to serve? The need to penetrate beyond Gandhi's idiom and symbols is particularly important in his economic writings. There, the village is assigned the stature of meeting economic necessity and providing moral purpose, and spinning becomes the important organizing principle in Gandhian economics.[13]

However, to assume that spinning in the late modern world can solve the problems of scarcity invites, at a minimum, serious skepticism. Why, then, even undertake to try to understand Gandhi's thoughts about economic modernization? There are several reasons why Gandhi, one of the most ardent, clear, and consistent critics of modernization in the twentieth century, has a claim on our attention. First, anyone who accepts the importance and even the necessity for modernization must also admit its disappointments even when it is successful on its own terms. If, for example, modernization leads to a longer life and a higher level of literacy for many but is often accompanied by continued civil strife, denials of basic rights, extensive poverty, pervasive alienation, new forms of inequality, and exploding rates of crime, then modernization cannot be judged to have been completely successful. In his criticism, Gandhi continually turns to the costs of modernization, not as unfortunate but tolerable side effects but as flaws that threaten everyone.[14] Interrogating modernization, he calls into question its fundamental principles as well as challenges a fatalism which holds that people can do nothing to change matters and are hostages to a process that is beyond their reach.

Second, Gandhi's economic theories need to be taken seriously because he is a writer from the third world. By this I do not mean that Western theorists have nothing to contribute to an analysis of third world economies or that third world observers are invariably correct.[15] Far from it. However, development occurs in a specific time and place and is not an abstraction but a series of specific policies that affect real people in real ways, build on existing opportunities, confront real obstacles, and alter a culture and its moral standards and traditional practices in often unexpected and sometimes unwelcome ways.[16] Knowing this, Gandhi provides a critique of modernization as an Indian who fears that it threatens important social practices and cultural values in his country.[17]

Another reason for reading Gandhi's economic theories seriously is that he attempts to provide alternatives to industrialization in the third world.[18] Although most observers would reject a literal reading of Gandhi's village economy, there is growing support for the idea that a vibrant economy in many developing countries requires a strong agrarian base and efforts to import Western models indiscriminately are frequently self-defeating and often harmful.[19] Rather than assuming that better opportunities await everyone in the city, Gandhi offers a reconstituted rural society to meet their multiple needs.[20] With the frightful poverty, unemployment, and despair that grip the urban centers of many countries of the third world, the need for a viable rural economy is matched by a need to protect the moral dignity and social status to rural life, and this Gandhi tries to do.[21] Moreover, we have discovered that a self-propelled, unrestrained economy of continued growth carries foreboding future environmental dangers for everyone, including affluent, postindustrial societies.

Finally, Gandhi claims the attention of anyone who is concerned about the move to industrialize the globe.[22] In addition to the threat this move poses to the environment, Gandhi fears that in a global, modernized economy, India will not be master of its own destiny but will find decisions that affect the country in the most profound ways are made elsewhere. Should this come to pass, the criteria to determine what will happen in India are not decided by Indians but by others. As it turns out, several observers find that the authority of the state in both developed and developing economies in the late modern world is declining as important decisions about government revenue and spending are made by global financial institutions.[23] Gandhi resists such a possibility because, he insists, if citizens are to be free, they and not external actors must control their government.

GANDHI AS A POLITICAL ECONOMIST

Gandhi's political economy is animated by his ethics.[24] As he understands matters, "True economics never militates against the highest ethical standard, just as all true ethics to be worth its name must at the same time be also good economics."[25] He takes this to mean that the principal ethical imperative of the economy must address real people in their actual lives. This is why Gandhi holds "The individual is the one supreme consideration."[26] When abstract principles, such as economic growth, become central, he fears human beings are lost, merely expendable means to some bright, elusive end.[27] Accordingly, he argues that the needs of individuals, not firms, must be the standard employed to judge any political economy.[28] For Gandhi, the greatest danger of the modern economy is not that it produces goods that quickly become obsolescent but that it makes people obsolescent.[29] With this standard in mind, he rejects machinery when it ceases "to help the individual and encroach[es] upon his individuality."[30] To provide more products for people who are out of work makes no sense to him.[31] The urgency of his concern stems partly from his appreciation that when traditional occupations disappear, they are not readily revived at will.

Another reason Gandhi believes the new technologies subvert his goals of the ethical economy is that they produce great wealth. The problem, as he understands matters, is that "wealth and truth have always been in conflict with each other and will remain so till the end of time."[32] Recognizing that something like money is necessary, Gandhi argues not for the elimination of commerce, property, or ownership but against the proclivity of individuals to make these the central aspects of their lives. On his account, the ethical person cannot make wealth his God. Money is welcome if one can have it consistently with one's pursuit of truth; otherwise one must not hesitate even for a moment to sacrifice it as if it were no more than dirt on one's hand.[33]

As in his use of nonscientific criteria to evaluate science, so Gandhi calls on noneconomic standards to judge the economy, and this creates problems for many.[34] Economics, like other academic disciplines, tends to be self-inclosed and its greatest explanatory and predictive powers come in simplifying reality and working with a limited set of variables that can illuminate the problems at hand. Gandhi, on the other hand, wants domains of inquiry to have porous boundaries, to carry invitations to myriad concerns, and to listen to voices other than the experts'. In this way, his political economy is messy, filled with considerations that unsettle and complicate standards of productivity and innovation. As with his other challenges to injustice, he means to make economic injustice visible.

GANDHI, ARENDT, AND LABOR

Gandhi fears that the new economy is becoming the organizing principle of the modern world, displacing not only traditional occupations without providing adequate work for everyone but destroying tradition itself and mounting a foreboding threat to autonomy. He believes work and consumption, important as they are, are becoming the primary way people understand themselves and each other, overpowering alternative constructions of the self.[35] On his account, whatever benefits modernization might have potentially offered are squandered when economics is elevated as the end of human activity and other goods become subordinate.

In important respects, Gandhi's arguments share the concern of various Western writers about the deleterious effects of modernization, especially Hannah Arendt's.[36] She sees the modern world preoccupied with economics and finds it has penetrated more and more enclaves of life. This is much different than what Arendt detects in ancient Greece where economics focuses on the management of the household. Its well-being and security enable citizens to escape necessity and attend to their civic life that assures their liberty. In her discussion of labor in ancient Athens, Arendt emphasizes its unavoidability, persistence, and servility. For her, the things we need most for our biological life are supplied by daily labor which is locked in an unending battle with the cycles of natural growth and decay. She shows how the citizens of ancient Athens rely on women and slaves to provide the household with the consumables that are necessary for life. Arendt's treatment of labor in ancient Athens reveals its paradox. At the very time she sees Athenian citizenship as creative and emancipatory, she is appalled that the good of a few depends on the degradation and humiliation of the many.

Today, she finds that the responsibility of the ancient slaves, "to carry the burden of consumption in the household," has shifted to an industrial economy, where laborers "produce for society at large."[37] In the modern world, slavery has been abolished, the industrial revolution provides more goods for more people, and we might think that we have been able to overcome necessity. But Arendt says no. For one, many people remain impoverished; moreover, we have developed a new, expanded sense of necessity which requires people to labor more and more.[38] Gandhi shares these views and is particularly concerned about the tendency of people to inflate the importance of consumption.[39] He complains that "The distinguishing characteristic of modern civilization is an infinite multiplicity of human wants."[40]

For her part, Arendt detects the same phenomena; laboring occupies "the highest position in the hierarchical order" of life.[41] The problem stems not merely from the character of consumer society, where the satisfaction of one desire (or consumer demand) leads to the thirst for new ones.[42] More than that, we think we "need" things in order to survive in our society, making everyone a laborer, that is, everyone is a slave. Today, work is not only about the repetitious replenishment of goods that are quickly consumed; today we also quickly collect new "needs" which replace many of the older ones that have become disposable. In the modern world, decay has become pervasive: "our whole economy has become a waste economy, in which things must be almost as quickly devoured and discarded as they have appeared in the world, if the process itself is not to come to a sudden catastrophic end."[43] On her account,

> The last stage of the laboring society, the society of jobholders, demands of its members a sheer automatic functioning, as though indi-

vidual life had actually been submerged in the over-all life process of the species and the only active decision still required of the individual were to let go, so to speak, to abandon his individuality, the still individually sensed pain and trouble of living, and acquiesce in a dazed, 'tranquilized,' functional type of behavior. . . . It is quite conceivable that the modern age . . . may end in the deadliest, most sterile passivity history has even known.[44]

Like Gandhi, Arendt abhors what she sees and, like him, challenges the idea that the moral and political costs are trivial next to their benefits.[45] Gandhi can agree with Arendt that desires have exploded in the modern world, that misery has not dissipated, and that labor continues to be unavoidable but has become the dominant source of identity. Because work is inescapable, Gandhi wants to return to practices and conceptions of work that are minimally nonalienating and nondegrading and optimally purposeful.[46] Moreover, he expects work to occupy an important but not the central place in the lives of men and women. To meet these goals, he reconceptualizes work, transforming it from a conventional expression of drudgery to a freely given expression of our humanity.[47] One of the things that is necessary for this to happen, Gandhi believes, is that the relationship between self-identity and consumerism must be disconnected.[48] If this happens, he thinks the economy can be structured in ways that enable people to have time for pursuits other than work.[49] His mortality tale is one where work is not the defining feature of a person's life; this occurs, however, only after work is available to all.[50] The paradox he finds in the modernized economy comes with "labor-saving production" that simultaneously throws many out of work while others labor more than ever.[51]

One of the marks of modernity that especially disturbs both Arendt and Gandhi is its propensity to commodify everything in its reach.[52] This can be seen in his complaint that railroads "had reduced holy places to unholy places." He remembers the holy city of Benares before "there was a mad rush of civilization" and a journey that had once been a spiritual experience has become trivialized and commercialized.[53] With this in mind, he wants India to avoid the fate he sees in "Western nations [which] today are groaning under the heel of the monster-god of materialism."[54]

Gandhi and Arendt give labor and modernization a political reading. They not only fear that the primary identity of people is coming from their location in the economy, both as producers and consumers; they also observe that individuals are now on their own. In modern economic thought, people are said to be economically rational when they determine what they want, know what they can get, scale back preferences that are unachievable, and then do what they must to get what is left.[55] As rational actors, each decision is said to be theirs alone and their personal preferences serve as their compass. No longer are they a part of the world, only of an economic process.[56] But human beings are more than processes for Arendt and Gandhi who find little in the modern world that is untouched by economics. In such a world, economic criteria are in a constant state of flux, and a person no longer has, as Arendt puts it, "permanent standards and measurements which, prior to the modern age, have always served him as guides for his doing and criteria for his judgment."[57] In their political readings, economics has become the center of life and this they mean to resist.

ECONOMICS, POLITICS, AND CIVIL SOCIETY

For purposes of this discussion, it is helpful to distinguish liberal and strong republican theories of civil society before embarking on Gandhi's own understanding.[58] The conventional liberal conception of civil society rests on a distinction between the state and society and holds that some social institutions (such as the family, religion, and private property) and activities (such as child-rearing and market relationships) ought to be free from government intrusion.[59] From this perspective, the institutions of civil society are the result of voluntary, spontaneous choices and actions. On this account, the traditional practices that have evolved in civil society reflect collective judgments about what is good for its members over time. Embedded in this conception of a voluntaristic civil society is a persistent suspicion of the role of an active state that is seen as a threat to freedom.[60]

The strong republican reading of civil society works with very different assumptions, finding that noncivic institutions and practices have the most profound influence not only on the identities and activities of citizens but also on the character of their politics.[61] In this account, a civil society marked by steep inequalities, a highly individualistic incentive structure, concentrations of private power, and a penchant for sweeping change develops a radically different form of politics than when these conditions are absent. While recognizing that the state can become a major obstacle to liberty, strong republicans appreciate that the institutions of civil society can also deny liberty to citizens. For this reason, strong republicans, unlike most liberals, pay considerable attention to the power that resides in civil society.

Gandhi's concerns about civil society often parallel the strong republican account. He finds that what happens there and in the economy has the most profound effect on the ways people meet necessity and think about themselves and others; how its institutional practices enrich or constrict their lives; and how concentrated private power seriously affects both politics and the autonomy of persons. For this reason, he cannot accept the classical liberal conception of civil society as benign. As presently constituted, he finds that many locations of power in civil society cancel aspirations for political equality and serve to favor some and degrade others. If India wins its political independence without reorganizing its civil society, including the ways people make a living, Gandhi expects the prize will be empty. This kind of thinking is reflected in his observation that "It would be folly to assume that an Indian Rockefeller would be better than the American Rockefeller."[62] Gandhi's ideal civil society has no Rockefellers and has no need of steep inequalities.

In his ideal society, tradition, politics, economics, social relations, and autonomy are tightly linked; but with modernization, he believes that any possible harmony is elusive. Much of Gandhi's critique of modernization parallels his criticisms of colonization and untouchability. Individually and collectively, these institutional practices generate imperatives that make their rules and goals appear appropriate or necessary and override alternatives.

GANDHI, CAPITALISM, AND SOCIALISM

When political philosophers turn to economics, distributive issues loom large. Although Gandhi is interested in the ways goods are distributed, he is primarily concerned with how they are produced. It makes no sense to him to build a theory concerning the fair distribution of goods if the goods come at the loss of the moral autonomy of individuals. For this reason, Gandhi holds that the most important problems of modernization are not whether the market or the state allocates but how goods are created in the first place.

Gandhi denies that either capitalism or socialism, the major competing modes of organizing the modern economy, adequately addresses the critical problems of production. Highly suspicious of capitalism with its emphasis on individual ownership, competition, and consumerism, he sees it neglecting the social and ethical consequences of the economy.[63] Given his ethical demands in evaluating an economy, he finds that entrepreneurs use others (their workers, suppliers, customers) as means to their ends. Within his framework, the private property rights–claims of owners ought never supersede the autonomy requirements of others.

However, he never considers state socialism to be an acceptable alternative.[64] Granting that many socialists are moved by generous instincts, he sees state socialism driven by a deterministic reading of history. It considers "materialistic advancement as the goal of life and . . . has lost touch with the final things in life."[65] Moreover, he believes that the inevitable regulatory control of state socialism diminishes the autonomy of individuals. For this reason, he looks

> upon an increase of the power of the State with the greatest fear because, although while apparently doing good by minimizing exploitation, it does the greatest harm to mankind by destroying individuality.[66]

Gandhi finds socialists and capitalists are drinking from the same fountain of progress, hoping to use technology and management to promote economic growth; each is confusing ends and means.[67] For him, the former can never justify the latter, and he holds that actions that are ordinarily inexcusable do not become acceptable because they serve some laudable end.[68]

SPINNING AND GANDHI'S IDEALIZED ECONOMY

For Gandhi, the major economic issue is whether people control the process of production or are controlled by it.[69] He is perplexed by claims that modern technology gives individuals more command over their lives than earlier technologies had. Readily admitting that people are now able to produce goods and provide services that were unavailable before, he goes on to insist that the mark of a good economy can never be measured in aggregate output or rates of growth. His idea of the good economy has three related but distinct properties: it provides work for everyone; the work enables everyone to subdue necessity; and the work is controlled by the workers, not by others.

When Gandhi surveys the India of his time, he finds these conditions absent: "If you [go to] some far-off village in the interior you . . . will find the people cheerless and fear-stricken. . . . They have no hope left in them." The reason is that they have been deprived of work and see no prospect of finding any.[70] Decisions affecting them have been made elsewhere; the new economic arrangements do not require their labor; and the goals of the new economy speak to productivity and not to their needs. This is why Gandhi is alarmed at cheap machine-made cloth that has been flooding India and drying up local markets for hand-spun cloth that had supplied a living (if austere) income to millions of Indians for centuries.[71] Jobs that once sustained entire communities have been eliminated with cheaper goods, and this Gandhi means to change with *khadi*, or hand-spinning.

Khadi, as Gandhi presents it, was once the universal employer in India, enabling people to work productively with readily available technologies. On his account, "every agricultural country requires a supplementary industry to enable the peasants to utilize their spare hours. Such industry for India has always been spinning."[72] To those who find his solution retrogressive, he asks: "Is it such a visionary ideal—an attempt to revive an ancient occupation whose destruction has brought on slavery, pauperism, and disappearance of the inimitable artistic talents?"[73] If nothing is done and independence comes amidst squalor, despair, and suffering, Gandhi fears that the prize will be hollow.

> Unless poverty and unemployment have been wiped out from India, I would not agree that we have attained freedom. Real wealth does not consist in . . . money, but in providing for proper food, clothes, education and creating healthy conditions of living for every one of us. A country can be called prosperous and free only when its citizens can easily earn enough to meet their needs.[74]

To achieve universal employment, Gandhi does not believe it is necessary for India to search for something new because it already has such a productive process in the hand-spinning. He recommends khadi not because he believes it has an inherent quality that makes it superior to any other form of work. Even though he sees something aesthetic and sublime in khadi, it is important to Gandhi because he thinks it works now for those who need it.[75]

> We may find remedies to prevent floods. That will take years. We may induce people to adopt better methods of cultivation. That must take still more years. . . . But these improvements will take generations. How are the starving millions to keep the wolf from the door meanwhile? The answer is through the spinning-wheel.[76]

The picture Gandhi paints of a robust India is one where poverty has been abolished and an austere life is assured, but for his vision to become a reality, he insists khadi is essential. From his vantage point, India will regain control over its own future when it enables its citizens to meet their own basic needs.

> I have not pictured a poverty-stricken India containing ignorant millions. I have pictured to myself an India continually progressing along the lines best suited to her genius. . . .
>
> If my dream is fulfilled, and every one of the seven lakhs of villages becomes a well-living republic in which there are no illiterates, in which no one is idle for want of work, in which everyone is usefully occupied and has nourishing food, well-ventilated dwellings, and sufficient Khadi for covering the body . . . such a State must have varied and increasing needs, which it must supply unless it would stagnate.[77]

For this to happen, Gandhi expects men and women to control production, but Gandhi's conception of control is much different from Marx's. When Marx talks about workers controlling the means of production, he focuses on ownership. Although this issue is important to Gandhi, he wants to see the process of production to be within the reach of ordinary people and responsive to their needs.[78] For him, the modern economy subverts that control in two ways: decisions about who is to work and at what compensation are made by persons other than the workers themselves. When Gandhi says he wants to "make every village self-supporting," he has in mind an ideal where the most fundamental decisions that affect people in their local situations are made by them and not distant strangers.[79]

The second reason he pays attention to production stems from his view that each economic arrangement has its own internal logic; in his ethical economy, autonomy is central but, he finds, the logic of the new economy speaks to other goals. In this way, he finds that the character of the new economy introduces standards that reduce the realm of freedom available to ordinary men and women. Accordingly, his alternative is a place where people are said to regain control of their lives and livelihoods because employment is widespread, power dispersed, and social relationships nonhierarchical.

MAKING A PLACE FOR MODERN TECHNOLOGY

Throughout his life, Gandhi recognizes some of the tangible benefits of many of the new technologies and holds that India needs to find an appropriate place for some of them.[80] However, as I have indicated, he insists that any use of new technologies must assure that people control the productive process and their own lives.[81] When he accepts modern technology, he does so with significant qualifications. If the villagers can find ways to control it, he has "no objection to villagers using even modern machines and tools."[82] He tells the readers of *Harijan* that "as a moderately intelligent man, I know man cannot live without industry. Therefore, I cannot be opposed to industrialization."[83]

Any industrialization in India, Gandhi insists, must find its place within a highly decentralized economy.[84] If new modes of production can reduce drudgery and improve the conditions of life while supplying everyone with work then, Gandhi concludes, such innovations have a place in his moral economy.[85] However, he quarrels with the modern idea that whenever new technologies appear in the world they need to be immediately incorporated without any explanation of how they will affect other goods. Gandhi refuses to accept the argument that the promises of the new technology cannot cover everyone until sometime in the future and, in the meanwhile, some will have to pay the price of poverty, humiliation, and domination. For him, the promises of a brighter future cannot exonerate suffering in the present and, before accepting new technologies, he wants men and women to determine the impact of technology on what should matter most to them: their autonomy.

By denying that modernization is inherently good and irrevocably necessary, Gandhi raises issues that do not surface until after India and other former colonies experiment with modernization and find many of its fruits bitter. Believing that traditional economies are universal providers and mesh with the many other facets of an individual's life, Gandhi wants to open a dialogue about economic arrangements. For him, what is introduced is less important than how new technologies are incorporated into society and who controls them.[86] His economic program is a part of his vision of a free India; it is to be independent not only of British imperial rule but also free of the modernized economy.

Gandhi finds some modern technology, such as railroads and hospitals, are "a necessary evil."[87] It is clear why he thinks they are evil. He complains, for example, that modern transportation crowds holy cities with people who treat them as an entertainment rather than places for devotion. And he thinks hospitals invite people to loosen their self-discipline because they expect doctors to cure them. However, why should Gandhi think they are necessary? One reason is that they can serve worthwhile functions even though they can be abused. He uses this reasoning to talk about lawyers who, he acknowledges, are necessary to secure local justice but have, in his reading, employed the law for their own benefit rather than justice.[88]

Another reason Gandhi sees some modern technology as "a necessary evil" is that he knows that the modern world has changed and will not return to a simple world. In a letter to Nehru, he allows that the simplicity he desires is no longer possible and that "a number of things . . . will have to be organized on a large scale."[89] He recognizes the elimination of "all machinery . . . requires a higher simplicity and renunciation than the people are today prepared for."[90] True to his own standards, he declines to impose his will on a reluctant or intransigent public. His responsibility, as he sees it, is to teach them to be suspicious about some of the things they sincerely want. By exposing the costs of the new technologies, he hopes to remind his readers what they risk losing and show them that the alternatives they are ready to discard are better defenders of their autonomy.

TWO MYTHS OF AGRARIAN LABOR

Gandhi sees the villages of India providing the ideal setting for maintaining traditional values and practices as well as defusing political power. It is to be the residence for a just, stable, and sufficient economy where work is available, desires contained, and elementary needs effectively met.[91] There, Gandhi expects to see a thriving community and satisfying economy continually reinforcing each other. His views seem too good to be true, and we are tempted to explain them as nostalgic lapses and consider his economic views as curiosities in his larger theory. Whether or not the villages ever resembled his ideal economic insularity, such an ideal seems neither welcome nor possible in the late modern world with its interlocking interdependencies, growing populations, and ecological interrelatedness. Gandhi's mythologized village economy not only reveals that odd mixture of conservatism and radicalism that marks so much of his thought; it also serves as a morality tale about control and autonomy. His metaphor of rural India as the ideal society is not meant to provide a determinant solution to the challenge of modernization. After all, he admits, "My ideal village still exists only in my imagination."[92] He knows that the forces of domination can arise in any society, the push for material satisfaction continually asserts itself, and the standards of efficiency, growth, and productivity incessantly subvert tradition. Gandhi offers his agrarian metaphor not as a weapon to conquer modernization but as an ideal with which to defend autonomy in a hostile world. He believes that the agrarian myth continues to embody what is important to rural India and has the ability to alert, nourish, and invigorate ordinary people there.[93]

While not common, criticisms of the modernizing economy and praise for a rural economy have been raised by others, including Thomas Jefferson.[94] Like Gandhi, Jefferson leans heavily on the agrarian myth to warn about what he takes to be the deleterious effects of modern commerce and industry. For him, the promise of the American experiment comes in its pledge of liberty and equality. On Jefferson's account, a society of yeoman farmers is the necessary foundation to keep this promise.[95] First of all, he sees it placing a premium on individual labor which enables farmers to be their own persons, and not the servant of others. Jefferson also holds that farmers are limited in what they can achieve. With their labor, they can provide for their families and be proud and satisfied with such accomplishments. His yeomen are not prone to corruption or seduced by the promise that they can live happier lives if only they can accumulate and consume more. Moreover, Jefferson's ideal is a one-class economy which forecloses the possibility that concentrated wealth can be converted into concentrated political power. Should this happen, Jefferson fears that his ideal of political equality will be subverted. For him, the great threat to the American republic comes not from alien powers but from the corruption it would visit on itself should it change from an agrarian society to a modernized one. If this comes to pass—and Jefferson is not at all optimistic that widespread commerce and industry can be arrested—the purpose of politics becomes defensive.

Like Gandhi's morality tales about Indian villages, Jefferson's myth of the yeoman farmer often rests on some shaky grounds. Most obviously, it ignores the large plantations of the South based on slavery. However, the story Jefferson means to tell is, in critical respects, the one Gandhi wants to disclose. Profound changes in the ways ordinary people routinely meet necessity alter their lives in ways that extend beyond their economic roles as producers and consumers. New institutional practices emerge; new patterns of reward, neglect, and penalty develop; and old forms of self-discipline give way to an externally enforced discipline. In Jefferson's and Gandhi's morality tales, the greatest dangers often come disguised as liberating but, if exposed, can be confronted.

For all their many differences, both Gandhi and Jefferson want to see a rough correspondence between what free people routinely do and what routinely happens to them, something they believe occurs in a simple economy but not a complex, modernized one. For Gandhi and Jefferson, intentionalilty and effort should count for something; a person's best efforts should not invariably be disregarded or lost; and what happens to people should not be continually determined by external actors.

When Jefferson's mythological farmers detect abuses of power, he imagines they gather together as equals to defend their liberty, arrest the tide of corruption, and defeat the temptation of some to use public power for their own purposes. For his part, Gandhi expects much the same from his idealized villagers. When they confront abuses of power, they do not face megainstituitons but other men and women much like themselves in their own communities. These villagers rely on nonviolent civil disobedience to challenge local abuses of power. In neither Jefferson's nor Gandhi's accounts of the simple, agrarian economy is life easy, politics perfect, or happiness guaranteed. What each account tries to promote is much different—a thriving autonomy.

Holding that no specific ethical solution fits every situation, Gandhi submits his rural myth as an outline for an ethical economy. How it takes on substance and particular meaning in specific settings must, in the last analysis, depend on the opportunities and constraints that await men and women in their individual and collective situations and how they develop a common solution.[96] In offering his metaphor, Gandhi means to challenge the idea that there is no alternative to modernity and modernization as they have developed and, in this way, resists the modern version of fatalism and helplessness. Just as Gandhi experiments with civil disobedience, he wants experiments with an ethical economy.[97]

CALLING UP REMAINDERS

Gandhi thinks we cannot help being affected by politics. Therefore, he reasons, we need to become political. He uses the same reasoning to apply to economics. For him, we must respond to politics to preserve our autonomy, and we must address economics for the same reason. At the same time, Gandhi recognizes that modernization is compellingly attractive and its most visible results convince more and more people that they need the new goods that crowd the market. He regards these newly constructed wants as often superfluous that become dangerous, particularly when men and women understand their own success and failure in terms of their possessions and wealth.[98] When the basis of identity and the standards of success and failure migrate to possessive, materialist terrains, Gandhi fears that spiritual and cultural values that once defined a society become increasingly irrelevant. If the trend continues, India will no longer be India but a copy of the West, a flawed one at that, according to Gandhi.[99]

Gandhi has often been seen as a utopian writer, and no more so than in his critique of the modernized economy and his rural alternative. A case can be made, however, that Gandhi carries a realistic edge in his economic writings. His economic realism is not the one associated with garnering higher growth rates and greater productivity; his realism stems rather from his insistent reminders that what is neglected or discarded in the modern economy is real and remains important to the human condition. He knows that the products and technology of the new economy are real, but Gandhi refuses to allow them to become the only reality. Repeatedly insisting there is another reality, he parades the unemployed, starving, illiterate, and vulnerable of India before his audience and asks about their real needs and the kind of economy most able to relieve their suffering now. He refuses to accept the heavy individual costs of modernization because of some measure of aggregate improvement. Averages tempt us to ignore individuals and overlook those who fall at the extremes, particularly at the lower end. Just as he castigates a narrow utilitarianism that celebrates the greatest good for the greatest number in politics, so he insists that any economy must be judged by ethical standards that focus on the least well-off.

Gandhi's realism also extends to his view that a voluntary movement to limit consumption is more likely to thrive if people have a cosmological outlook rather than a narrowly individualistic one. From his perspective, the person who sees interconnectedness and interdependency is more likely to understand that both necessity and personal interests are served by limiting consumption than someone whose primary point of reference is the isolated, independent self.[100] The moral demands that he makes on individuals to curb their consumption are levied after they have overcome acute scarcity and insecurity. Then, Gandhi believes, he can approach his vision of a community of caring and service where autonomous men and women are not proceeding alone but are part of overlapping networks.[101] There, his self-sufficient person is neither destitute nor dependent on the charity of others or the good will of the state.

Gandhi's economics builds on the vulnerabilities and developmental capacities of individuals. To concentrate only on the former offers us a dark, pessimistic reading of the human condition; the danger of focusing only on the latter is not so much that it is utopian but that it leaves individuals defenseless against those practices that threaten to undermine their autonomy. In joining the dark and the bright, Gandhi attempts to provide a framework for autonomy. To do this, he refuses to take the world as he finds it, but challenges it to address the elementary needs and inescapable vulnerabilities of ordinary people.

His economic texts, as is the case with most of his other writings, are about struggle. Believing that inequality and domination are always

ready to assert themselves and that efforts to achieve equality and freedom will always find resistance, he argues that it is essential to dispute
claims that economics has its own internal standards and is not subject
to external standards of evaluation.[102] In his interrogation, he is worried
about remainders; not only what is neglected but also who is neglected
because they do not contribute to the economic process and have become irrelevant in the modern economy.[103]

NOTES

1. Kothari, *Footsteps into the Future,* 92.
2. The modernized economy has been justified by reference to dramatic
increases in productivity, yet criticized because of inequitable distributions.
Some see abundance but others find exploitation. Gandhi works with many
conventional criticisms about distribution and acquisition but moves beyond
them; he is particularly concerned about issues of production.
3. Chatterjee, *Nationalist Thought and the Colonial World,* 99–100.
4. "Advice to Construction Workers," May 13, 1947, in Iyer, *Writings,* 3:
221.
5. *Harijan,* March 31, 1946.
6. See Gandhi, *Constructive Programme* (Ahmedabad: Navajivan Publishing
House, 1945).
7. Max Weber, *The Protestant Ethic and the Spirit of Capitalism* (New York:
Scribner's Sons, 1958), 181.
8. Max Weber, *The Interpretation of Social Reality* (London: Eldridge, 1971),
104–16.
9. *The Hindu,* January 26, 1946 in *Collected Works,* 83: 27.
10. Gandhi argues that some of the most significant casualties of the ravages
of poverty are self-confidence, personal dignity, and faith. Talk about morality
or God to the destitute, and they "will call you and me fiends. . . . They know,
if they know any God at all, a God of terror, vengeance, a pitiless tyrant. They
do not know what love is" (*Young India,* September 15, 1927).
11. *Young India,* March 18, 1926. On another occasion, he writes that "to
those who are hungry and unemployed, God can dare reveal Himself only as
work and wages as the assurance of food" (February 25, 1939, in Iyer, *Writings,*
3: 537).
12. See Indira Rothermund, "The Gandhian Pattern of Mass Communication," *Gandhi Marg* 8, 12 (1987); and Rudolph and Rudolph, *Modernity of Tradition.*

13. For a brief review of criticisms of Gandhi's idealization of traditional, rural India, see Buddhadeva Bhattacharyya, *Evolution of the Political Philosophy of Gandhi* (Calcutta: Calcutta Book House, 1969), 197–200; Chatterjee, *Nationalist Thought*; and Parekh, *Colonialism, Tradition, and Reform.*

14. For Gandhi's argument that whenever we look at any economic arrangement, we must privilege individual autonomy, see *Young India*, November 13, 1924.

15. Gandhi writes he is "humble enough to admit that there is much we can profitably assimilate from the West. Wisdom is no monopoly of one continent or one race. My resistance to Western civilization is really a resistance to its indiscriminate and thoughtless imitation based on the assumption that Asiatics are fit only to copy everything that comes from the West." *Young India*, August 11, 1927.

16. "European writers . . . cannot guide us beyond a certain measure if they have to generalize from European examples which cannot be on all fours with Indian conditions because in Europe they have nothing like the conditions of India. . . . What may be, therefore, true of Europe is not necessarily true of India. We know, too, that each nation has its own characteristics and individuality. India has her own; and if we are to find out a true solution for her many ills, we shall have to take all the idiosyncrasies of her constitution into account, and then prescribe a remedy. I claim that to industrialize India in the same sense as Europe is to attempt the impossible." *Young India*, August 6, 1925, in Iyer, *Writings,* 1: 317.

17. "If the village perishes, India will perish too. It will be no more India" (*Harijan*, January 20, 1940). He also finds that "Western observers hastily argue from Western conditions that what may be true of them must be true of India where conditions are different in so many material respects. Application of the laws of economics must vary with varying conditions" (*Young India*, July 2, 1931).

18. "Sparsely populated, America may have need of machinery. India may not need it at all. Where there are millions and millions of units of idle labor, it is no use thinking of labor-saving devices." *Harijan*, November 2, 1934.

19. The titles of the works of Richard B. Norgaard, *Development Betrayed* (London: Routledge, 1994); Michael Edwards, "The Irrelevance of Development Studies," *Third World Quarterly* 11, 1 (January, 1989), 116–135; and Michael Redclift, *Sustainable Development: Exploring the Contradictions* (London: Methuen, 1987) indicate the character of some recent critiques of the dominant models of development which favor large-scale industrialization and other forms of capital-intensive programs in third world economies. For his part, Gandhi wants a labor-intensive economy that builds on local skills and resources.

20. Gandhi reminds Indians that they are "the inheritors of a rural civiliza-

tion. . . . Its defects are well known but not one of them is irremediable. To uproot it and substitute for it an urban civilization seems to me an impossibility, unless we are prepared by some drastic means to reduce the population from three hundred million to three or say even thirty." *Young India*, November 7, 1929.

21. For Gandhi's discussion of his idealized village economy and politics, see *Rebuilding Our Villages* (Ahmedabad: Navajivan Publishing House, 1952) and *Panchayat Raj* (Ahmedabad: Navajivan Publishing House, 1959).

22. See William Connolly, *Identity/Difference* (Ithaca: Cornell University Press, 1991), 24–25.

23. Susan Strange argues that "the authority of the governments of all states, large and small, strong and weak, has been weakened as a result of technological and financial change and of the accelerated integration of national economies into one single global market economy" (*The Retreat of the State* [Cambridge: Cambridge University Press, 1996], 13–14). For her part, Saskia Sassen finds "Central banks and governments appear now to be increasingly concerned about pleasing the financial markets rather than setting goals for social and economic well-being. . . . Do we want the global capital market to exercise this discipline over our governments? And to do so at all costs—jobs, wages, safety, health— and without a public debate?" (*Losing Control? Sovereignty in an Age of Globalization* [New York: Columbia University Press, 1996], 50–51).

24. "I must confess that I do not draw a sharp line on any distinction between economics and ethics. Economies that hurt the moral well-being of an individual or a nation are immoral." *Young India*, October 13, 1921.

25. In the same piece, he argues "All economics that inculcates Mammon worship and enables the strong to amass wealth at the expense of the weak, is a false and dismal science." *See also Harijan*, October 9, 1937.

26. *Young India*, November 13, 1924.

27. The modern economy—whether market or socialist—is preoccupied with growth. However, growth seldom comes without a price, and its costs are often discounted or ignored, sometimes because they are hidden and sometimes because they are assessed on the people who are least likely to be heard when they complain. For a classic discussion of some of the costs, see Fred Hirsch, *The Social Limits of Growth* (Cambridge: MIT Press, 1976).

28. "It is beneath human dignity to lose one's individuality and become a mere cog in the machine. I want every individual to become a full-blooded, fully developed member of society." *Harijan*, January 28, 1939.

29. Gandhi finds that "machinery . . . is harmful when the same thing can be done easily by millions of hands not otherwise occupied." *Young India*, July 2, 1931.

30. *Young India*, November 20, 1924.

31. Gandhi says he refuses "to insult the naked by giving them clothes they do not need instead of giving them work which they sorely need." *Young India*, October 13, 1921.

32. *Indian Opinion*, May 29, 1909, in Iyer, 3: 37.

33. *Indian Opinion*, May 29, 1909, in Iyer, 3: 37.

34. Ashis Nandy is particularly helpful in putting Gandhi's method of inquiry into perspective with his observation that "Gandhi's anti-technicism seems so devastatingly retrograde because it seeks solutions to the technological problems of our times partly outside technology." *Traditions, Tyranny, and Utopias*, 137.

35. Gandhi is also concerned with the propensity of people to think of the goods they buy only in economic and not social terms. They seek the best price for cloth, for example, even if that means eliminating traditional occupations and devastating local communities.

36. Arendt, *Human Condition*.

37. Arendt, *Human Condition*, 119.

38. The abolition of slavery and arrival of new technologies "did not simply result in new property or lead to a new redistribution of wealth but were fed back into the process to generate further expropriations, greater productivity and more appropriations." Arendt, *Human Condition*, 255.

39. "Civilization, in the real sense of the term, consists not in the multiplication, but in the deliberate and voluntary restriction of wants. This alone promotes real happiness and contentment and increases the capacity for service." *From Yeravda Mandir*, ch. VI.

40. *Young India*, June 2, 1927.

41. Arendt, *Human Condition*, 306.

42. Arendt, *Human Condition*, 126–35. Arendt is extremely severe about consumption. Attacking Marx's view that the emancipated person will reach for "higher" activities, she writes that we find "the spare time of the *animal laborans* is never spent in anything but consumption, and the more time left to him, the greedier and more craving his appetites. That these appetites become more sophisticated, so that consumption is no longer restricted to the necessities but, on the contrary, mainly concentrates on the superfluities of life, does not change the character of this society, but harbors the grave danger that eventually no object of the world will be safe from corruption and annihilation through consumption." *Human Condition*, 133.

43. Arendt, *Human Condition*, 134. This is amplified by Agnes Heller who observes, "The modern world is the cemetery of things that had been used but not used up, just replaced and thrown away." *A Philosophy of History in Fragments* (Oxford: Blackwell, 1993), 231.

44. Arendt, *Human Condition*, 322. This is Nietzsche's fear regarding the last man in *Thus Spake Zarathustra*, 128–31.

45. Both fear that a preoccupation with economics means people withdraw from other areas of life, particularly political ones, and make prosperity and not their liberty their priority.

46. For a discussion of Gandhi's argument on the dignity of labor, see his *Bread Labour*.

47. For Gandhi, labor, particularly manual labor, is not a sign of our weakness but of our humanity, yet he finds it is continually disparaged: "In our country manual labor is regarded as a low occupation. . . . We should spin, therefore, if only to guard against the pernicious tendency of regarding the toilers as being low in the social scale." *Young India*, May 20, 1926.

48. See *Young India*, April 4, 1931. Hirsch finds that an "increase in resources does nothing to increase welfare, since wants increase correspondingly. The extent to which existing demands are satisfied may never increase because wants rise commensurable with resources" (*Social Limits*, 122).

49. Gandhi finds that the consumer products of the modernized economy become new needs that threaten to exhaust us, depleting us of the energy and attention once devoted to traditional duties. He reports that when he looks at Britain, he is "disillusioned," seeing people who "seem half-crazy. They spend their days in luxury or in making a bare living and retire at night thoroughly exhausted." They have nothing else in life but consumption or work (Letter to H. Polak, October 14, 1909, *Collected Works*, 9: 479–81; see also *Young India*, July 24, 1924).

50. "The saving of labour of the individual should be the object" of the modernized economy. *Young India*, November 13, 1924.

51. *Young India*, November 13, 1924.

52. For example, Gandhi complains that people now believe they can buy what once required self-discipline (such as good health).

53. Speech, *India*, October 22, 1909, in Iyer, *Writings*, 1: 325.

54. Speech, December 25, 1916, in Iyer, *Writings*, 1: 359.

55. What is left after people use their reason to determine what they can get may not be much, and what it takes to get it may be very expensive to their autonomy.

56. See Arendt, *Human Condition*, 257.

57. Arendt, *Human Condition*, 307.

58. I discuss strong republicans in *Republican Paradoxes and Liberal Anxieties*, ch. 2.

59. Many, but not all, contemporary liberals hold that the state may properly regulate one or another institution or practice in civil society, but, they go on to argue, the basic distinction must be respected.

60. See Friedrich Hayek, *The Political Order of a Free People* (Chicago: University of Chicago Press, 1979); and Michael Oakeshott, *Rationalism in Politics and Other Essays* (Indianapolis: Liberty Press, 1962).

61. Representatives of the strong republican tradition are Aristotle, Machiavelli, and Rousseau.

62. *Hind Swaraj*, ch. 19.

63. For representative selections of Gandhi's belief that class conflict is not inevitable, see *Harijan*, October 19, 1935 and December 6, 1936. "I do not believe that capitalists and the landlords are all exploiters by an inherent necessity or there is a basic or irreconcilable antagonism between their interests and those of the masses. All exploitation is based on the cooperation, willing or forced, of the exploited" (*Amrit Bazar Patrika*, August 3, 1934). However, he favors privately owned small holdings and offers his theory of "trusteeship" to control large, industrial holdings. See his *Trusteeship* (Ahmedabad: Navajivan Publishing House, 1960).

64. "Pandit Nehru wants industrialization because he thinks that if it is socialized, it would be free from the evils of capitalism. My own view is that the evils are inherent in industrialism, and no amount of socialization can eradicate them." *Harijan*, September 29, 1944.

65. *Young India*, December 4, 1924.

66. D. G. Tendulkar, *Mahatma: The Life of M. K. Gandhi* (New Delhi: Ministry of Information and Broadcasting, 1961), 4, 15.

67. See *Harijan*, March 23, 1947, for his attack on Nehru's efforts to industrialize India. For him, any plan "which exploited the raw materials of a country and neglected the potentially more powerful man-power was lop-sided and could never establish human equality."

68. See *Young India*, January 20, 1927.

69. He argues the villagers "cannot retain [their] freedom . . . if they do not control the production of the prime necessaries of life." *Young India*, July 2, 1931.

70. *Young India*, June 17, 1926. In detailing the effects of acute poverty, Gandhi sees people who "had resigned themselves to death by slow and painful starvation. They had become so accustomed to living on charity doles that they almost refused to work. They had become less than animals, they were living sepulchers." *Young India*, September 4, 1924.

71. *Industrialize and Perish* (Ahmedabad: Navajivan Publishing House, 1966), 24.

72. *Young India*, February 16, 1921.

73. *Young India*, February 16, 1921.

74. "Advice to Construction Workers," May 13, 1947, in Iyer, *Writings*, 3: 221.

75. "Khadi is the only economic proposition in terms of the millions of villagers until such a time, if ever, when a better system of supplying work and adequate wages for every able-bodied person . . . is found" (*Harijan*, June 20,

1936). In an article defending spinning, Gandhi observes that people should "burn [the spinning] wheel if you find a better substitute" (*Young India*, September 15, 1927).

76. *Young India*, October 31, 1924. For Gandhi, spinning is not an end but a means to address the basic needs of the poor and unemployed. He claims that spinning is the "only hope" for these people. "What is claimed for spinning is that (1) it supplies the readiest occupation to those who have leisure and are in want of a few coppers; (2) it is known to the thousands; (3) it is easily learnt; (4) it requires practically no outlay of capital; . . . (7) it affords immediate relief in times of famine and scarcity; . . . (10) even the smallest success means so much immediate gain to the people; and (11) it is the most potent instrument of securing co-operation among the people" (*Young India*, August 21, 1924).

77. *Harijan*, July 30, 1938. Several years later, he offers a shorter version of his ideal: "Everyone must have a balanced diet, a decent house to live in, facilities for the education of one's children, and adequate medical relief" (*Harijan*, March 31, 1946).

78. When asked whether he is opposed to all machinery, Gandhi answers that he is opposed to its abuses and favors scientific and technological "discoveries" to help laborers (*Young India*, November 13, 1924).

79. *Young India*, July 17, 1924; also see *Harijan*, July 26, 1942.

80. See Pantham, "Gandhi, Nehru, and Modernity." Gandhi claims he has "no quarrel with steamships or telegraphs. They may stay, . . . [but] they are not an end" (*Young India*, October 7, 1926).

81. "Question: Then you are fighting not against machinery as such but against its abuses which are so much in evidence today?"

"Answer: I would unhesitatingly say, yes. I am aiming not at the eradication of all machinery, but limitation." *Young India*, November 13, 1924.

82. *Harijan*, August 29, 1936. Ten years earlier he observes, "Now that we know the use of steam and electricity, we should be able to use them on due occasion and after we have learnt to avoid industrialization" (*Young India*, October 6, 1926).

83. *Community Service News*, September–October, 1946. "I have not contemplated, much less advised the abandonment of a single healthy, life-giving industrial activity for the sake of hand spinning. The entire foundation of the spinning wheel rests on the fact that there are crores [tens of millions] of semi-unemployed people in India" (*Young India*, May 27, 1926).

84. "I am personally opposed to great trusts and concentrations of industries by means of elaborate machinery" (*Young India*, July 24, 1924). On another occasion, he observes, "If India is to evolve along non-violent lines, it will have to decentralize many things. Centralization cannot be sustained and defended without adequate force" (*Harijan*, December 30, 1939).

85. "I would favour the use of the most elaborate machinery if thereby India's pauperism and resulting idleness be avoided" (*Young India*, November 3, 1921).

86. "I do visualize electricity, ship-building, ironworks, machine-making, and the like existing side by side with village handicrafts. But the order of dependence will be reversed. Hitherto the industrialization has been so planned as to destroy the villages and village crafts. In the State of the future, it will subserve the villages and their crafts. I do not share the socialist belief that centralization of the necessities of life will conduce to the common welfare when the centralized industries are planned and owned by the State." *Harijan*, Jan. 27, 1939.

87. "A Word of Explanation," in *Hind Swaraj* (Ahmedabad: Navajivan, 1938), 16.

88. See *Hind Swaraj*, ch. 11.

89. Letter to Jawaharlal Nehru, October 5, 1945, in *Collected Works*, 81: 319–20.

90. "A Word of Explanation," *Hind Swaraj*, 16.

91. Although Gandhi believes that the promise of making more money coaxes some to abandon traditional Indian culture, this is not the central aspect of his critique. If it were, a strong moral educational campaign can theoretically reverse the process. But because necessity, not avarice, drives most people to industrial centers in search of jobs, the problem is not mainly motivational but is deeply structural.

92. Letter to Jawaharlal Nehru, October 5, 1945, in *Collected Works*, 81: 319–21.

93. See *Hindu Standard*, October 28, 1944.

94. For a discussion of Gandhi's and Jefferson's views on politics, see Lucien Buck, "Gandhi and Jefferson on Democracy and Humanism," *Gandhi Marg* 16, 3 (July-September 1995): 175–192. Some of the political parallels between Gandhi and Jefferson are their support for decentralized power, their endorsement for participatory politics, and their celebration of local government (Gandhi's panchayats and Jefferson's wards).

95. For a discussion of Jefferson's populist economics, see Joyce Appleby, *Liberalism and Republicanism in the Historical Imagination* (Cambridge: Harvard University Press, 1992), 253–76, 291–319. Appleby and Richard Matthews, in *The Racial Politics of Thomas Jefferson* (Lawrence: University Press of Kansas, 1984) argue that Jefferson is not opposed to modernity. Nevertheless, he continually warns about its dangers to liberty and political equality.

96. Letter to Jawaharlal Nehru, October 5, 1945, in *Collected Works*, 81: 319–21.

97. For a discussion of Gandhian economics and politics as utopian experiments, see Richard Fox, *Gandhian Utopia: Experiments with Culture* (Boston: Beacon Press, 1989), esp. 54–58.

98. See *Young India*, June 2, 1927; also see Bondurant, *Conquest of Violence*, 168–69.

99. See *Young India*, October 7, 1931.

100. "Man is a social being. Without interrelation with society, he cannot realize his oneness with the universe or suppress his egoism. . . . If man were so placed or could so place himself as to be absolutely above all dependence on his fellow-beings, he would become so proud and arrogant as to be a veritable burden and nuisance to the world. Dependence on society teaches him the lesson of humility." *Young India*, March 21, 1929.

101. "Individual liberty and interdependence are both essential for life in society. Only Robinson Crusoe can afford to be all self-sufficient" (*Harijan*, Mar. 31, 1946).

102. "Indian society may never reach the goal [of economic equality] but it was the duty of every Indian to set his sail towards that goal and no other if India was to be a happy land." *Harijan*, March 16, 1947.

103. Kothari is representative of those who find a deleterious side of modernity. He sees the new, dynamic technologies leading "not only to a growing marginality of man as a producer; he will also be forced to live under conditions of stress, overcrowding, and despair" (*Footsteps into the Future*, 91–92). In a later book, Kothari worries that there is "a growing amnesia towards the poor everywhere" (*Poverty*, 29).

5

GANDHI'S POLITICS

Today, in politics, democracy is the *name* for what we cannot have—yet cannot cease to want.[1]

Politics is unavoidably about power and people: about how power can enable or disable people. With this in mind, Gandhi observes that "political power is not an end but one of the means of enabling people to better their condition in every department of life."[2] Working with this perspective, he seeks to understand the nature of power, how it is expressed in rhetoric and practice, and the ways, if any, it might be legitimated and limited. In unfolding his answers, Gandhi shares and departs from liberal-democratic views on politics as well as blends political realism and idealism to his view of what a good polity should be all about. He insistently challenges standard conceptions of power and invites his readers to question familiar approaches to the subject. To do this, Gandhi denies the conventional liberal distinction between civil society and the state and liberal claims to neutrality in order to disclose the many sites of power in both the public and private realms and how power often favors some at the expense of others. He sees power residing not only in the state but also in social practices (such as untouchability), ideology (the authority of modernity), the structure of the economy, and the myriad ways that ideas and people are organized. All the while, he challenges an activist state, finding it pretentious in what it thinks it can accomplish and dangerous in the way it uses people to achieve its objectives.

The problems of political power are lessened but not solved by democratizing it, according to Gandhi. Distrusting the adequacy of standard ideas about democracy, he denies that voting and elections are sufficient either to assure a government based on popular consent or to

139

safeguard the autonomy of everyone. Representative democracy is important to Gandhi, but he argues that popular rule requires even more.[3] Holding that any state reflects the configurations of power that exist in society, he wants to promote a regime where significant economic, social, and political inequalities have been reduced and where all forms of power are dispersed. For him, the ideal democracy protects and reflects plurality, most especially responding to those who have been excluded in the past. In this spirit, Gandhi sees "This age of awakening of the poorest of the poor" is the "age of democracy."[4] To make it a reality, he urges democrats to struggle to make government simple and avoid hierarchy and domination. Even should this succeed, Gandhi finds an ideal democracy can make mistakes, and he invests his citizens with civil disobedience to confront injustice that might arise there.

Gandhi's conception of power is intimately tied to his radical views of freedom and autonomy.[5] For him, individuals not only carry duties and deserve freedom but also are the ultimate source of power. In locating power in individuals, Gandhi wants them to know that they can govern themselves. Attempting to be self-governing, of course, can bring harsh penalties, and we typically say that someone who is punished lacks power. Gandhi denies this, holding that defiant persons no longer allow fatalism or fear to be their governors. He sees people surrendering their power when they refuse to assert their convictions, leading him to claim that "no man loses his freedom except through his own weakness."[6]

HIND SWARAJ

The way that the cosmos, duties, power, and autonomy come together for Gandhi can be seen in his view of *Hind Swaraj* or Indian self-rule. Gandhi seeks to make *swaraj* a concept that not only brings self-rule to the country and its people but also unites Indians to one another. For Gandhi, India once enjoyed self-rule, but that was before the advent of colonialism and "modern civilization."[7] To regain its freedom, Gandhi insists, requires all Indians to resist domination and to rule themselves. For him, this means not only empowerment but also "self-control."[8] This will occur, on his account, not because India has its own flag, army, and centralized state which exercises an unlimited sovereignty over citizens but because all Indians treat each other with equal regard and respect, are able to subdue necessity, and see themselves related in a cosmos.

In this respect, Gandhi's sense of Indian independence diametrically differs from conventional understandings of national self-determination. As nationalism develops, claims of territorial sovereignty are extended not only to control the resident population but to everything under its jurisdiction. On this view, the sovereign determines which policies enhance its understanding of the security, well-being, and development of the nation. With modern sovereignty, constitutionally designated officials claim the right to arrange and rearrange their priorities at will, constrained only by competing centers of power and by technology (with the idea that with less political opposition and more sophisticated technology, they can rearrange more). This is what characterizes most anticolonial movements whose goal is to wrest sovereign control from alien hands and place it under indigenous control.[9]

Gandhi disputes this view, finding that such movements unwittingly trap themselves when they accept the definition of victory set by their former colonial masters, namely that the winner exercises unhindered sovereign control. From Gandhi's perspective, such a victory not only severs the harmony of the community, it also permits officials to ignore autonomy, tradition, and the environment. He sees claims to modern sovereignty consigning these latter goods, now remainders, to a subordinate and expendable position. From Gandhi's perspective, if national independence is exercised apart from a cosmological outlook, the very purpose of Indian independence is defeated. National independence is no improvement for him if Indians replace colonial officials and dominate their fellow citizens or destroy their own civilization, society, and environment.

Gandhi's *Hind Swaraj* is about the ability of ordinary Indians to rule themselves. For this reason, Gandhi holds that an India independent of imperial rule but steeped in internal domination and poverty has no real self-governance.[10] For him, both the whole and the parts must be free, and each must reflect a sense of interdependence and cooperation. Among other things, this means to Gandhi that citizens ought not have their lives scripted and directed by others. The vision Gandhi holds for an independent India of self-governing men and women is not only about goals but also about the ways those goals are pursued. For this reason, he insists that politics must be primarily about means; change must come nonviolently, and he warns that "if our political condition undergoes a change, irrespective of the manner in which it is brought about . . . the change will not be in the direction of progress but very likely the opposite."[11]

GANDHI'S MULTIPLE MEANINGS OF POWER

Gandhi finds conventional meanings of power are incomplete. In the standard account, power is the ability of one actor to cause others to behave in ways they would not have otherwise chosen. On this account, power can be either positive or negative. With the former, power-holders promise some good to induce others to act in particular ways. For example, parents promise a treat to their children, interest groups offer contributions to political candidates, or governments offer subsidies to businesses to get the recipients to act in a particular way. The inducements are negative when some harm is threatened, as when parents threaten to punish their children, interests groups oppose a candidate, or governments penalize certain conduct. Whether positively or negatively expressed, such expressions of power are usually directed at overt behavior.

Gandhi recognizes that these are palpable, consequential expressions of power that cannot be ignored. But he has several complaints about the adequacy of such constructions of power. In the first place, the emphasis is on active rather than latent power; as a consequence, power that is quiet is disregarded and Gandhi wants to rouse quiet Indians to express their power. Conventional expressions also disregard the potential power that lies with the quiet and complacent. Moreover, the empirical emphasis of power frequently loses sight of the often unexpected and unwelcome consequences of applied power which can harm not only others but also the power-holders. Gandhi also finds that standard views of power tend to be static and take current power arrangements to be natural and settled.

Another problem he has with much contemporary political analyses is that the state is the focus of power and little attention is given to sites of power in civil society. What is overlooked is the way that nonpolitical institutions and practices enlarge, shift, contract, or close the choices of individuals and define, redefine, locate, and relocate meanings of the good, necessity, success, and harm. Moreover, a state-focused view of power ignores how private power invades the public realm to use public power for private purposes. For this reason, Gandhi wants to confront not only the state but the other locations of power that he finds hierarchical, asymmetrical, and dominating.

Especially unusual in the literature, Gandhi invests individuals with extraordinary power. He does this in two very different ways. First, he argues that what individuals accept or tolerate serves to perpetuate institutions and practices that would otherwise languish and disappear. He holds that individuals, having transferred their power, can recover it when they wish, with civil disobedience if necessary.[12] In reclaiming their power, people "nearly establish their own government" and rule themselves.[13] If agents are to be autonomous and remain loyal to their moral commitments, Gandhi wants them to see they cannot transfer responsibility to institutions that act in their name but in ways that deny their own moral commitments. On his account,

> Most people do not understand the complicated machinery of the government. They do not realize that every citizen silently but none the less certainly sustains the government of the day in ways of which he has no knowledge. Every citizen therefore renders himself responsible for every act of his government. And it is quite proper to support it so long as the actions of the government are bearable. But when they hurt him and his nation, it becomes his duty to withdraw his support.[14]

With this in mind, Gandhi insists that no government exists independently of what the people accept. They may accede to their government because they genuinely support it. Or they may disagree with the state's conduct but nevertheless acquiesce because the costs of dissent are high, because they are fatalistic, or because they are preoccupied with their own individual concerns. Whatever the reason, Gandhi argues, government rests on their sufferance, even though the state or individuals might deny the relationship. By making power visible and by teaching people they are the basis of power, he thinks he can domesticate it and make it accountable to clear-sighted citizens.

The second way Gandhi credits individuals with power appears in his call for the individual to stand alone, if necessary, to reclaim power. On his account, lonely assertions of power can have a powerful demonstration effect as others come to see their complicity in their own domination and understand that they can recover the power they ceded to others.[15] One reason he pushes this argument is that he wants to empower those on the periphery who are told they have no power and believe it.

In what follows in this chapter, I will be using the varied understandings Gandhi credits to power, some conventional and some uniquely his. In doing so, I mean to show that he broadens standard meanings of power to include more phenomena than is usually the case and that part of his reconstruction of power involves positions that are ordinarily thought to be contrary to power, such as Gandhi's view of the power of love.

THE POWER OF LOVE

Gandhi claims he can change attitudes over the long term by mobilizing the power of love. Because this reading of power is distant from the way we normally think about either love or power, it is helpful to talk first about some non-Gandhian approaches to empowerment and conversion before approaching his conception of power as love. When we talk about the way that literacy or education empowers people, we mean that literate or educated persons have the ability (or power) to see things they would have not otherwise seen, are freed from ignorance and superstition, and are no longer dependent on those who are literate or educated. Much of the push for literacy in sixteenth-century Europe, for example, stems from the aspiration of individuals to read the Bible in the vernacular so that they, and not others, can determine the meaning of the sacred texts. Today, parents typically believe a solid education provides their sons and daughters with abilities and aspirations to do things they would not have otherwise had imagined.

We can also take the religious conversion or awakening of some adults or the rejection of religion by other adults as expressions of new outlooks as well as forms of empowerment. In the first case, religious conversion is said to free men and women from their old, derelict ways; in the second case, adults are said to be no longer dependent on a religious orthodoxy and are now free to decide things on their own. In each of these examples, individuals are said to see and do things differently than if they had remained glued to their former understandings.

Gandhi's view of love reflects some of these expressions of changed outlooks. Because he seeks to alter both attitudes and behavior, he asks how people who are committed to particular ideas about what is real, possible, and good can voluntarily come to a different understanding. If individuals are ambivalent or unsatisfied about their current views, then they are open to solid, rational arguments to change. But Gandhi recognizes that those he wants to convert usually carry their own strong convictions and are not readily open to alternative, particularly conflicting, standards. Therefore, he reasons, he must appeal to their "heart," and he does this through love. Then, he believes, his opponents are open to the possibility of seeing the world in a different way. Once this happens, he thinks they are ready to hear rational appeals and conversion is possible.

Gandhi knows that conventional applications of power have incredible abilities to change behavior because of the rewards and penalties they carry. But such inducements do not necessarily convince people to genuinely want what they are commanded to do. Moreover, when the inducements are lifted, many return to their earlier ways of thinking and acting, making the effects of power only temporary. Gandhi holds that love is different; it is a force for lasting change which breaks down resistances. For him, love creates the basis for trust rather than the suspicion that accompanies conventional uses of power. It does this by speaking to a transcendent, rather than to an instrumental self, and disclosing what people share.

In the first chapter, I discussed Gandhi's view of ahimsa or love, and it is helpful to notice how he translates this conception into politics. Holding that everyone has the capacity to love and everyone can respond to love, he argues that it is love that holds people together, not their interests. Moving as it does beyond particularities, love is said to appeal to what is best in persons and when love is operative, bonds of friendship and community can thrive. Although others have called for strong civic attachments to form a national bond, Gandhi wants to do much more. He intends to universalize love, roaming beyond conventional boundaries and reaching for those who have significantly different ways of looking at the world. Moreover, Gandhian love is expressed nonviolently and, in this way, treats everyone as worthy of respect. Finally, Gandhi holds that because love can melt hatred and anger, it is possible to forge agreements and evolve outlooks that enable different men and women to live together amicably.

By asking people to love their opponents, and even suffer for their commitments, Gandhi wants to avoid what Nietzsche calls resentment.[16] Resentment is born out of the hatred and fear we have of those we think are responsible for harming us. It rests on the assumption that if the other is conquered, we are released from its torment and now free to make our own choices. Gandhi sees this as a delusion. Recognizing that others are often a source of injustice and need to be resisted, he wants such resistance to avoid two common mistakes embedded in a politics of resentment. One is the idea that the contest must be fought on the terrain defined by others because such a move means that any victory will mimic the standards of success predetermined by the other. For Gandhi, part of the struggle is to locate the field that speaks to our needs and is not hostile to our autonomy. The second mistake Gandhi wants to avoid is the idea that once we have defeated the other, the task of liberation is complete and all good things will follow.[17] This ignores the fact that in accepting the terms of the other, we repress our own aspirations, which have now become remainders as we adopt the terms defined by the other to describe us and what is important. Gandhian love seeks to defeat resentment and open new ways of thinking how we can live harmoniously with the other.

HOW DOES GANDHI UNDERSTAND POLITICS?

There once was a time, Gandhi argues, when politics were relatively unimportant. Life was simple and people led coherent lives.[18] On his account, politics seldom intruded into the lives of ordinary people and demanded little from them. At most, rulers exacted some tribute, but this imposition did not disturb the lives of ordinary people. What transpired in palaces or on battlefields little affected stable self-understandings and routines. Satisfied with their tribute, rulers did not generally disturb the rhythm of everyday life, and the traditions of local communities guided conduct rather than the state. This, Gandhi contends, changes in the modern age.

Today, he finds that it matters to ordinary people what happens in the corridors of power; it affects how they meet their multiple needs and the identity they are assigned. On Gandhi's reading, the modern state penetrates into basic, ordinary routines and invades what was once private. It does this not only by coercively extending state power into private space but also by legitimizing new institutional practices which, he believes, redefine the good, diminish the need for cooperation, and alter the ways men and women make a living. As Gandhi sees it, we have not asked to become political; rather politics compels our attention because it continually and profoundly intrudes into our lives today. In the modern

> age, our degradation reveals itself through our political condition. . . .
> In the olden days, our peasants, though ignorant of who ruled them, led their simple lives free from fear. They can no longer afford to be so unconcerned.[19]

For Gandhi, politics is unavoidable in the modern age and state power is seen as particularly dangerous. In some important ways, Gandhi's argument corresponds to St. Augustine's. Sharing the view that power cannot justify itself, both part company with efforts to legitimate power on substantive or procedural grounds.[20] For Augustine and Gandhi, there is no legitimate reason why some people should force their will on others or why some should use the violence of the state to choose what others may choose. For each, no person or state has an inherent right to compel others to do what they would not have freely chosen for themselves. Augustine sees the state appropriating a power that is properly God's and making legitimacy into a secular principle born out of the necessity for order. Although Gandhi does not share Augustine's preoccupation about order, he agrees that necessity cannot be converted into morality. Power is important to both Augustine and Gandhi who see individuals drawn in two very different directions. Augustine sees the choice between virtue and sin and finds that the latter has an unshakable presence, tied as it is to human pride. For Gandhi, people can develop morally or regress to the state of the "brute," and individuals "must choose" which course they will take.[21]

Augustine and Gandhi see pride at work in our various efforts to graft our conceptions of justice to political power and, in doing so, to justify the coercion of some over others. The search for secular justice is sometimes a well-intentioned effort to move beyond the contingent and pursue a conception of the good and partly a reflection of pride. However, Augustine finds efforts to legitimize coercive power as the great human conceit, mimicking the divine in claiming knowledge about what constitutes the good and the ability to achieve it. Armed with these deceptions, the proud believe they can exonerate their use of power over others. With similar arguments, Gandhi finds that any claim to the truth is, at best, partial and unavoidably tainted with our pride, and he seeks to disable arguments that exonerate political coercion for the sake of a higher good.

Although Gandhi's critique of politics parallels much of Augustine's, their views rest on very different premises. Even though both believe that human reason is frail and can never fully understand a comprehensive truth, Augustine confidently concludes that we can approach the truth through Christian faith. For his part, Gandhi believes that essential elements of the truth are captured only incompletely by any particular religious or secular position; at best, each embodies a slice of the truth but none can claim a comprehensive understanding of the truth because each is partial. More than that, Gandhi places much more emphasis on the autonomy of individuals and the power of love as a brake on political power than Augustine who emphasizes eternal salvation. While Augustine believes we are at our best when we follow God's word through a life of prayer and devotion, Gandhi argues that we are at our most religious when we actively confront injustice in the world.

Gandhi's reading of politics is based on his understanding of the pervasiveness and unavoidability of power, and he seeks to confront, diffuse, and challenge it and expose the pride that often drives it. On his account, pride is always ready to assert itself, whether in the state or civil society, and always ready to hunt for more power to implement its plans. For this reason, Gandhi reasons, politics in the modern era especially must be about clear-sightedness and nonviolent struggle.

CIVIC EDUCATION

Gandhi finds that most people commonly misunderstand the nature of power and politics, limiting their political attention to formal institutions, laws, and rituals and usually taking little notice of how power pervades society.[22] He seeks to educate his fellow citizens about the nature of power, its myriad sites, its dangers, and how it enables or disables them. Armed with such an understanding, he believes that people are better equipped to detect and challenge abuses of power and make it responsible.[23]

Popular conceptions of power and politics typically reflect the civic education and socialization of citizens. This education covers not only what is taught at home and in schools but also the lessons attached to political activities and rituals, such as with elections or civic commemorations. When this kind of civic education takes hold, it serves to legitimize both political power as constituted and the basic laws governing behavior and property. The lessons citizens learn usually give an important place to the goodness, legitimacy, and appropriateness of their regime and its ideas of fairness and equity. However, the focus of conventional civic education on governmental arrangements and rules has the effect of concealing other sites and practices of power located throughout society. In the process, it conceals the ways that many forms of power direct choice and assess costs.

Gandhi is particularly concerned about the hidden character of much contemporary power. For him, conventional political education is misleading not only because its formalism conceals much power but also because individuals do not understand they are the basis of political power and are implicated in its uses. Learning about the formal obligations and rights allotted to them, they also typically accept the limits assigned to them and the need to defer and acquiesce. For Gandhi, most of what we learn about power and politics is incomplete and unrealistic. To talk, as he does, about our "hallucination about titles, law courts, schools, and councils"[24] means that people invest an aura in them that is unreal. Titles are said to bring authority, courts justice, schools a neutral education, and councils fair laws. For his part, Gandhi wants to problematize these practices and make them observable sites of power.[25]

THE NEW IDOL

Gandhi finds that many place an unwarranted faith in the state, either the current or a reformed one. They fail to see the causes of their discontents often lie elsewhere as they call on the state to strike out at the objects of their resentment. In doing so, he thinks they elevate the state to a position that is based on a dangerous deception that it represents the people, acts on their behalf, and can cure what ails them. In this respect, Gandhi's concerns parallel Nietzsche's observation that "coldly [the state] tells lies too; and this lie crawls out of its mouth: 'I, the state, am the people.' That is a lie!"[26]

With Nietzsche, Gandhi sees the pretentiousness of the modern state as menacing. Rising from the ashes of religion and tradition that aimed at the good, the modern state fills a vacuum, promising to replace neglected gods and discarded traditions. For his part, Nietzsche finds that the modern state "lures them, the all-too-many—and . . . devours them, chews them, and ruminates! 'On earth there is nothing greater than I: the ordering finger of God am I'—thus roars the monster."[27] Nietzsche laments that today even "great souls" are prey to its seductive claims. Those with "rich hearts" believe they have no recourse but to turn to the state; in doing so, they become its creatures and not their own masters. Again Nietzsche, "It will give you everything if you will adore it, this new idol: thus it buys the splendor of your virtue and the look of your proud eyes."[28]

To explore Gandhi's critique of the pretentiousness of the modern state, including those that are democratic, I take up several themes in his work which question the necessity and desirability of a superintending state as well as what passes for the legitimacy of the democratic state.[29] When Gandhi initially raises questions about the adequacy of democracy, both fascism and communism are threatening political movements and his criticisms are taken at the time as wrong-headed and beside the point. Since the destruction of fascism and the collapse of Soviet communism, democracy has become the nominal legitimizing principle of government. At the same time, many who are highly committed to democracy have argued that the actual practices of Western politics are pale copies of what democracies should look like in practice.[30] In many ways, their criticisms reflect elements of Gandhi's earlier challenge to Western democratic theories and practices, and I will scan some of their critiques in order to situate Gandhi's own position. In what follows, I concentrate on Gandhi's arguments with the democratic state as we have come to know it.

Problematizing Democratic Politics

Gandhi attempts to decenter claims that a universal franchise and majoritarian procedures are sufficient to legitimize power. He thinks the extension of the franchise is necessary but insufficient for a robust democracy, particularly in the face of countertendencies in complex, modern societies to dedemocratize the polity. One of the major impediments to democratizing any regime is the tendency of public officials simultaneously to display and hide their power.[31] By concentrating on the ceremonial, the monumental, and the martial, they seek to invest themselves as the carriers of the nation's best interests and security and to legitimize their use of power and the political institutions they manage. At the same time, those with power rarely bargain publicly about who is to get and who is to pay. The public debates in which they engage seldom reflect the rational, dispassionate search for solutions that is celebrated in classical conceptions of democracy but serve instead as rhetorical devices to reinforce supporters and embarrass opponents. Moreover, the debates that appear open and spontaneous often mask prior decisions that are made by oligarchs, far from the gaze of the public.[32]

The tendency of power to hide itself behind the ceremonial, to become hierarchical and concentrated, and to avoid accountability are the very things Gandhi wants India to avoid in its construction of democracy. In his search for a responsive, nonviolent mode of popular government, he insists India must move beyond the competitive elections and pluralism that mark Western democracies, and he urges participatory, decentralized modes of politics.[33] Even with these reforms, he sees future dangers because of the inherent dangers of power and the unavoidability of pride. To domesticate power in order to make it fit for human society requires that power be continually exposed and scrutinized. Otherwise, it has a tendency to hide and become dangerous, not hospitable, to democracy.

Gandhi is also concerned with the tendency in modern democracy to be satisfied with the proposition that formal political equality assures everyone the same voice in public space and ensures popular accountability. He wants a more expansive sense of equality, one that enables all to stand on the same solid footing when they face their government. A democracy that is built on steep economic and social inequalities is one that is apt to be more responsive to those with more and indifferent to those with less. As Gandhi sees matters, this cannot qualify as a real democracy.[34]

The Issue of Majoritarianism

In contemporary democracies, competitive elections provide an accepted way of determining the will of the majority and investing government with legitimacy. However, it is not always clear what is meant by the term "majority" or how it operates in democratic practice. Contemporary democratic theorists have discussed how the term is fungible, how different decision rules reveal very different outcomes, how some are included in the democratic process but others are not, how the scale and complexity of modern society reduces citizen control, and how other institutions—such as bureaucracies, interest groups, and corporations—undermine democratic accountability.[35]

Even when democratic decision-making represents the majority, Gandhi asks about the status of the minority. Sometimes, losing affects matters of convenience or issues of marginal concern. Gandhi is not particularly interested in these losses because the essential autonomy of individuals is not affected. However, he finds that if human beings are degraded by the rules of the majority, losing is something quite different than with the earlier case. Here we encounter Gandhi's suspicions of claims that democratic governance is an adequate check on the abuse of power. Unlike William Jennings Bryan who thinks the voice of the people is the voice of God, Gandhi holds the voice of the people is the voice of voters, a fallible collection of often well-meaning (but sometimes indifferent or self-interested) people who constitute something over fifty percent of the population. While the democratic process eliminates the tyrannical rule of one or a few over the majority, Gandhi believes that it cannot overcome human fallibility and, he concludes, cannot legitimately coerce a minority to obey laws contrary to its deepest principles.[36] Not surprisingly, he readily concludes that "In matters of conscience, the law of majority has no place."[37] With this in mind, he observes the

> majority vote . . . does not cancel the minority vote. It stands. Where there is no principle involved and there is a programme to be carried

out, the minority has got to follow the majority. But where there is a principle involved, the dissent stands, and it is bound to express itself in practice when the occasion arises.[38]

Gandhi does not expect his position will lead to a flood of objections to majority decisions. However deeply suspicious he is of government, he grants that it is necessary to provide a minimal order in social life and thinks most citizens accept this position. In assigning a duty to citizens to be vigilant about abuses of power, he does not want them to inflate every grievance into a matter of conscience and claim an exemption from any rule that is inconvenient or disagreeable. In this regard, Gandhi writes, he would "be deeply distressed, if on every conceivable occasion every one of us were to be a law unto oneself and to scrutinize in golden scales every action of our future National Assembly."[39] For him, mistakes might be made by the government, and the issue is whether these errors rob persons of their autonomy. Gandhi finds it just as repugnant to be apathetic about serious injustices coming from the majority as it is to elevate personal interests over democratically enacted rules.

Political Interests

Gandhi recognizes that most people do not shake their concerns about themselves. The way they make a living, raise a family, and interact with others, and the way their background empowers or degrades them are important to ordinary people and, Gandhi thinks, they should be. The perennial danger for Gandhi is that people frequently make their own interests their primary standard for judging politics. For many, politics becomes a means to enhance their well-being, even if that means others must pay for their benefits or others are injured by their claims. For this reason, Gandhi wants to make politics safe from interests, not hospitable to them.[40]

In the modern world, Gandhi believes, interests have assumed unwelcome dimensions. Most obviously, they have multiplied, and many have little or nothing to do with exercising a person's autonomy or meeting necessity. For this reason, Gandhi challenges the pluralist position that no interest should count for more than another interest and everyone should be free to advance his or her interest, however defined.[41] Gandhi wants to rank interests, making the well-being of the most destitute the highest one. On his account, "every [other] interest, therefore, that is hostile to their interest, must be revised or must subside if it is not capable of revision."[42]

Gandhi denies the pluralist view that politics is a vast market, with candidates and parties acting like firms, seeking to win votes (or customers) for their product. In the pluralist account, winning is what counts, and it becomes necessary to build a coalition with promises of individual advantage. In this setting, any coalition that is formed may or may not be coherent, may or may not interfere with the minority, and may or may not endanger the group's or the community's long-term welfare.[43] With its emphasis on constructing a winning coalition with promises of short-term gains, the market model of politics does not and (according to such defenders as Anthony Downs and Robert Dahl) cannot speak to a common good or general welfare.[44] The foundation of this form of politics is not the citizen but the organized interest group.[45] This Gandhi rejects as vigorously as he can.[46] For him, "ultimately, it is the individual who is the unit."[47]

For Gandhi, we need a different conceptual language to think about democracy than can be supplied by political pluralism. One reason is its penchant to concentrate on immediate benefits for strategic publics. With this in mind, he criticizes the narrow, short-term focus he detects in British parliamentary politics in his time. While it hardly resembles the vote-trading and coalition-building that has come to characterize modern political pluralism, Gandhi sees the British model unable to speak to a general good. Political favors are widely dispersed, not in the forms of "what are generally known as bribes," but as a "subtler influence" that steers elected officials away from a search for the common good.[48] He also fears that speech is distorted in pluralist democracy; it has become primarily cathartic and not communicative. But if voters can only hear how something affects their interests, they will be deaf to the concerns and needs of others. As he understands it, the

> evolution of democracy is not possible if we are not prepared to hear the other side. We shut the doors of reason when we refuse to listen to our opponents, or having listened make fun of them. If intolerance becomes a habit, we run the risk of missing the truth.[49]

Gandhi attempts to secure a different kind of pluralism in India, one that is attentive to and protective of the multiple traditions and practices that mark the country. He sees different local customs providing people with their own particular modes of understanding, making a living, raising a family, and meeting their multiple needs. To assume that out of the welter of differences, one state-imposed solution should crowd out all alternatives denies standing to other practices and logics. Distinguishing between political and cultural pluralism, he finds that in pursuing the former, the latter is discounted and becomes lost.[50] One reason Gandhi continually returns to the villages of India is that he considers them to be havens for the diverse moral practices and traditions that demonstrate the mutual dependence of ordinary men and women on one another.[51]

Challenging Bureaucracy

Bureaucracies in the modern democratic polity commonly develop in response to popular pressures for state action. Today, the public expects government to provide public education and health services, assure safe drinking water and sanitation, and license health professionals, to name just a few of the tasks citizens routinely assign to the modern state. But modern democracies appear unable to tame the administrative and regulatory organizations they have created to perform these tasks. One reason is that citizens want efficiency in the delivery of services, and bureaucracies take on hierarchical forms that promise to increase both control and efficiency.[52] This drive for the timely, efficient delivery of services masks the high price that Max Weber has shown bureaucracy to charge for its services:

> the more it is "dehumanized," the more completely it succeeds in eliminating from official business love, hatred, and all purely personal, irrational, and emotional elements which escape calculation.[53]

For Weber, the rule-governed nature of bureaucracies that are said to assure the fair and neutral application of law comes with a heavy cost. One reason is that bureaucratic neutrality emphasizes that officials set aside personal or partisan considerations when they regulate or administer. This means not playing favorites and speaking in an impartial voice. However, the bureaucratic process is marked with all sorts of assumptions that are far from impartial. For Foucault, it "ceaselessly characterizes, classifies, and specializes" and engages in "surveillance, continuous registration, perpetual assessment and classification" in ways that are "both immense and minute."[54] From this perspective, the modern bureaucratic state is not neutral when it assigns identities to others who are now known by the requirements of state policy and not by their character or needs. Because bureaucratic classifications are not benign but carry power that can affect individuals in the most profound ways, Gandhi is suspicious of claims to neutrality that sanction the use of power over others. For him, the partiality of any truth and the criticality of autonomy mitigate against the bureaucratic impulse to classify and categorize individuals. Moreover, Gandhi finds the bureaucratic proclivity to rest on expertise means it does not have to listen but merely applies its version of the truth; for this reason, he wants specialists to stop, listen, and be accountable.[55]

Bureaucracies are highly technical affairs, and specialists carry a knowledge and competency not available to the lay public. Lacking technical proficiency, ordinary citizens are shut out of the process of policy formation and implementation, and democratic control is undermined. To challenge this tendency, Gandhi seeks to diffuse power and uncomplicate things so that people can take charge of their lives rather than have others take charge of them.[56] He warns that independence "will be a sorry affair if people look up to [the government] for the regulation of every detail of life" and quarrels with the propensity to accept new forms of control and regulation.[57]

Gandhi's critique of bureaucracy takes on a special poignancy today, applying not only to the centralized bureaucracies of the nation-state but the bureaucracies of private megainstitutions. Deregulation gives a wider role to nongovernmental institutions, but the structures and dangers of bureaucracy are not transformed when they migrate from governmental to private settings. They remain impersonal, hierarchical, and specialized and continue to challenge the democratic process and individual self-rule. As the welfare state recedes in many places, the institutional power of the megainstitutions of corporate bureaucracies and mass associations often fills the vacuum left by a retreating government. Gandhi would not find these shifts in power salutary because he wants to challenge all forms of concentrated power whether in the public or private sectors. His criticisms of physicians and lawyers in *Hind Swaraj* carry many of the same kinds of complaints that are directed at bureaucracy. Gandhi finds that they depersonalize relationships, privilege the knowledge of the expert, create dependency relationships, and compartmentalize the life of persons. His ideal society would "obviate the necessity for highly specialized talent; it would place the destiny of the masses, as it were, in their own hands."[58]

With its claims to neutrality, instrumental reason, and efficiency, bureaucracy depoliticizes the world, and we encounter fewer sites of contested power and more locations for problem solving. This Gandhi wants to resist, not because he equates the good life and the good community with continued conflict but because he sees that claims that promise to settle issues through technical solutions frequently mask configurations of power that shape social relationships and, thereby, leave steep inequalities and institutionalized indignities undisturbed.

Political Complexity and Control

One of the sharpest differences separating Gandhi's view of democracy and most contemporary accounts fixes on the way we respond to the complexity of modern society and government. However much we may want to return to a more simple time, the modern argument runs, the realities of our era compel us to take complexity into account when we design and manage public institutions. This means that earlier conceptions of a simple accountability need to be reassessed and replaced by new ones that respond to a world that has greatly changed.

Several critics have noticed a tendency to respond to complexity by seeking to simplify popular ideas of politics and to approach politics symbolically and not substantively. Indeed, with growing complexity, the need for ritual, thought by some to be an outmoded relic of the past, intensifies in the late modern world as the basis for understanding politics. In discussing the replacement of substance with symbolism, Murray Edleman warns that political ritual "involves its participants symbolically in a common enterprise," and he goes on to argue that it "promotes conformity and evokes . . . joy in conformity."[59]

For his part, Gandhi argues that manipulation and democracy are contradictory terms. As he sees matters, "Democracy is not a state in which people act like sheep. Under democracy individual liberty of opinion and action is jealously guarded."[60] He fears that complex institutions threaten to overwhelm individuals caught in legitimizing rituals.

How the potency of political ritualism works in modern democracies can be seen in the observations of David Kertzer:

> Through participation in the rites [of voting], the citizen of the modern state identifies with larger political forces that can only be seen in symbolic form. And through political ritual, we are given a way to understand what is going on in the world, for we live in a world that must be drastically simplified if it is to be understood at all.[61]

Kertzer finds that the invisible state "must be personified before it can be seen, symbolized before it can be loved, imagined before it can be conceived."[62] Gandhi recoils at the personification and symbolization of the state. Should this come to pass, people no longer judge but acquiesce, and obedience becomes the automatic response to the benevolent state. Then, citizens forget that the state never escapes its coercive properties.[63] Gandhi wants to remind people that

> The State represents violence in a concentrated and organized form. The individual has a soul, but as the State is a soulless machine, it can never be weaned from violence to which it owes its very existence.[64]

To humanize the state and make it the object of love is to put people off guard. To address this problem, Gandhi calls for a comprehensive education in politics, not just a formal one, and he wants to exchange symbolic simplification for real simplification by radically decentralizing government and dispersing power to local communities.[65] There, he expects people to encounter a government they can understand and control. The language they use to judge government comes from their own experiences and is not manufactured for them elsewhere.

Even if we cannot (or do not want to) return to a simple society, Gandhi's critique of democratic politics is informative. He continually insists on the need to develop criteria beyond the conventional ones to judge the state, its policies, and its politics. He strives to show that any regime that claims to be democratic must be open, responsive, and accountable to a far greater extent than is now the case. For him, institutions are valuable only if they promote the autonomy of persons and if they do not, he wants to explore alternative forms of governance, not just alternative policies.

The opaqueness of modern politics undermines Gandhi's struggle to expose power and its uses; its oligarchic character subverts his efforts to move power back to ordinary citizens, and its substitution of groups for individuals jeopardizes his commitment to self-rule. For this reason, Gandhi urges Indians to build a politics that aims at simplicity, openness, and accountability in a world that is growing more complex.[66] For him, the need for a critical spirit intensifies in such a setting. When power is hidden, the need for exposure intensifies. When oligarchs replace citizens, the more the latter must be assertive. The more government power is presented as benevolent, the more its inescapably coercive properties must be uncovered. On his account, the need for struggle does not lessen because a state takes on new forms; rather, he wants to continue the struggle within the opportunities and constraints that accompany complex democracy.

GANDHI'S IDEAL DEMOCRACY: THE PANCHAYAT RAJ

In developing his theories of popular government, Gandhi returns to the villages of India where, he believes, people are less vulnerable to the control of others and better positioned to challenge abuses of power. Gandhi's ideal political arrangement for the village is the Panchayat, an ancient form of governance with a five-member assembly elected by the villagers.[67] There, he expects power to flow from the base. This is possible, Gandhi thinks, because the social and economic conditions that favor autonomy are in place: every citizen is able to earn a living and steep inequalities have been eliminated.[68]

Gandhi assigns the *panchayat raj* a limited but what he considers an important list of duties it can readily accomplish and which cannot be adequately addressed by individuals on their own: "the education of the boys and girls in its village; its sanitation; its medical needs; the upkeep and cleanliness of village wells or ponds; and the uplift of and daily wants of the so-called untouchables."[69] Given his abhorrence of violence, Gandhi deprives the *panchayat raj* of the authority to punish; rather it is expected to rely on "its moral authority, strict impartiality, and the willing obedience of the parties concerned" to assure its smooth operation.[70] As he sees it, the success of the panchayat leadership comes not in solving disputes, but avoiding them.[71] When this conflict does occur, he calls on public opinion to "do what violence can never do."[72]

In Gandhi's version of democracy, "the weakest should have the same opportunity as the strongest."[73] To achieve his vision, he calls for economic floors and ceilings to assure that the range of inequalities is narrow.[74] For him, steep inequalities make it difficult for citizens to understand each other and thereby reduce the chances of finding mutually satisfying agreements.[75] On his account, the ideal village republic will

> be a structure on sand if it is not built on the solid foundation of economic equality. Economic equality must never be supposed to mean possession of an equal amount of worldly goods for everyone. It does mean, however, that everyone will have a proper house to live in, sufficient and balanced food to eat, and sufficient *Khadi* with which to cover himself. It also means that the cruel inequality that obtains today will be removed by purely non-violent means.[76]

Gandhi's "perfect democracy [is] based upon individual freedom. The individual is the architect of his own government. The law of non-violence rules him and his government."[77] Acknowledging that many see his goal as "utopian," he insists that politics needs standards and he offers the highest standard he can imagine. Even though he knows his "picture" of India is not completely "realizable," the country "must have a proper picture of what we want before we can have something approaching it."[78] Gandhi's effort to restore the panchayat raj can be read as another of his morality tales, this one designed to show the importance of decentralized government.[79] As with his other tales, he seeks to disclose the importance of people taking charge of their lives, and for this to happen, they must be part of a cooperative, participatory community.[80] Gandhi's democracy is not primarily about a set of procedures or institutions but about sites of self-conscious action. In constructing his political ideal, he offers not another interest to pluralist politics but a different way of thinking and talking about politics and the state and, in this way, to recall what are becoming remainders in modern politics.

POLITICS AND RELIGION

Gandhi is intensely spiritual and, he claims, reluctantly political.[81] He participates in politics, "only because politics encircle us today like the coil of a snake from which one cannot get out, no matter how much one tries. I wish, therefore, to wrestle with the snake."[82] In his wrestling match, he calls on religion to animate him and seeks to join it with politics.[83] However, his fusion of the two departs from either of the forms familiar in the West. In one, the state retains sovereignty and favors one religion over others or approves a particular church as the official religion as with the Orthodox Church of Imperial Russia. The other is where the church determines some public policies or the state and church are combined under the jurisdiction of religious officials, as with the Papal States. Gandhi's linkage of politics and religion has a radically different character. He does not want the state to become involved in what he calls "denominationalism."[84] Paralleling the liberal effort to separate church and state, Gandhi writes that "The State has nothing to do with [religion]. The State would look after your secular welfare, health, communications, foreign relations, currency, and so on, but not your or my religion. That is everybody's personal concern."[85]

What then does Gandhi mean when he says he wants to join politics and religion?[86] From his perspective, we do not make civic institutions spiritual by making them holy (which puts them beyond criticism) or having them enforce a particular religious ideal (which makes them coercive). On his view, institutions have a spiritual dimension when their own internal practices and external effects enhance, rather than demean, the dignity of persons.[87] For this reason, Gandhi thinks that if the internal practices of an institution diminish autonomy, it is "irreligious."

Emphasizing that politics should be driven by moral principles, he strenuously objects to views of politics that hold moral principles and virtues are appropriate to private but not public life. This position is epitomized by Niccolo Machiavelli's famous aphorism that the prince must learn how not to be good if he is to remain a prince.[88] Gandhi fears that when private and public life have their own distinct and sometimes contradictory moral foundations, there is the constant danger that public officials, however selected, treat citizens as means to political ends. Arguing that "political life must be an echo of private life and there cannot be any divorce between the two," Gandhi wants each to be morally directed.[89] He maintains that citizenship depends on a morally coherent life, that no good citizen fails to practice the ordinary virtues, and that politics must be informed by moral standards, not by interests.[90]

This line of thinking leads Gandhi to insist that an individual's reli-

gion must be expressed in "service to the helpless."[91] Although meditation and prayer are important to him, if this is all that describes a person's
religious commitments, Gandhi finds them woefully inadequate.[92] For
this reason, he insists that "religion which takes no account of practical
affairs and does not help to solve them, is no religion."[93] Insisting that
religion is more than talk, ritual, and meditation, he observes that:

> It is good enough to talk of God whilst we are sitting here after a nice
> breakfast and look forward to a nicer luncheon, but how am I to talk
> of God to millions who go without two meals a day. To them God
> can only appear as bread and butter.[94]

For Gandhi, the destitute need work, and the highest spiritual exercise in India is to promote the conditions that enable everyone to work
for a living.[95] For him, the spiritual life is not concentrated on the future
and the distant but on the present and the local.[96] His reformulations of
service touch many realms, and what he says about service not only
undermines traditional, particularly Brahminic, views of religion but also
conventional ideas about political participation, the topic of the next
section.[97]

REDEFINING POLITICAL PARTICIPATION

In thinking about an ideal mode of politics, Gandhi seeks to empower citizens rather than the state. He goes about this by radically
redefining political participation in ways that not only depart from mini-
malist modes, such as voting, but also from more energetic modes, such
as participatory democracy where citizens are active in more sites.[98] Gandhi finds these modes are important but inadequate, and he offers three
new understandings of participation. One involves politicizing ordinary
Indians and showing them politics continually intrudes into their everyday lives. Second, Gandhi believes people act politically when they engage in service, such as working to eliminate untouchability. Each
activity is democratic in the broadest sense because, Gandhi insists,
everyone can participate in them, with different people deciding which
is the best expression for them. Gandhi's third form of participation

concerns leaders who dedicate their lives to the well-being of their communities and express their politics through service.

Gandhi wants Indians to understand that their everyday decisions ought to reflect their political and ethical commitments. This is what lies behind his call to Indians to resign from the British civil service and leave British schools. The issue for Gandhi is not so much about hurting the British as it is keeping Indians from contributing to their own domination.[99]

Gandhi's effort to politicize what had been taken to be nonpolitical can be seen in his championing of *khadi*, or spinning homemade cloth.[100] Khadi is so important to Gandhi that, at one point, he makes it a requirement for the franchise, a move that seems bizarre.[101] Its prominence reflects Gandhi's view of full citizenship as a broad, participatory identity rather than one that is procedurally designed to be inclusive. Spinning for Gandhi is not simply a manual activity but a moral, political, and economic project. He credits it with contributing to full employment, diminishing dependencies on other nations, enabling people to take responsibility for themselves (because they now have a living income that they have earned), and promoting a sense of self-worth.[102] From his perspective, those who think spinning is irrelevant or beneath them reject their responsibility to their community and their duties to the most vulnerable members of society. For Gandhi, this kind of detachment disqualifies someone from full citizenship; here and elsewhere, he denies citizenship is adequately conceptualized as a universal entitlement and insists that it must always be tied to concrete responsibilities.

Gandhian service is based on the premise that people are able to "renounce self-interest" and act on behalf of the good of the community.[103] This can be seen in the advice he offers a group of male students at Pachaiyappas College regarding the "hardships of child widows."[104] Because of the heavy hand of superstition, child widows are destined to remain unmarried and become destitute and lonely. To challenge this injustice, he asks the students "to make this sacred resolve that you are not going to marry a girl who is not a widow, you will seek out a widow girl."[105] For Gandhi, this is not an act of charity by the students; rather, it is an act of their humanity and stems from the duties they owe others in an interconnected cosmos. And it is political because it challenges patterns of power and practices that disable some in the most degrading ways. Moreover, he is telling the students that it is not good enough for them to condemn unjust, hurtful practices; they are responsible for alleviating suffering now, not just criticizing it and waiting for others to challenge it actively.

Gandhi's reconceptualized political participation is also addressed to those who aspire to be leaders and dedicate their lives to service to the public.[106] Unlike professional politicians who make laws, Gandhi's political leaders are to be "Servants of the People" who teach people how to become autonomous rather than legislating for them. They are expected to engage in education, economic self-help, social work, and political mobilization and, in these ways, assist members of their communities to take charge of their own lives.[107]

Gandhi's views of service and leadership appear in his Constructive Program in 1922, and he repeats them frequently. In addition to calling for communal unity between Hindus and Moslems, the abolition of untouchability, and the establishment of khadi, his Constructive Program is meant to foster local industries, improve sanitation, educate all children as well as adults, promote provincial languages as well as Hindi, and emancipate women. As independence approaches, he calls on the Congress Party to disband and its members to become Servants of the People and promote the Constructive Program.[108] Because of its prominent role in the independence movement, Gandhi thinks Congress is uniquely fitted for the tasks of moral regeneration and voluntary social reconstruction.[109] If his supporters become preoccupied with power and office in New Delhi, he fears they will misunderstand the nature of democratic leadership and neglect their obligations to their fellow citizens.[110]

In his reconstructed meaning of political leadership, Gandhi's ideal leaders abandon conventional power and are said to gain or rather earn their authority within their local communities through sacrifice, work, and disinterest about their own situations. Because this occurs in a local setting, the actions and intentions of any potential leader can be judged more accurately and confidently by prospective followers than when aspirants to leadership are distant and removed. For this reason, Gandhi holds that the authority of the ideal leader voluntarily flows from citizens who have not been manipulated.

On his reading, legitimate leadership is more likely to evolve in a community where men and women can reliably test the sincerity of the leader. Partha Chatterjee has argued that this amounts to replacing politics with morality, but it is more apt to say that Gandhi cannot conceptualize politics without morality. His version of the ideal Servant can be seen in his own life. He is someone who owns no private property, possesses few personal possessions,[111] spins khadi daily, and spends time working and living with ordinary Indians to empower them.[112]

FROM A MINIMAL STATE TO A LIMITED STATE

Gandhi sees the state unavoidably relying on coercion, including violent coercion. And he finds the modern state embodying centralized, hierarchical, bureaucratized structures that are particularly dangerous to individual self-governance. Not surprising, he attacks the state as a "soulless machine."[113] However, Parekh shows that from the 1930s onward, Gandhi alters his view of the state, increasingly seeing it as a vehicle for change, better equipped than public opinion to right deep-seated, institutionalized injustices, such as untouchability.[114] While still of great value to Gandhi, public opinion and other non-state remedies sometimes seem too halting and unreliable to serve as the only means to effect the changes he considers most essential. His move to accept state action discloses a Gandhi who is willing to tolerate coercion for limited, specific goals; his circumscribed endorsement of state power is not meant to promote justice but to dismantle injustice.[115]

Injustice can be understood as the reverse of justice. In many ways it is. Standards of justice are highly specific: we can think of Aristotle's conception of distributive justice; a Lockean conception of rights as a reflection of justice; or Marx's classless society as the just society. With each standard, injustice is the negation of a positive theory of justice. Each conception of justice comes with its own construction of injustice. The Lockean liberal, for example, finds that state expropriation of private property is unjust and a Marxist sees private property, particularly concentrated capital, is unjust. At this point, identifying injustices becomes an extension of the question "What is justice?"

Gandhi wants to reverse the way we talk about justice and injustice and make injustice the primary basis for judgment and action.[116] He thinks diverse men and women can agree that particular forms of domination and suffering are unjust, whether they are liberals or Marxists, Indians or British, even though they share little understanding of what the just society might look like.[117] Emphasizing injustice also keeps us in the present and localizes our concerns. Gandhi sees people preoccupied with justice fixing their gaze on the future where they imagine the final conquest of good over evil. Fortified with their perfectionist ends, there is the danger that they find little need to consider the harms they cause others in their march to a future good.[118] An opposite danger in focusing on future justice is that people do nothing about correcting the injustices of the present because they are unprepared to settle for anything less than a perfectionist outcome.[119] Gandhi constantly challenges this kind of political lethargy just as he complains about Indian nationalists who are so focused on national independence that they do not recognize and respond to the other injustices in their own society. In placing his politics firmly in the present, Gandhi continually asks about such costs and insists people are responsible for the pain they tolerate or cause today in their quest for a better tomorrow. Concentrating on injustice introduces urgency and constraint on the use of power and lays the basis for his support for limited state action. For Gandhi, injustice is tangible and observable and not imagined (as future justice is), and he offers support for state action to relieve suffering and subordination but seldom for more.

For his part, Gandhi does not believe the state *qua* state can overcome its reliance on violence, and therefore he continues to approach it skeptically. When he calls for state action, he holds that it must be always accompanied with a "minimum of violence," and he assigns it limited tasks.[120] Gandhi's discussion of an enlarged state is usually tied to eliminating untouchability, encouraging employment, and providing an equitable distribution of land for the peasants.

Even though Gandhi gives the state a wider role to play as India approaches independence, he continues to rely primarily on public opinion and never repudiates his observation of 1927 that "Government cannot afford to lead in matters of reform. By their very nature Governments are but interpreters and executors of the expressed will of the people whom they govern."[121] For all of his cautious acceptance of the state, Gandhi continues to work for decentralization, warn about political abuses, and offer his "Servants" as a way of addressing local problems without having to rely on the state. In sanctioning limited state power, Gandhi means to narrow its scope of action to combat the most severe forms of injustice that are visited on the most vulnerable members of society. And he attempts to bring it under the same unconventional methods he mobilizes against British colonial rule: popular pressure and civil disobedience.

EXPERIMENTAL POLITICS

Gandhi offers a view of politics that is local, simple, and participatory, and many criticize his vision as distracting. For them, his theory of politics misses the mark.[122] This is the case if we focus on how we can specifically apply his various theories in the late modern world with all of its complexity. However, the real issue ought to be about his aspirations for a politics dedicated to enhancing the autonomy of everyone. For Gandhi, politics and the state are unavoidable in the modern world; he never presents his idealized regime as one where power has disappeared or the state has withered away. He acknowledges that even in the best political arrangement, power can be abused and must be resisted.[123] To achieve his goals, Gandhi weaves together several requirements for the good polity. One concerns decentralizing and simplifying government and rendering it accountable. The second theme focuses on a civic education that recognizes the various, often opaque, locations of power and the ways it can be abused and the ways people can expose and challenge power. Third, he wants individuals to escape acute dependencies in order to govern themselves. Fourth, he expects citizens to become active in their society, often as an alternative to state action. Finally, he offers nonviolence as a way of proceeding politically.

Set at this level of generality, Gandhi's ideal politics retains its utopian flavor and also carries a sense that this is the kind of politics that many desire. They do not want to live in a regime where power is hidden except when it is abused, and they want to be autonomous rather than frightened or fatalistic. For Gandhi, claims such as order, efficiency, growth, and productivity carry insufficient purchase to override the claims for individual self-governance. He wants to rob such claims of their self-importance and show they ought not routinely trump a politics that aspires to be open and accountable. Popular control of government is always elusive, but it is surely not enhanced when efforts to undermine it are ignored or when the friends of democracy decline to acknowledge that contemporary democracy can generate its own abuses of power.[124]

In mounting his attack on the centralized, bureaucratic state and interest group politics, Gandhi seeks both to problematize the modern state and politics and experiment with alternatives. His formulation of politics is not meant to settle political questions but to keep them alive, and his experiments are not meant to discover perfectionist solutions but to be resilient to diversity and openness. In this way, Gandhi hopes to protect the goods that he fears are becoming lost in modern, mass, complex democracy. The problematizing impulse that Gandhi carries to his discussions of violence and to economics also finds a place in his view of politics. Holding that we cannot escape state power, he wants us to tether it because, even with its limited capacity to do good, it has an extraordinary aptitude to do great harm.[125]

Gandhi says he enters politics because it has become unavoidable, and he does not expect to retreat to some quiet, tranquil place where politics can be ignored. Efforts to return to a mythic past that bypasses politics is a dangerous stance to Gandhi because it leaves power unattended except by those who would use it for their own advantage. For him, the danger in contemporary politics is a new fatalism which denies that people can either control the institutions of modern society or recover what is valuable from the past and that they ought not to try. To be political, in Gandhi's reading, means that people come equipped with a broad understanding of power, judge the uses of power with the materials of their own reformed tradition, demonstrate the courage to act nonviolently to remove injustice, and engage in service.

In the end, Gandhian politics is about struggle. The very goals he offers cannot fit comfortably in the modern world and, from a Gandhian perspective, they ought not be expected to. His goals serve as reminders about what is important but in danger of being lost. Gandhian struggle is not only against the entrenched power of the state; it is also a struggle with concentrations of private power in civil society. Each of these struggles precludes discovering a new, harmonious cosmos because Gandhi wants constantly to disturb any arrangement that fosters its own forms of domination and humiliation.

NOTES

1. John Dunn, *Western Political Theory in the Face of the Future* (Cambridge: Cambridge University Press, 1979), 27.

2. *Young India*, July 2, 1931; see also Bondurant, *Conquest of Violence*, 184.

3. See *Nonviolence in Peace and War*, 1: 22–23.

4. *Democracy: Real and Deceptive*, ed. R. K. Prabhu (Ahmedabad: Navajivan, 1961).

5. For a further discussion of Gandhi's views on democracy and autonomy, see Ronald Terchek, "Gandhian Politics," in *New Dimensions and Perspectives in Gandhism*, ed. V. T. Patil (New Delhi: Inter-India Publications, 1988).

6. Cited in Nirmal Bose, ed. *Selections from Gandhi* (Ahmedabad: Navajivan Publishing House, 1957), 122.

7. *Hind Swaraj*, ch. 8.

8. *Hind Swaraj*, ch. 20.

9. In responding to those who want to wrest sovereignty from the British and place it in Indian hands, Gandhi retorts, "you want English rule without the Englishman. You want the tiger's nature, but not the tiger, that is to say, you would make India English. . . . This is not the *swaraj* that I want." *Hind Swaraj*, ch. 4.

10. If independence means "a change from white military rule to a brown [one], we hardly need make any fuss. At any rate, the masses then do not count. They will be subject to the same spoliation as now if not even worse." *Young India*, December 19, 1929.

11. Foreword, *Gokhale's Speeches*, Iyer, *Writings*, 1: 138.

12. "Submission to the State law is the price a citizen pays for his personal liberty. Submission, therefore, to a State wholly or largely unjust is an immoral barter for liberty." *Young India*, November 10, 1921.

13. *Young India*, November 10, 1921.

14. *Young India*, July 28, 1920.

15. See his justification to engage in civil disobedience on his own during World War II after the Working Committee of the Congress Party rejects his appeal to support a nationwide campaign of civil disobedience. *Harijan*, June 19, 1940.

16. Nietzsche holds that "every sufferer instinctively seeks a cause for his suffering . . . .

"The suffering are one and all dreadfully eager and inventive in discovering occasions for painful affects." *On the Genealogy and Morals*, 127.

17. This is one of the central arguments of *Hind Swaraj*. Gandhi argues against accepting British terms of engagement and offers his own mode of response politically, economically, and socially.

18. Gandhi acknowledges that prior periods carry their own forms of subordination, as in the case of untouchability, and they must be resisted. However, he thinks the rhythm of life is not greatly altered when one prince replaces another in the premodern era.

19. "Foreword," Gokhale's Speeches, in Iyer, *Writings,* 1: 137–38.

20. This stands in opposition to Aristotle's ideal state as pursuing the common good, Locke's assignment to the state to act as an "impartial umpire" to protect rights, or Rousseau's social contract as embodying the general will. For Augustine and Gandhi, each of these goods represents an inadequate justification of power. None of them, by itself or in tandem with other principled standards, can vindicate the use of force by some over others.

21. *Harijan,* June 7, 1940.

22. Gandhi also thinks that a proper understanding of politics is stymied by the tendency of people to concentrate on the formal institutions of government or for them to assume a fatalistic view that nothing can be done to affect change. Another obstacle to a Gandhian conception of power comes with a narrow conception of what politics can accomplish. He continually complains that many think that if India gains its independence from Britain, the great task of politics is finished. However, he insists, this is based on a misunderstanding of what politics can and cannot accomplish. See *Hind Swaraj.*

23. In this vein, he writes, "Swaraj is to be attained by educating the masses to a sense of their capacity to regulate and control authority." *Young India,* January 29, 1925.

24. *Young India,* April 20, 1921.

25. In the modern world, much that we see is filtered through the mass media. What they choose to ignore and what to emphasize structure our own sight and understanding of politics. See Gandhi, *An Autobiography or the Story of My Experiments with Truth* (Ahmedabad: Navajivan Publishing House, 1972), Part II, ch. 28.

Gandhi fears that the mass media are replacing reliable sources of knowledge. "Unfortunately, the newspapers had become more important to the average man than the scriptures . . . and other good literature" (*Harijan,* April 27, 1947). His own view of what constitutes an editor's responsibility comes in the opening pages of *Hind Swaraj*: "One of the objects of a newspaper is to understand popular feeling and to give expression to it; another is to arouse among the people certain desirable sentiments; and the third is fearlessly to expose popular defects. . . . To the extent the people's will has to be expressed, certain sentiments will need to be fostered, and defects will have to be brought to light" (*Hind Swaraj,* ch. 1). Also see Sailendr Bhattacharyya, *Mahatma Gandhi: The Journalist* (Bombay: Times of India Press, 1962).

26. Friedrich Nietzsche, *Thus Spake Zarathustra,* in *Portable Nietzsche,* ed. Walter Kaufmann (New York: Penguin, 1976), 161.

27. *Zarathustra,* 161. Compare with Hobbes's Leviathan who is called the "mortal God."

28. *Zarathustra,* 161–62.

29. See Thomas Pantham, "Thinking with Mahatma Gandhi: Beyond Liberal Democracy," *Political Theory* 11, 2 (May 1983): 165–88.

30. See Norberto Bobbio, *Future of Democracy* (London: Polity Press. 1987); and Danilo Zolo, *Democracy and Complexity* (University Park: Pennsylvania State University Press, 1993). Similar criticism comes from other quarters as well: Parekh, *Gandhi's Political Philosophy*; Nandy, *Traditions, Tyranny, Utopia*; Jurgen Habermas, *Legitimation Crisis* (Boston: Beacon Press, 1976); and Claus Offe, *Contradictions of the Welfare State* (Cambridge: MIT Press, 1984).

31. Bobbio finds that "one of the cliches heard in all past and present debates on democracy is the assertion that it is 'open government' by a 'visible power.' " But he discovers an "invisible power" lurks in the background, unnoticed by many commentators who insist that what they see (rather than what is hidden) is what counts. *Future*, 79.

32. See Friedrich Hayek, *Political Order of a Free People*, for a conservative critique along these lines; for a neo-realist critique, see Bobbio, *Future of Democracy*; for a similar critique from the left, see Offe, *Contradictions*.

33. See Gandhi, *Democracy: Real and Deceptive*.

34. See *Democracy, Real and Deceptive*.

35. On the fungibility of majorities, see Kenneth Arrow, *Social Choice and Individual Values* (New Haven: Yale University Press, 1951); on the role of decision rules, see E. E. Schattschneider, *The Semisovereign People* (New York: Harcourt Brace Jovanovich, 1975); on complexity, see Zolo, *Democracy and Complexity*; and for a discussion of accountability, see Robert Dahl, *Dilemmas of Pluralist Democracy* (New Haven: Yale University Press, 1982); Theodore Lowi, *The End of Liberalism* (New York: Norton, 1969); and Charles Lindbloom, *Politics and Markets* (New York: Basic Books, 1977).

36. "I do not believe in the doctrine of the greatest good for the greatest number. It means in its nakedness that in order to achieve the supposed good of fifty-one percent, the interest of forty-nine per cent may be, or rather should be, sacrificed." "Letter to an Indian Friend," July 4, 1932 in Mahadev Desai, *The Diary of Mahadev Desai* (Ahmedabad: Navajivan Publishing House, 1953), 149.

37. *Young India*, August 4, 1920.

38. *Harijan*, August 11, 1940, in Iyer, *Writings*, 2: 248. From Gandhi's perspective, "The rule of the majority has a narrow application, i.e., one should yield to the majority in matters of detail. But it is slavery to be amenable to the majority, no matter what its decisions are" (*Young India*, March 2, 1922).

39. *Nonviolence in Peace and War* 1: 22–23.

40. In this regard, Gandhi echoes the concerns of many democratic theorists who often disagree among themselves about other matters. See, for example, Rousseau's apprehension about particular wills crowding out the general will in

The Social Contract as well as Madison's distrust of factions dominating government in *Federalist No. 10.*

41. See Arthur Bentley, *The Process of Government* (Evanston: Principia Press, 1908) for the classical formulation of pluralism. For two of the most influential accounts, see David Truman, *The Governmental Process* (New York: Knopf, 1951), and Dahl, *Who Governs?* (New Haven: Yale University Press, 1961).

42. *Young India,* September 17, 1931.

43. For a critique along these lines that remains highly influential in American democratic theory, see Joseph Schumpeter, *Capitalism, Socialism, and Democracy* (New York: Harper & Brothers, 1942).

44. Anthony Downs, *An Economic Theory of Democracy* (New York: Harper and Row, 1957), and Dahl, *Who Governs?*

45. Bobbio reflects a common observation when he writes that in "democratic states . . . it is less and less the individual who is the most influential factor in politics and more and more it is the group: large organizations" (*Future of Democracy,* 28).

46. Consider Gandhi's opposition to a separate electoral list for the Untouchables in legislative bodies. He wants them represented as individuals not as members of a group. See Gandhi, *The Nation's Voice* (Ahmedabad: Navajivan Press, 1932), 40.

47. *Harijan,* July 28, 1946.

48. *Hind Swaraj,* ch. 5.

49. *Harijan,* May 31, 1942.

50. Gandhi appreciates that India is a mosaic of diverse cultures, languages, and religions. No centralized formula can respect this plurality, and to try to impose one means destroying what is distinctive in each. To make universalizing binding rules is to rob the world of its diverse groundings.

51. For a further discussion of the contrast between Gandhi's democratic politics and pluralism, see Ronald Terchek, "Gandhi's Democratic Theory," in *Political Thought of Modern India,* ed. Thomas Pantham and Kenneth Deutsch (New Delhi: Sage of India, 1986).

52. Max Weber observes that "in its most rational development, [the bureaucratic state] is precisely characteristic of the modern state." *From Max Weber,* 82.

53. *Economy and Society* (Berkeley: University of California Press, 1978), 975.

54. Michel Foucault, *Discipline and Punish: The Birth of the Prison,* trans. A. Sheridan (New York: Vintage, 1979), 209, 212.

55. See *Young India,* August 11, 1921.

56. When political power is widely dispersed, "the interference with the freedom of the people is reduced to a minimum." *Harijan,* January 11, 1936.

57. *Young India,* August 6, 1925.

58. *Harijan,* October 9, 1937.

59. Murray Edleman, *The Symbolic Uses of Politics* (Urbana: University of Illinois Press, 1967), 16. Edleman extends this argument in a later book, arguing that "everyone who grows up in our society is bound to become aware, at some level of consciousness, that an individual vote is more nearly a form of self-expression and of legitimation than of influence" (*Constructing the Political Spectacle* [Chicago: University of Chicago Press, 1988], 97).

60. *Young India*, March 2, 1922.

61. David Kertzer, *Ritual, Politics, and Power* (New Haven: Yale University Press, 1988), 1–2.

62. Kertzer, *Ritual, Politics, and Power*, 6.

63. For Gandhi, conventional politics is about power and coercion, and the phenomena Kertzer describes mask these realities.

64. Bose, *Selections from Gandhi*, 41.

65. Gandhi also wants individuals to develop more "simple tastes" and move away from a "multiplicity of material wants" which add to the complexity of contemporary society. See *Young India*, September 3, 1925.

66. Gandhi insists that because society is losing its simplicity is no reason for it to lose its standards, particularly those attached to the autonomy of persons. Complexity makes autonomy more difficult to achieve but can never, he reasons, serve as an excuse for ignoring it.

67. See *Harijan*, July 26, 1942.

68. *Harijan*, January 18, 1948.

69. *Young India*, June 5, 1931.

70. *Young India*, June 5, 1931.

71. *Harijan*, June 4, 1948.

72. *Harijan*, June 1, 1947.

73. Gandhi, *Nonviolence in Peace and War*, 2: 269.

74. He holds that his version of a democracy "is clearly an impossibility so long as the wide gulf between the rich and the hungry millions persist." *Democracy*, 68.

75. In societies where there are great disparities of wealth, the rich and poor assign different meanings to common words. What the rich mean by justice or rights is not what the poor mean by these terms. The meanings are not only disparate but often discordant.

76. *Harijan*, August 18, 1946.

77. *Harijan*, July 26, 1942.

78. *Harijan*, July 28, 1946.

79. On Gandhi's reading, "True democracy cannot be worked by twenty men sitting at the centre. It has to be worked from below by the people of every village." *Harijan*, January 18, 1948.

80. For him, politics is best approached in a circular rather than linear or

hierarchical way. Gandhi sees a united India "composed of innumerable villages [where] there will be ever-widening, never-ascending circles. Life will not be a pyramid and the apex sustained by the bottom." *Harijan*, July 28, 1946.

81. It is helpful to notice that Gandhi is not particularly religious. Although he attended temple as a child out of respect for his mother, he is not a temple-goer as an adult and he never builds a temple in any of his ashrams. Nevertheless, he is deeply spiritual.

82. *Young India*, May 23, 1920.

83. "Quite selfishly, as I wish to live in peace in the midst of a bellowing storm howling round me, I have been experimenting with myself and my friends by introducing religion into politics." *Young India*, May 12, 1920,

84. "I do not believe that the State can concern itself or cope with religious instruction. I believe that religious education must be the sole concern of religious associations. . . . We have suffered enough from State-aided religion and a State Church. A society or a group, which depends partly or wholly on State aid for the existence of its religion . . . does not have any religion worth the name." *Harijan*, March 23, 1947.

85. *Harijan*, September 22, 1946. Compare with Locke's *Letter on Toleration*. Gandhi also observes that even if "the whole community had one religion," it is a mistake for the state to become involved because there are "as many religions as minds. Each mind had a different conception of God from that of the other" (*Harijan*, March 16, 1947).

86. For a further discussion of the relation Gandhi draws between politics and religion, see *Young India*, June 18, 1925. Also see V. T. Patil, "Gandhi and His Ideas on Religion and Politics," in *New Dimensions and Perspectives in Gandhism*, V. T. Patil (New Delhi: Inter-India Publications, 1988), 169–80; Chatterjee, *Gandhi's Religious Thought*; Iyer, *Moral and Political Thought*, 38–51; and Parekh, *Gandhi's Political Philosophy*, 65–109. Also see Thomas Pantham, "Indian Secularism and Its Critics," *Review of Politics* 59, 3 (Summer 1997): 523–40.

87. Gandhi's understanding of spirituality does not carry the transcendent character conventionally attributed to the term. Margaret Chatterjee remarks that "Gandhi drew no distinction between spirituality and social involvement" (*Gandhi's Religious Thought*, 175). Earlier in her book, she observes that "Gandhi made no distinction between the sacred and the profane" (149).

88. "It is necessary for a prince, who wishes to maintain himself, to learn how not to be good, and use this knowledge or not use it, according to the necessity of the case" (*The Prince* [New York: Modern Library, 1950], 58). What Machiavelli says to the prince can be applied to ambitious state officials, interest groups, and citizens as well.

89. Speech, May 8, 1915, in Iyer, *Writings*, 1: 375.

90. See speech, April 27, 1915, in Iyer, *Writings*, 1: 373–76.

91. *Young India*, August 14, 1924.

92. On Gandhi's account, "The Brahman who has understood the religion of today will certainly give Vedic learning a secondary place and propagate the religion of the spinning wheel, relieve the hunger of the millions of his starving countrymen, and only then... lose himself in Vedic studies. ". . . If I have to make the choice between counting beads or turning the wheel, I would certainly decide in favor of the wheel, making it my rosary, so long as I found poverty and starvation stalking the land." *Young India*, August 14, 1924.

93. *Young India*, June 7, 1929.

94. *Young India*, October 15, 1931.

95. In emphasizing service, Parekh sees Gandhi replacing "the traditional repertoire of spiritual exercises with a wholly new set of his own, including cleaning latrines, living and working among the untouchables and nursing the sick." *Gandhi's Political Philosophy*, 106–7.

96. One of the highest forms of religious activity for Christians comes with the work of missionaries Christianizing unbelievers. Gandhi, for one, does "not believe in people telling others of their faith, especially with a view to conversion. Faith does not admit of telling. It has to be lived and then it becomes self-propagating" (*Young India*, October 29, 1927). For Gandhi, religion becomes "self-propagating" when its members continually apply their ideals in their own local community, addressing the suffering of its most vulnerable members, and responding to the injustices that reside in their own society. For Gandhi, people who are sincerely religious should address injustice at home.

97. See Gandhi, *Constructive Programme*, 58.

98. There are several kinds of participatory models in democratic theory. The developmental approach claims citizens are extended by participation, learning not only about issues but how much they depend on others and others depend on them in their common projects. Another model concentrates on how community effectiveness is enhanced through widespread, intense activity. In these renditions, the participatory democrat stands in sharp contrast to the interest-carrying citizen who sees democratic politics as a competitive game and not a cooperative activity.

99. See *Hind Swaraj*.

100. See *Harijan*, April 10, 1937.

101. *Young India*, November 27, 1924.

102. For a selected collection of Gandhi's writings on spinning, see *Spinning and Khadi* (Lahore: Gandhi Publications League, 1943).

103. *Harijan*, June 29, 1935. In the same piece, Gandhi holds that "service, like virtue, is its own reward and [the person engaging in service] will rest content with it."

104. In some areas of India during Gandhi's lifetime, marriages are arranged between children, to be consummated years later. In the meantime, each child lives with his or her parents. If the boy dies under this arrangement, the girl is considered a child widow.

105. *Young India*, September 15, 1927.

106. "I felt compelled to come into the political field because I found that I could not do even social work without touching politics. I felt that political work must be looked upon in terms of social and moral progress." On his reading, "No part of life is untouched by politics" in the modern era and one "cannot sit still while the people are being ravaged." *Harijan*, October 6, 1946.

107. "The *Gandhi Seva Sangh* [Gandhi's voluntary service organization] has come into existence for the purpose of carrying on the constructive programme. That alone is real politics. . . . What do we care if they do not call it politics? We shall remain within the Congress fold, but keep ourselves away from power and elections." Gandhi, Speech at Gandhi Seva Sangh, February 22, 1940, in Iyer, *Writings*, 1: 425.

108. He admits that he and his supporters "used politics to put our principles into practice. Now, after some experience, we are renouncing politics" (Speech, February 22, 1940, in Iyer, *Writings*, 1: 423). Also see Gandhi, *Constructive Programme*. However, Gandhi does not advocate disbanding the state. Rather, he wants a parallel structure in place which carries political functions and is close to and controlled by local publics.

109. Throughout his career in India, Gandhi's relationship with Indian politicians in the Congress was often uneasy. He was suspicious of efforts to socialize the economy, build up the military forces, and create a strong central state; yet this is the direction of the Congress leadership. Whatever the practical, political consequences of his call for the disbanding of Congress, Gandhi's theoretical position is unmistakable. The political parties and the state are simply unable and incompetent to accomplish certain tasks, and when it tries, it often injures.

110. Gandhi grows increasingly impatient with many office-holders in the Congress. He finds it is "fast becoming an organization of selfish power-seekers and job-holders. Instead of remaining the servants of the public, Congressmen had become its lords and masters. The Congress was, moreover, torn by petty intrigues and group rivalries." *Harijan*, June 1, 1947.

111. The personal belongings consist of his clothes, eye-glasses, books, a watch, and a few other items.

112. See Gandhi, "The Village Worker," in *Rebuilding Our Villages*. Also see Dalton, *Mahatma Gandhi*, 191. On one occasion, Gandhi talks about the way he would conduct himself as a Servant. He expects the village families to ask him to teach their children, but he thinks he will be otherwise busy with other local projects and unable to devote the time to this request. He will offer to find a

teacher and the families to bear the expense. Later, they will learn "the importance of hygiene and sanitation, and when they come and ask for a sweeper, I will tell them: 'I will be your sweeper and I will train you all in the job' " (*Harijan*, March 17, 1946).

113. Bose, *Selections from Gandhi*, 41. Earlier, Gandhi observes that people "cannot be made good by law. . . . I would prevent people from drinking and smoking. . . . But to regulate these things by law... would be a remedy probably worse than the diseases. . . . There is no law against using kitchens as closets or drawing rooms as stables. But public opinion, that is, public tastes will not tolerate such a combination. The evolution of public opinion is at times a tardy process but it is the only effective one" (*Young India*, July 9, 1925). Even after he gives the state more room for action than he did in the 1920s, he continues to have doubts about how far it can reconstruct attitudes and never leaves the idea that widescale conversion is necessary in India if the untouchables are to be free.

114. Parekh, *Gandhi's Political Philosophy*, 118–21.

115. Service, always important to Gandhi's views of politics, assumes a larger presence in his writings after he gives the state more room to act. If citizens rely only on the state to address injustice, then it is the state that becomes autonomous, and not citizens. His version of service extends to personal activities aimed at relieving and eliminating the suffering of the most vulnerable members in society.

116. See Judith Shklar's *The Faces of Injustice* (New Haven: Yale University Press, 1990), for an extended discussion of the different phenomenologies attached to justice and injustice.

117. Gandhi does not expect everyone simultaneously to discover that a particular practice is unjust. However, he believes that over time, everyone will respond to voluntary suffering.

118. This is one of Gandhi's major objections to state socialism. See *Harijan*, July 14, 1947.

119. *Young India*, June 28, 1928.

120. When he occasionally talks about the government owning industry and land, he insists that this will be accomplished nonviolently. However, he is vague and laconic as to how this will be done. See Jayantanuja Bandyopadhyaya *Social and Political Theory*, 114–15.

121. *Young India*, October 20, 1927.

122. These are the objections of Parekh, *Gandhi's Political Philosophy*, and Chatterjee, *Nationalist Thought*.

123. This is why he wants the Servants to teach civil disobedience.

124. Gandhi claims that power always reappears and can never be completely restrained by liberal constitutionalism. At this point, the issue for Gandhi is how individuals confront power they take to be used for an unjust purpose.

125. "I look upon the power of the State with the greatest fear, because, although while apparently doing good by minimizing exploitation, it does the greatest harm to mankind by destroying individuality." Interview, 1934, in D. G. Tendulkar, *Mahatma*, IV, 15.

6

CHALLENGING VIOLENCE AND DENYING PERFECTIONISM

Standing on the very brink of social disaster in our western world, it would be a rather glorious thing if we could humble our pride sufficiently to appropriate from the east what we need most desperately in the west, a strong enough faith in the efficacy of ethical forces to achieve social justice without wading through blood to get it.[1]

More than most, the twentieth century has been incredibly violent. Two world wars, innumerable regional conflicts, countless instances of civil strife, and wars of national liberation are familiar in the historical account of the era. And so are the disturbing means of violence that are continually introduced into national arsenals. Yet this is also a century when what appeared to be great, invincible empires collapsed without the weight of violence bringing them down. The British and Soviet empires, which appeared secure, invulnerable, and interminable, collapsed without the help of widespread armed conflict. Moreover, extensive and enduring changes have come through nonviolent action; the politics of both democratic and nondemocratic states have been marked by countless protests, some by individuals, some by small groups, and some large ones—ranging from calls for an expanded franchise, trade union recognition, and rights for minorities and women to environmental integrity and an end to war. These and other cases illustrate extra-institutional politics at work, a politics coming from below when conventional politics are unresponsive to the deeply felt distress of people. Gandhi is the major contributor to theories of nonviolent political change, challenging conventional ideas that violence is politically efficacious and can be morally justifiable. He offers his theory of civil disobedience as a nonviolent way of confronting injustice and of enabling those on the margin to express their deepest concerns. But Gandhi's civil disobedience is more than a political statement; it is a moral one as well; it is a protest against "an unwitting and unwilling participation in evil."[2]

Gandhi's popular reputation rests on his theory of nonviolent resistance or what he calls *satyagraha* or "truth force." For him, truth is embodied in the dignity, worth, and equality of everyone, that is, their autonomy. What animates the *satyagrahi* (or practioner of nonviolence) is that denials of autonomy must be publicly, nonviolently challenged. Gandhi's satyagrahi believes that what happens to any one person is important to everyone because we are all interrelated. From his perspective, people can never morally separate themselves from their society and its institutional practices or shed moral responsibility for the injustice that resides in their community. What people tolerate, much less support, makes them complicit in what happens in their society.

However, the role of nonviolence for Gandhi is often overstressed. It is not the highest good for Gandhi; autonomy is, that is, governing oneself honestly and courageously.[3] For Gandhi, civil disobedience is one aspect of nonviolence and is not higher than other forms of nonviolent conduct; it stands alongside service as one of the best expressions of human conduct.[4] Seeing men and women as part of an interdependent cosmos, Gandhi expects them to act on the responsibilities they have to one another. Working with this perspective, he sees autonomous persons expressing their duties in freely assisting the most vulnerable members of their community.

Satyagraha is inseparably linked to Gandhi's efforts to resist domination nonviolently. In this chapter, I lay out Gandhi's efforts to demonstrate why nonviolence is superior to violence and then show that violence is not the greatest evil for him. Fatalism, cowardliness, and harming or allowing harm come to others are just as formidable evils for Gandhi because they deny one's own autonomy or the autonomy of others.[5] I then show that just as he interrogates the efficacy and morality of violence, Gandhi problematizes nonviolence as a universally valid standard for all ethical conduct.

WHY NOT VIOLENCE?

As much as most of us want to avoid violence, it sometimes seems necessary. This seems especially to be the case when the strong employ violence to dominate the weak or attack the vulnerable. In such cases, resistance in kind seems to need no justification. Gandhi disagrees.[6] He offers a comprehensive critique about the inferiority of violence as a way of proceeding. The exceptions I show later in this chapter do not disturb Gandhi's central condemnation of violence but rather show the limited cases where he thinks it can be justified.[7]

Gandhi sees a violent society unwilling to acknowledge the essential dignity and worth of each of its members and finds the violent life is at war with itself. In such a society and for such people, fear and suspicion are widespread, and speech is used not to uncover commonalities but to intimidate and terrify. When this occurs, Gandhi sees individuals stuck at the stage of the "brute," unwilling to develop morally.[8] Such people, Gandhi holds, are fighting "an imagined enemy without" and neglecting "the enemy within."[9]

Violence, as Gandhi sees it, respects no boundaries and becomes self-justificatory. In this way, the violent person plays at being god, not a loving or forgiving god but an angry one, a just one, an avenging one, a purifying one or a jealous one. In trading places with the divine, the violent person pretends to possess the truth about good and evil and to determine who should be punished and who spared. Not only does such pride contradict Gandhi's view of the partiality of any truth, it claims a dangerous omnipotence for itself when it decides what limits, if any, will restrict its use of violence and when it sets rules for itself that are designed to hurry victory regardless of its effects on others. In this way, the violent person treats other human beings as means, as things to be used, overcome, controlled, humiliated, frightened, or silenced.[10] For his part, Gandhi wants to see conflict initiated against what he takes to be injustice, but he wants it to be self-limiting, something he thinks is inherent in nonviolence but not violence.

Set at this abstract level, Gandhi's opposition does not convince those who hold that the blatant use of violence by an aggressor can sometimes only be met with the violence of the victim. Such critics hold that there are some evils that are greater than violence, and the refusal to employ violence only invites greater injustice and evil. One reason that Gandhi quarrels with this position is that he finds in the long run violence does more harm than good. For him, the good it appears to serve "is only temporary, the evil it does is permanent."[11]

Gandhi is particularly concerned with how violence affects those who rely on it routinely. As violence becomes habitual, Gandhi reasons, the goals for which it is initially employed are lost as people become preoccupied about its uses and about the ways they can find new sources of power while limiting or reducing the power of their opponents. Spreading like a virus, Gandhi sees the initial use of violence infecting a widening range of people. Increasingly, it becomes an ordinary tool to settle conflicts and assure compliance. Feeding on itself, once morally objectionable actions become acceptable.[12] Familiarity with violence eventually invites its use against anyone who stands in the way.[13] For his part, Gandhi expects that when violence becomes institutionalized, it will be readily directed at former friends and allies. It becomes "an easy step from employing violence on foreign rulers to using it on our own people whom we consider obstructing the country's progress."[14] He fears that "Once the custom of effecting reforms by force gets established, the people tend to become dull and lifeless."[15] One reason Gandhi is so concerned about violence is that it can appear anytime and anywhere.[16]

WHAT IS GANDHI'S TRUTH FORCE?

Gandhi holds that satyagraha is universally applicable in three senses: everyone can practice it,[17] everyone can respond to it,[18] and it can be applied in all of the spheres of life.[19] For Gandhi, it is not meant to be a political tactic but a moral force. He explains that the "equivalent" of satyagraha

> in the vernacular rendered into English means Truth Force. . . . Violence is the negation of this great spiritual force which can only be wielded or cultivated by those who will entirely eschew violence. It is a force that may be used by individuals as well as by communities. It may be used as well in political as in domestic affairs. Its universal applicability is a demonstration of its permanence and invincibility. It can be used alike by men, women and children. . . . It is impossible for those who consider themselves to be weak to apply this force. Only those who realize that there is something in man which is superior to the brute nature in him, and that the latter always yields to it, can effectively be passive resisters.[20]

Gandhi initially equates nonviolent action with passive resistance but later repudiates the connection.[21] He finds that the term "passive" connotes fatalism and an acceptance of injustice and thereby diminishes the power captured in the word "resistance."[22] On his account, resistance requires courage and strength rather than passivity or withdrawal.[23]

Gandhi wants nonviolence to be a way of life and infuse all social relations: familial, political, economic, and educational. There is no room for selective nonviolence in Gandhi's theory: a person who is nonviolent at home or with friends but has no patience or respect for others is not truly nonviolent.[24] "It is no non-violence if we merely love those that love us. It is non-violence only if we love those that hate us."[25] If men and women are to live peacefully together in a democratic society, Gandhi reasons, they must be tolerant and open and foreswear violence.

In presenting satyagraha as the only reliable means of disabling injustice, Gandhi insists that he is aiming at changing both the outlooks and behavior of his opponents.[26] For this reason, Gandhian nonviolence is more than a strategy for peaceful change; it is "a program [for the] transformation of relationships."[27] How does one convert opponents who are morally certain about their position and whose power is substantial? Gandhi believes we are able to change our opponents, not because we have struck a mutually satisfactory bargain or credibly threaten them, but by reaching them through public suffering. To do this, he reconceptualizes suffering.[28] Seeing a profound difference between voluntary and involuntary suffering, Gandhi finds a nobility in the former and seeks to make it into "the badge of the human race."[29] At the same time, he holds that certain forms of voluntary suffering are illusionary, such as the hermit's "quest of self-perfection."[30] What Gandhi wants is a voluntary suffering that is public, this-worldly directed, and devoted to relieving involuntary suffering, whether one's own or another's. In this sense, voluntary, public suffering is an affirmation of the principle of autonomy. It takes on this character because the voluntary sufferer struggles against domination, challenges fatalism, and affirms one's own dignity and strength in a hostile environment.[31] Involuntary suffering for Gandhi does not have redemptive value; it is visited on people because of their human vulnerabilities (as with sickness and accident) or their social and political vulnerabilities (as with colonialism, gender, or caste). Gandhi wants to resist the latter forms of suffering and not make them into virtues when people quietly accept their indignities.

He holds that others are moved by voluntary suffering because it speaks to them in ways that reason, by itself, cannot: "Suffering is infinitely more powerful than the law of the jungle for converting the opponent and opening his ears, which are otherwise shut, to the voice of reason."[32] From his perspective, voluntary suffering conveys a sense of urgency that abstract reasoning does not.[33] Gandhian suffering opens matters up, dissolving previous indifference or callousness and providing a readiness to hear the concerns of others and weigh them in a fresh way.[34]

Voluntary suffering weaves together several themes that are central to Gandhi. It is active, requires courage, defies fatalism, and entails personal engagement. In addition, it requires detachment from the temporal and material in the sense that the voluntary sufferer is willing to forgo security and advantage and endure pain for the sake of some moral good. Finally Gandhi's view of voluntary suffering is based on a trust that people do not relish witnessing suffering in others and will eventually do what they can to bring it to end.

Gandhi's repeated emphasis on conversion, love, and suffering helps to distinguish his theory of satyagraha from *duragraha* or "stubborn persistence."[35] With both, nonviolent power is mobilized, but with the latter, we encounter a tactic to force targets to respond to the demands of the protesters. As Bondurant notices, strikes and demonstrations "are nothing more than the action which each respective name signifies and so should not be called *satyagraha*."[36] To qualify as the latter, Gandhi insists that nonviolent actions should not be adversarial but should seek to transform relationships.[37] One way Gandhi wants to promote trust is to reduce the hardships of the targets as much as possible, not increasing them as in the case of duragraha.[38]

THE UNAVOIDABILITY OF COERCION

In spite of Gandhi's repeated efforts to distinguish conversion and coercion and his insistence that his opponents will respond to the power of voluntary suffering, several of his targets have thought otherwise, finding that his civil disobedience campaigns are unavoidably tied to coercion. The South African leader General Jan Smuts, for one, insists that Gandhi's fasts were political methods whose success depends on emotional appeals and veiled threats of violence. Smuts thinks that if

Gandhi dies from his fast, widespread violence will follow. Intimidated by this possibility, Smuts accepts Gandhi's demands.[39] And many who have been sympathetic to Gandhi, like Joan Bondurant, have also seen satyagraha as coercive, although she emphasizes its nonviolent character. Bondurant finds that nonviolent coercion results in indirect or unintended injury, and that both the nonviolent activists and their opponents pay the price.[40] Nirmal Kumar Bose acknowledges as much when he writes that satyagraha is "a way of conducting 'war' by means of nonviolence."[41] A similar view comes from the American political realist Reinhold Niebuhr who sees in Gandhi both a highly idealistic, religious, and ethical thinker as well as someone who astutely knows the nature of power and how to deploy it nonviolently. Discussing his civil disobedience campaigns against British colonialism, Niebuhr finds that Gandhi

> knows that he cannot win freedom for India merely by appealing to the sense of justice of a community which probably has a stronger sense of justice than any other nation. He does use force. But he uses it without violence and without hatred, and he robs the privileged group of its moral pretensions.[42]

Gandhi's satyagraha may aim at moral conversion but, by these accounts, power is inherent in the process as well.[43] This is something Gandhi readily accepts, but he refuses to make power the central dimension of his conception of satyagraha.[44] He seeks to mobilize power to reorder the conventional agenda and introduce new issues by those who have been consigned to positions at the margin. In this way, Gandhian campaigns rely on power to unsettle and disturb, but Gandhi expects that any lasting changes will come from voluntary suffering and conversion.

AHIMSA

Hinduism has traditionally held a nonperfectionist view of violence. It is condemned for what it does to both the objects and users of violence. The former are denied their dignity and worth and the latter, driven by hatred and anger, refute the peace and harmony that is necessary for their own full lives. For all their misgivings about violence, most Hindu thinkers accept the view that it is unavoidably necessary to preserve the cosmic order. In doing so, they do not mean to give a ready justification of violence but to restrain it and keep it to a minimum.[45] For his part, Gandhi sees violence playing an ambivalent role in Hinduism, and he thinks that its best expression lies not in "historical Hinduism" but in his reading of the *Gita*. He reports that

> when I was in detention in the Aga Khan Palace, I once sat down to write a thesis on India as a protagonist of non-violence. But as I proceeded with my writing, I could not go on. I had to stop. There are two aspects of Hinduism. There is, on the one hand, the historical Hinduism with its untouchability, superstitious worship of stocks and stones, animal sacrifice and so on. On the other, we have the Hinduism of the *Gita*, the Upanishad and Patanjali's *Yoga Sutra* which is the acme of *ahimsa*. . . . *Ahimsa*, which to me is the chief glory of Hinduism, has been sought to be explained away by our people as being meant for *sannyasis* only. I do not share that view. I have held that it is *the* way of life [for everyone].[46]

Reconstructing Hinduism in ways that build on what he takes to be its positive, liberating qualities, Gandhi places ahimsa at its core.[47] For him, ahimsa makes social life both possible and worthwhile. "The principle of ahimsa," he writes, "is hurt by every evil thought, by undue haste, by lying, by hatred, by wishing ill of anybody."[48] To become an active force, Gandhi insists that ahimsa must mean more than avoiding harm which is the "least expression" of the term. For Gandhi, ahimsa is "the largest love, the greatest charity. If I am a follower of ahimsa, I must love my enemy."[49]

Gandhi's conception of love is not an expression of intimacy or passion but has a spiritual cast to it.[50] In this way, it parallels some of the attributes that Martin Buber sees in *I-Thou* relations where persons move beyond narrow constructions of themselves and others.[51] In distinguishing *I-Thou* from *I-It*, Buber means to show there are two kinds of relationships that persons develop with their external world. *I-It* is a relationship between a rational self and an object that has its own particular content and takes on an instrumental dimension. Buber's *I-Thou* is a relationship characterized by love between persons and moves beyond the cognitive and utilitarian. The *I* in his *I-Thou* relationship loses itself in the other, leading Buber to observe, "Love is responsibility of an *I* for a *Thou*. In this lies the likeness . . . of all who live, . . . to love *all men*."[52]

Buber knows that people do not constantly live on the plain of *I-Thou*. For him, *I-It* is pervasive and unavoidable. He holds that "the melancholy of our fate" is that every *Thou* becomes an *It*, that is, "the *Thou* becomes an object among objects—perhaps the chief, but still one of them."[53] The reason this is so, according to Buber, is that *Thou* is born out of and reflects love, but we cannot continually leave behind the rational, cognitive, and utilitarian aspects of our daily lives, and thus we invariably subvert the permanence of a transcendent love. According to Buber, "Without *It* man cannot live; but he who lives with *It* alone is not a man."[54]

Because the *Thou* does not endure and the *It* continually asserts itself, Buber does not despair that human beings are destined to live only in an objectified world, bereft of love. For him, everyone is capable of love and developing this capacity means, to Buber, that persons become human as they move beyond the material and instrumental and live outside and beyond themselves.[55] Then, they are ready to love, something that is not possible when individuals are fixed on their own interests and see others as objects to be used or manipulated.

Gandhi takes a parallel position in his discussion of ahimsa. Gandhian love builds on an openness that enables individuals to discover their unity and mutuality.[56] In this sense, one person does not love fragments of another person; Gandhian love is totalizing both for the lover and the loved one. Perfect love, as Gandhi would have it, means transcending one's own ordinary concerns and engaging with others as equals. With Buber, Gandhi does not expect perfect love to emerge "so long as we exist physically. Perfect non-violence whilst you are inhabiting the body is only a theory . . . but we have to endeavour every moment of our lives" to strive for this ideal.[57]

Gandhi's call for ahimsa also shares several attributes with Aristotle's "moral friendship." For Aristotle, we can have friendships of utility, reflecting the benefits we derive from our friends; or we can fashion friendships of pleasure, based on the enjoyment that flows from our relationship; or we can have moral friends. This latter expression of friendship moves beyond utility and pleasure and looks at our moral friend as "our other self." In laying out his theory of friendship, Aristotle makes three important claims. One is that moral friendship is one of the greatest goods a person can experience. Second, moral friendship can occur only among equals; we cannot see our friends as our other self if we regard them as superior or inferior. Third, we have a limited number of friends because we are able to suspend our own particularities and interests for only a few persons, not indiscriminately for many.[58]

It is on this last point that Gandhi parts company not only with Aristotle but with most who write about love. Gandhi wants to make it universal not only in the sense that anyone is capable of loving and worthy of love but in the sense that anyone can love everyone, including those who cause harm and suffering. With this move, Gandhi seeks to make love political as well as spiritual and moral. He believes that if love can be transported to the political terrain, new possibilities present themselves for openness and mutuality, for moving beyond particularities, and for nonviolently discovering what the participants share. Gandhi's reformulation of love does not deny disagreement or even conflict but rejects resentment and vengeance as the ways to settle differences.[59] In politicizing love, he seeks to transform conventional political relationships based on conventional power and self-interest and make love a way of sharing a common life.

Gandhi's effort to make love into something political appears to disfigure love (from something that is intimate and special to something that is universal and routine) and to misunderstand politics, stripping politics of power. For his part, Gandhi expects his reconstituted, politicized love to enable people to live together as equals, not under a truce between winners and losers. When ahimsa animates, Gandhi sees people understanding one another differently than they conventionally do—as strangers, as useful, as sources of pleasure or displeasure, or as enemies. He expects women and men to see others as they see the best in themselves, of being worthy of respect and able to make choices for themselves. Although such dispositions have a cognitive element in Gandhi's writings, he makes them rest primarily on noncognitive properties: compassion, humility, openness, and love.[60]

MEANS AND ENDS

Gandhi holds that the way to achieve a wider love is to pay attention to the "means" we apply in our relations with others.[61] For him,

"Means and end are convertible terms in my philosophy of life."[62] Throughout his discussions of nonviolence, he seeks to place moral constraints on conflict and he does this by continually returning to the importance of means.

> They say 'means are after all means.' I would say 'means are after all everything.' As the means so the end. There is no wall of separation between means and end. [Human beings have] control (and that too very limited) over the means, none over the end. Realization of the goal is in exact proportion to that of the means. This is a proposition that admits of no exception.[63]

Gandhi holds the view that our partial understanding of the truth should remind us of our fallibility and restrain us from taking our fragments as the whole truth.[65] In asking us to recognize our own partiality and fallibility, Gandhi pushes beyond mere tolerance of diverse conceptions of the truth. He claims that both he and those who grasp different fragments of the truth are deserving of mutual respect.

> I know that we are both right from our respective points of views. And this knowledge saves me from attributing motives to my opponents or critics. . . . I very much like the doctrine of the manyness of reality. It is this doctrine that has taught me to judge a Mussulman from his own standpoint and a Christian from his.[66]

To acknowledge the partiality of one's own truth does not minimize a person's moral commitments but leads to humility. In aborting claims of absolute certainty, Gandhian humility emphasizes the need for self-limiting applications of power.[67] When people claim that they own the absolute truth, they are apt to believe they are justified in imposing it on others, without any restraints. Such an epistemological and moral selfconfidence requires no dialogue or love, only revelation.

THE OTHER SIDE OF AHIMSA

In presenting ahimsa as his ideal, Gandhi argues for a disposition that nonviolently assists the vulnerable and challenges domination. It might appear that what he expects to follow is a society whose members have learned to live in peace and harmony while respecting the dignity and worth of each other. Living in such a world seems too good to be true, and no one appreciates this more than Gandhi. For him, the human condition denies the possibility of a perpetual cosmic harmony because *himsa*, the negation of ahimsa, continually stalks the human condition. It is impossible to avoid harming others, he reasons, not because we are evil but because human life rotates around both our spiritual and biological natures. Each set draws individuals in different, and sometimes contrary, directions. When Gandhi warns that the "world . . . is full of *himsa*," he not only has in mind the cruelty and violence that continually assert themselves but also the tendency of all human beings to care about themselves and not see others apart from the ways they can help or hurt us. At such times, we are prepared to use others for our own benefit.

> Strictly speaking, no activity and no industry is possible without a certain amount of violence, no matter how little. Even the very process of living is impossible without a certain amount of violence. What we have to do is to minimize it to the greatest extent possible. Indeed, the very word non-violence, a negative word, means that it is an effort to abandon the violence that is inevitable in life.[68]

Gandhi holds that himsa cannot be banished from the world or any single person once and for all. No courageous act, moral commitment, or amount of service can obliterate the inevitable concerns about the self that return again and again to any society and every person. The reason he gives is that all human life "exists by some *himsa*. . . . The world is bound in a chain of destruction. In other words, *himsa* is an inherent necessity for life in the body." Because we "never completely renounce the will to live," Gandhi wants us to "make a ceaseless endeavour to reduce the circle of *himsa*."[69]

Denying perfectionism, Gandhi emphasizes the importance of striving toward moral ideals and struggling against the gravitational force of himsa. To recognize that life unavoidably entails violence means that individuals must determine whether violence will define them or whether they will resist it. He wants people to make nonviolence their ideal, knowing that they "shall ever fail to realize it, but [should] never cease to strive for it.''[70] For Gandhi, the human condition is marked neither by perfectionism nor fatalism but by struggle.[71] He wants to free people from the force of gravity that continually pulls them back to their unavoidable pride.[72]

For Gandhi, himsa is not merely a defect in character, although it is that. It is more than the will to dominate for the sake of some personal or ideological good, as with the revolutionary, although it is that. Each of these expressions of himsa, Gandhi holds, can be more or less overcome. He thinks that we can become sufficiently detached and compassionate to see the harm we cause others; we can, as he understands matters, confront injustice without becoming unjust ourselves. But when himsa stems from the natural concern individuals have for themselves, it is more difficult to domesticate. That others are harmed unintentionally is, for Gandhi, not the point. He wants to show people that they cannot completely and permanently escape the self-interested side of their lives, but they can continually resist it. Everyone, he claims, should recognize that the "ego cannot be wholly gotten rid of," but, he claims, it can be challenged.[73] In this sense, Gandhian struggle is not only directed at the injustices and cruelty that he sees embedded in many social practices and the state; Gandhian struggle is also internal.

COURAGE, FORGIVENESS, AND ACTION

Gandhi continually and insistently links nonviolent civil disobedience with courage and a readiness to suffer.[74] Moral courage is no ordinary virtue for Gandhi; it is one of his touchstones.[75] He expects that every life will encounter obstacles, some large and painful, others small and negotiable. To lack the courage to proceed, Gandhi reasons, means persons are no longer honest to their convictions. Indeed, he believes that cowards do not govern themselves but transfer their power elsewhere. This move, he believes, contradicts our own dharma which should not be denied in the face of danger.[76] According to Gandhi,

> *dharma* does not under any circumstances countenance running away in fear. In this world which baffles our reason, violence there will then always be. The *Gita* shows the way which will lead us out of it, but it

also says that we cannot escape it simply by running away from it like cowards. Anyone who prepares to run away would do better, instead, to kill and be killed.[77]

The nonviolent person is "fearless. . . . The practice of ahimsa calls forth the greatest courage."[78] For Gandhi, "cowards can never be moral" because they are uncommitted to their own integrity or moral projects, unless it is safe or convenient.[79] Insisting that a person's autonomy is always paramount, Gandhi repeatedly argues that open, straight forward violence on behalf of one's own integrity is preferable to running away but nonviolence is superior to both.[80]

> Where there is only a choice between cowardice and violence I would advise violence. Thus when my eldest son asked me what he should have done, had he been present when I was almost fatally assaulted in 1908, whether he should have run away and seen me killed or whether he should have used his physical force which he could and wanted to use, and defended me, I told him that it was his duty to defend me even by using violence.[81]

This approach can be seen in Gandhi's ready admission that soldiers are courageous. Nevertheless, he insists that their bravery is inferior to that of the satyagrahi.[82] Granting that the courageous resolve of the armed solider is superior to passivity and cowardliness, Gandhi finds the soldier's courage is defective and incomplete because the "possession of arms implies an element of fear . . . but true nonviolence is an impossibility without the possession of unadulterated fearlessness."[83] Moreover, the violence of the solider is available only to those with the requisite physical strength, training, and weapons but, Gandhi reasons, anyone can be nonviolent. Gandhi's satyagrahi requires no weapons and asserts his own autonomy by courageously governing himself.[84]

The central importance of moral courage in Gandhi's theory can be seen in his anguished report of how nonviolence can be misunderstood and how some try to make a virtue out of passivity and fear. He recalls,

> The people of a village near Bettiah told me that they had run away whilst the police were looting their houses and molesting their women folk. When they said they had run away because I had told

them to be non-violent, I hung my head in shame. . . . I expected them to intercept the mightiest power that might be in the act of harming those who were under their protection, and draw without retaliation all harm upon their own heads even to the point of death, but never to run away from the storm center. It was manly enough to defend one's property, honour, or religion at the point of the sword. It was manlier and nobler to defend them without seeking to injure the wrongdoer. But it was unmanly, unnatural, and dishonorable to forsake the post of duty and, in order to save one's skin, to leave property, honour, and religion to the mercy of the wrongdoer. I could see my way of delivering the message of *ahimsa* to those who knew how to die, not to those who were afraid of death.[85]

Gandhi's criticism of the coward is unrelenting: such a person is a hypocrite, "who, being afraid to die, takes flight before any danger, real or imaginary, all the while wishing that somebody else would remove the danger by destroying the person causing it."[86] Gandhi's courageous persons leave behind fear and hatred and empower themselves, even if the rest of the world sees them unarmed, poor, and weak, and they walk with the confidence that they can effectively confront injustice.[87]

Insistently challenging fatalism, Gandhi hopes to show the efficacy of courage. He sees too many people accepting the lots dealt them by others and pleased with the small favors that come their way at the expense of their autonomy. They fear unsettling the present arrangement where they have found their place, however confining it may be. For his part, Gandhi thinks that such people do not understand that what should be most important to them is their own dignity and integrity. For them to see this, Gandhi wants people to become discontented and shake their fatalism in order to take control of their own lives. Then, they will recognize that they have been sacrificing their dignity with their steady lethargy and blind compliance born out of their fear. With this in mind, Gandhi observes that "As long as a man is contented with his present lot, so long is it difficult to persuade him to come out of it."[88]

It turns out that Gandhian courage opens up the possibility to develop other virtues. Gandhi expects that the person defined by fear and suspicion will have little room for love, compassion, or generosity. Rather than extend themselves to others, frightened people withdraw from the world to avoid any risk. He finds that

Fear and love are contradictory terms. Love is reckless in giving away, oblivious as to what it gets in return. Love wrestles with the world as with itself and ultimately gains a mastery over all other feelings.[89]

In staking out his claim that everyone can be courageous, he means to show that anyone can be a hero. Indeed, Gandhi continually retells the exploits of the heroes of the *Gita* and other sacred texts in ways that make their encounters with danger and resistance to domination into morality tales that can be transported into the lives of ordinary Indians in his own time. He means to show them that they can resist domination if they overcome their own fear.[90] Holding courageous action is within anybody's province, Gandhi democratizes conflict. It is not to be restricted to a few with special training and resources but is available to everyone. The satyagrahi can be anyone because any person's "strength does not come from physical capacity. It comes from an indomitable will."[91]

Along with courage and love, forgiveness is a central element in Gandhi's conception of nonviolence[92] and, in critical ways, parallels Hannah Arendt's political discussion of forgiveness. To forgive, Arendt observes, is to begin again; in putting aside the wrongs of the past, it allows people to settle differences and find ways that former adversaries can live together.[93] Gandhi holds that in forgiving our opponents, we are no longer entrapped by the past. By this he does not mean that we should forget about suffering and humiliation but that in confronting injustice, it is the act and not the actor that needs to be challenged. In forgiving the actor, Gandhi asks not for retribution but a new beginning that is free of prior injustice. The important issue for him is not how we punish past injustices but how we eliminate present injustice.[94]

RESPONSIBILITY AND THE MORAL AGENT

Gandhi's argument for responsibility carries a heavy burden for men and women. From his perspective, we are responsible not only for what we do but also for what we tolerate. The reason is that he finds the state and social practices are not free-standing but exist only because they are supported by individual citizens. "Even the most despotic government," he writes, "cannot stand except for the consent of the governed which

. . . is often forcibly procured. . . . When . . . the subject ceases to fear the despotic force, the power is gone."[95]

Gandhian responsibility implicates us in the actions of the institutions around us, whether or not we derive some benefit from them.[96] From his perspective, anyone who tolerates injustice nourishes and exonerates it.[97] To deny our culpability in institutional practices, Gandhi argues, means that we surrender our autonomy and live our lives according to a script written by others and not by ourselves. He sees this is always a danger but one that has become particularly acute where the modernized economy and centralized state diminish the role of individuals. For Gandhi, modern complexity confuses the issue of responsibility by assigning it to impersonal institutions where no one seems accountable or masking power and domination with the imperatives of efficiency or productivity. However, Gandhi claims, complexity can never repeal personal responsibility, at least if we want to continue to govern ourselves. When he asks why British colonialism prospers in India, Gandhi wants to make both the British and Indians responsible. In his account, colonialism is thriving because Indians allow it to.

> It is as amazing as it is humiliating that less than one hundred thousand white men would be able to rule three hundred and fifteen million Indians. They do so somewhat undoubtedly by force but more by securing our cooperation in a thousand ways and making us more and more helpless and dependent on them as time goes forward.[98]

So long as people refuse to challenge domination, Gandhi holds that they make themselves subordinate to others. When this happens, he sees individuals allowing themselves to be fashioned by others, daring not to act in ways that disturb their superiors and spending their time anticipating what will please and displease their overseers. Gandhi wants to show his fellow citizens that they are contributing to their subordination but can regain their dignity by courageously taking an active responsibility for themselves.[99] Gandhian autonomy comes not as a gift bestowed by the state but comes from each individual deciding on whom to become and what to choose. For him, the burden of freedom is an inescapable part of the human condition. Freedom for Gandhi does not mean being left alone or making choices from a prescribed list but taking responsibility for one's self and one's society, even when it is painful.

DEMOCRACY AND CIVIL DISOBEDIENCE

We often detect situations that we find are unjust and wonder how to respond. The quick answer for someone such as Gandhi might appear to be that people should nonviolently disobey whenever they observe injustice, but he is far from recommending such a step until several prior conditions are met.[100] In addition to exhausting other possible remedies,[101] Gandhi insists the person contemplating disobedience must be convinced a moral issue is at stake.[102]

> I pride myself on my yielding nature in non-vital matters. . . . I have found by experience that, if I wish to live in society and still retain my independence, I must limit the points of utter independence to matters of first rate importance. In all others which do not involve a departure from one's personal religion or moral code, one must yield to the majority.[103]

How do we know if we are asserting claims to disobedience based on principled standards or are pursuing some self-interested or vindictive goal? How can we tell whether our own particular understanding is sufficiently valid to break the law, particularly in a democracy? What is involved, after all, is the active assertion by individuals who claim that their moral knowledge justifies breaking a law that is supported by the majority. Gandhi does not expect that many will publicly disobey the law when it seems advantageous to them, given the penalties they face. Disobedience occurs, he argues, when principles are at stake. The problem in modern democracies is that people are often morally unsure of themselves when their moral standards conflict with the majority's, and then they are apt to allow majoritarian principles to carry the day.

In some important ways, his concern about democratic lethargy for assuming moral responsibility parallels Alexis de Tocqueville's. Each fears that citizens are apt to look to the majority to supply them with appropriate standards of behavior. For both Gandhi and Tocqueville, this is a case of a phenomenally derived principle judging the phenomena itself and leaving us with a self-justifying standard to decide what is right and wrong. According to Tocqueville the reason this has become commonplace is that tradition, which once served as a source for judging, has now grown weak. Without such a standard, he holds that modern democratic citizens find it difficult to appraise the validity of a law except to ask whether it has met the test of majority proceduralism.

The urgency of the problem can be seen in Tocqueville's question about obedience and disobedience to the law in the democratic age.[104] How does someone know when the law is deserving of compliance and when it is not? If someone relies on a majoritarian standard to legitimize law, then laws that meet the test should always be obeyed and independent standards to judge the law are considered inapplicable. However, Tocqueville thinks the issue is too important to be left there, and he appeals to natural law, tradition, and religion to help him judge positive law. For this to happen, he argues, moral standards must be convincingly internalized rather than stand as a nostalgic relic.

Even though he significantly departs from Tocqueville in many ways, Gandhi nevertheless carries the Frenchman's concern about the effects of democracy on autonomous judgment. They share the apprehension that in the modern world once robust traditions have grown mute and the prospects that people will develop an autonomous conscience are weakened. Each is deeply concerned that when traditional standards decay and social bonds weaken, people look to the majority to fill the void. From the perspective of Gandhi and Tocqueville, the modern self comes equipped with instrumental standards to evaluate what is useful but is often unsure about the moral worth of their own moral commitments.

CHALLENGING AUTHORITY: SOME COMPARISONS AND CONTRASTS

Gandhi and Antigone

Sophocles' tragedy, *Antigone,* provides us with one of the earliest and strongest accounts of nonviolent disobedience to civil authority. Her brothers have killed each other in combat, one defending and the other attacking their native city of Thebes. Creon, now king, declares the brother who defended the city a hero and decrees a ceremonial burial for him; the other is labeled a traitor and denied the customary proper rite. Anyone breaking his decree, Creon warns, faces death. Nevertheless, Antigone is determined to follow the traditional burial rites because her religion holds that the soul is condemned to roam endlessly and never comes to rest unless the dead are buried. She tells Creon that as long as her brother's soul wanders because he has been refused a proper burial, she has a responsibility to a higher law to bury her brother. For her, divine law takes precedence over human, positive law.

> For me it was not Zeus who made that order. . . .
> Nor did I think your orders were so strong
> that you, a mortal man, could over-run
> the gods' unwritten and unfailing laws (450–56).[105]

Unmoved, Creon dismisses pleas from numerous quarters to listen to positions different from his own.[106] When his son Haemon insists that certainty can never be absolute, Creon responds that the law must be steady and unbending.[107] To accept arguments to annul his decree, the king argues, would undermine the order and security of the city. For Creon, the power of office obligates rulers to remain steadfast and its subjects to be obedient.

> The man the state has put in place must have
> obedient hearings to his least command
> when it is right, and even when it's not (666–68).

Creon is certain he knows the truth and he expects obedience to his law, not discourse about it.[108] Gandhi would see in Creon a deserving target of civil disobedience, with his abuse of power, his refusal to listen, and his sponsorship of suffering. He would admire Antigone's courageous affirmation, her allegiance to a higher law, and her refusal to be governed by fear. However, Gandhi would find her position troublesome. She does not know how to deliberate or love. Even though her position is incomparably preferable to Creon's, her single-minded determination, bereft of love, contributes to more death and suffering in Thebes.[109] Moved by contempt, she traps Creon in his own arrogance. When he finally recognizes his mistakes, it is too late to repair them both because of his own prior blindness and because Antigone has given Creon no way out.

Gandhi and Locke

The differences between Gandhi and Locke are deep and numerous. Locke, for one, makes rights stand at the center of his theory in comparison to Gandhi's argument that rights are derivative from duties. Moreover, Locke's individualism conflicts with Gandhi's view about an interdependent cosmos. However, they share an important principle in their calls to resist tyranny.[110] For his part, Locke holds that everyone is a rights-carrier and that when individuals form a government they surrender their powers to make, interpret, and enforce laws but not their natural rights. Based on the consent of the governed, Locke's state is designed to protect rights. However, for all of his efforts to mute state power and make law dependent on legislative majorities, Locke acknowledges the state can usurp legitimate power and become tyrannical. At this point, he presents a theory of rebellion that rests on majority concurrence, not on an individual assessment that power has been dangerously abused.[111]

Locke's rejection of the individual's right to rebel stems from his apprehension that rights-claims are not readily self-limiting; some may claim a right for themselves that is really a narrow interest and use their understanding to revolt. But even when Lockean natural rights are at stake, Locke denies that the solitary person has warrant to rebel. He expects aggrieved individuals to wait until a majority agrees with them. On his account, majorities will not disturb the civil peace and endanger their own life, liberty, and property over petty issues but will rebel only when they agree that their basic rights are severely threatened. In this way, he seeks to defeat subjectivity.

Although Gandhi acknowledges that subjectivity is an inescapable and serious problem when individuals decide whether to obey or disobey the law, he would find Locke's solution too restrictive. In the first place, Gandhi argues that public disobedience accompanied with a readiness to suffer and accept punishment reduces the chances of narrowly inspired disobedience. People are not apt to disobey the law and face jail or worse simply to promote an interest. They are likely to disobey because they sincerely believe that moral principles are at stake and that they cannot be honest to themselves if they continue to obey. Another reason Gandhi would find Locke's justification of resistance too limiting is that it is exclusively tied to rights and to legislative proceduralism. For Gandhi, rights are too narrow a concept to cover his priority of autonomy for everyone.[112] He also wants people to examine not only their own situation but also the situation of the most vulnerable members of society and would find Lockean rights fail to address the injustice meted out to others.

He also departs from Locke over the issue of an individual's right to resist. Although Gandhi clearly prefers a majority to resist injustice, he would find Locke's claim that we must wait for majorities to decide is unacceptably restrictive. Gandhi does not want someone who conscientiously believes injustice has occurred to wait for the majority to catch up. For him, injustice must be challenged whether a majority agrees or not.[113] For Gandhi, no person's moral commitment should be suspended until supported by a majority.

Gandhi and Marx

In important ways, Gandhi and Marx share much. Both mount strong criticisms of capitalism, finding it exploitative, degrading, and hostile to the autonomy of persons. Moreover, neither believes that injustice will be eliminated without a self-conscious struggle. However, these and other similarities cannot hide their profound disagreements.[114]

There is the obvious one that Gandhi flatly, continually, and passionately rejects violence while Marx holds that only violence can dislodge the ruling class that has every incentive to resist challenges to its power.[115] Their disagreements about nonviolence and violence flow, in part, from their differing positions regarding the role of judgment. For Marx, the will is determined by the class structure in which people are located. In this sense, our individual identities are reflective of our locations within the class arrangements of our society and are not autonomously willed. For this reason, Marx finds the claim of accepting personal responsibility for one's actions as problematic, at best.

Gandhi rebels against Marx's determinism and its conclusions. For him, the will can always transcend time and place; and understandings of the good, while contextualized by tradition and social location, are not determined by either. In Gandhi's account, persons are able to penetrate beyond their particularities to understand their responsibilities to themselves and others. From his perspective, people do not have to wait for the appropriate structural conditions to know and act on what Gandhi calls the truth. They can see suffering regardless of historical period, social arrangements, or their own backgrounds and need neither special training nor the right environment to know when they or others are seriously injured. Moreover, he does not see traditions as fetters but as empowering. At the same time, Gandhi denies that individuals can ever excuse their inattention to, much less their complicity in, injustice because of the structural conditions of their society. He also claims individuals can incorporate the principles of *sat* or truth into their daily lives, even in a corrupt, colonial society. Indeed the pages of *Young India* and *Harijan* are filled with advice and examples of how very ordinary people can individually take charge of their own lives. Gandhi's individualistic and meliorist positions are simply antithetical to Marx who would find them illusionary and diversionary, and worst of all, reactionary.

Marx's emancipated self seems to have escaped contingency, duty, and politics in a classless society where everyone freely acts on real human needs. For his part, Gandhi holds that even in the best society, the emancipated self is embedded in contingency (which provides the person with both an identity and vulnerabilities), is conscious of extended duties to others, and finds that social relations are always subject to a corruption that needs to be resisted. In these ways, Gandhi denies Marx's assumption that politics and conflict can be overcome once and for all. Marx, unlike Gandhi, does not confront the role of power and politics in his version of the good society and seems to expect them to disappear or at least become benign. Although Gandhi's good society promises to expose power, diffuse it, and make it accountable, he knows that neither power nor pride can be conquered once and for all. Recognizing that even in the best regime power is subject to abuse, Gandhi argues that civil disobedience must remain a viable form of politics to challenge injustice.

Gandhi, Thoreau, and King

Gandhi shares much with Henry David Thoreau, who is one of the first writers to articulate a theory of civil disobedience, and with Martin Luther King, Jr., who mobilizes nonviolent civil disobedience to challenge racial segregation and advance the cause of racial equality in the United States. Thoreau, with whom Gandhi is often compared,[116] sees the American tolerance of slavery and its war with Mexico as morally unjustifiable and resists being a party to these policies in any way. For him, his conscience, not government, must be his moral arbiter.[117] Government "can have no pure right over my person and property but what

I concede to it," he claims.[118] His refusal to be implicated takes the form of withholding his taxes. For this, Thoreau is sent to jail. In his now famous essay *Civil Disobedience*, he reports that he "quarrel[ed] not with far-off foes, but with those who, near at home, co-operate with, and do the bidding of, those far away, and without whom the latter would be harmless."[119] Like Gandhi, Thoreau finds no reason to suspend his moral judgment to government because it is democratic. "The majority are permitted," he argues, "to rule . . . not because they are most likely to be in the right, nor because this seems fairest to the minority, but because they are physically the stronger."[120]

Thoreau challenges Americans to ask what it means to them to be free; to raise this question is to ask whether they obey themselves or others. In this way, he shares Gandhi's belief that individuals cannot escape responsibility for the policies of their government, that in opposing injustice it is necessary to offer public witness, and that resistors must be prepared to accept punishment for their commitments. What is the purpose of Thoreau's civil disobedience? It turns out that he wants to have no hand, however indirect, in harming others and to separate himself from a government that does harm others. As he understands it, "it is his duty . . . to wash his hands" of an unjust regime.[121] He also wants to be left alone.

> It is not a man's duty, as a matter of course, to devote himself to the eradication of any, even the most enormous wrong. . . . If I devote myself to other pursuits and contemplations, I must first see, at least, that I do not pursue them sitting upon another man's shoulders. . . .
>
> I have other affairs to attend to. I came into this world, not chiefly to make this a good place to live in, but to live in it, be it good or bad.[122]

Once released from jail, Thoreau returns to the wilderness where he seeks to disassociate himself from injustice and to construct his own life.[123] Thoreau's disobedience is that of a radical individualist who wants to be unencumbered by either an unjust government or what he takes to be involuntary duties.[124] In his ideal society, autonomous persons stay out of one another's way, not hurting others but not necessarily helping them. Thoreau and Antigone represent a first step in a Gandhian understanding of civil disobedience—the refusal to cooperate with evil, and Martin Luther King reflects the other step that is so essential to Gandhi, namely accepting responsibility to challenge unjust practices and promote the autonomy of everyone.[125]

Drawing on Western philosophy, scripture, natural law, and American constitutional and common law as well as Gandhi's teaching and example, King challenges the practices of racial segregation and inequality in America.[126] It is wrong, he insists, to relegate some to subordinate positions because of their backgrounds. He takes it to be his personal responsibility both to challenge injustice and to work for a society that respects the essential dignity and worth of all persons. Thoreau's withdrawal from combating injustice after he has separated himself from it is an insufficient response for King who reasons that "Injustice anywhere is a threat to justice everywhere." Claiming that we are responsible for our personal conduct as well as the institutions we tacitly accept, King argues, "We are caught in an inescapable network of mutuality, tied in a single garment of destiny. Whatever affects one directly, affects all indirectly." Like Gandhi, he takes civil disobedience to be not only a right but a duty and seeks to mobilize others to advance conditions that protect their own dignity and that of others. King also reflects the Gandhian position that he is fighting "evil rather than . . . persons who happen to be doing the evil."[127]

Gandhi and King each carry a comprehensive view of autonomy and makes it the standard to judge practices, laws, and institutions. In King's case, "any law that uplifts human [beings] is just. Any law that degrades human [beings] is unjust."[128] For him, every individual deserves to be free, and freedom means "the capacity to deliberate or to weigh alternatives, . . . expresses itself in decisions . . . [and entails] responsibility" for one's choices.[129] Departing from those who assume that reason or science can show the way out of our problems or that God will eventually obliterate injustice, King insists that people need to take charge and actively confront it.[130]

In challenging injustice, King argues that an important reason to proceed nonviolently stems from the incompleteness of anyone's knowledge.[131] From this perspective, human knowledge is not only inherently insufficient but "reason is darkened by sin."[132] Because everyone is vulnerable to sin, people delude themselves when they believe they can repeal their own pride. At such a time, King fears people believe they have a warrant to employ violence.

Although others in India and abroad have pursued a self-conscious Gandhian politics, few embody his principles and translate them into action as persistently and consistently as King. Both are highly spiritual; each translates his spirituality into concrete service designed to remove subordination and humiliation; each is deeply suspicious of conventional politics as an adequate mode of transformation; each insists that those who want change need to be prepared to share the suffering that accompanies it with their targets; and both find that nonviolence and individual autonomy are inexorably linked.

COMPLICATING NONVIOLENCE

Gandhi stakes out two claims about the applicability of nonviolence. The first is its global character; he insists that nonviolence can be applied anywhere at any time.[133] His second claim concerns its unique expression in India. He continually understands himself as an Indian, coming from the Hindu tradition and living in Indian society with its great strengths and disabilities. His Hindu version of nonviolence poses no inherent conflict with his global theories of nonviolence; one need not accept his Hindu commitment to prize both human and nonhuman forms of life in order to accept nonviolence with other persons. Here I want to consider his Indian version to show how Gandhi complicates his own theory in order to make nonviolence a continued search rather than an end-state and to show that Gandhian nonviolence is not based on perfectionism.

Gandhi's Nonviolence in India

When Gandhi talks about the unity of life, he means all biological life that he sees as part of the cosmos. For this reason, he offers a comprehensive view of nonviolence that covers every form of life. However, he is acutely and painfully conscious that he regularly compromises his comprehensive principle of nonviolence in practice. In discussing his argument that it is often necessary to take lower forms of life, I mean to show that Gandhi rejects a purist position regarding nonviolence.

Gandhi, a committed vegetarian,[134] understands that his vegetarianism must always be a limited expression of nonviolence because, he reasons, any form of agriculture and any vegetarian diet inescapably harms some living organism.[135] When farmers clear the land to plant a new crop, Gandhi sees them doing violence to the living organisms in the earth and, he reasons, the necessary activities of farming and eating undermine any one's best intentions to be nonviolent.[136] He insists, however, that the limitations of nonviolence in practice do not falsify the theory because it does not require a perfectionist application to be valid. The illusiveness of nonviolence reminds Gandhi that we are all locked in a constant struggle with necessity but that we need not be defined by necessity.[137] "All life," he tells us, "exists by some *himsa*. . . . The world is bound in a chain of destruction. In other words, *himsa* is an inherent necessity for life in the body."[138]

Gandhi's anti-perfectionism in regards to nonviolence emerges in his account of killing a wounded monkey in his ashram. He explains that taking the animal's life is a greater expression of care than keeping the suffering animal alive for a short time.[139] For Gandhi, the issue is whether one should allow the animal to suffer. To avoid taking the animal's life, Gandhi reasons, is to sanction cruelty. He works with the same perspective when he reports that

> Mad dogs are killed in the Ashram, the idea being that they die after much suffering and never recover. [Some Indians do not kill] them and deceive themselves into thinking that they observe nonviolence. As a matter of fact, they only indulge in great violence.
>
> Non-violence sometimes calls upon us to put an end to the life of a living being.[140]

Countless letters indicate the distress of many Indians at Gandhi's willingness to take the lives of animals. In response, Gandhi complains that formalistic applications of nonviolence betray an "ignorance of the nature of *ahimsa* which has for us long ceased to be a living faith, and has been degraded into formalities complied with when not very inconvenient."[141] Here and elsewhere, he argues that persons must not be bound by an inflexible proceduralism or a universal logic in order to respond to suffering and to understand the meaning of nonviolence in practice.

He regrets that his critics forget that "subhuman life is . . . but still only one aspect of [the] comprehensive principle" of nonviolence. Gandhi reminds his perfectionist readers that "our dealings with our fellow-men are still more important than that."[142] Continuing to assert his belief in the essential unity of all life, he holds that unlike lower forms of life, only human beings are capable of improving morally. However, Gandhi reasons, this does not give human beings warrant to destroy other forms of life for their own convenience.

Gandhi appreciates that his arguments about his defense of lower forms of life and his own justification of killing some animals are framed within his Hindu commitments and not particularly compelling to those from other traditions. These commitments are central to Gandhi, and he wrestles with how he can reconcile his discordant loyalties. For him, others need not accept his own views about the unity of all biological life in order to recognize the validity of his arguments against employing violence against other human beings. As he puts it, "my message and methods are, indeed, in their essentials for the whole world."[143] However, it turns out that Gandhi insists that there are not only some compelling reasons to take lower forms of life but also there are some limited, justifiable reasons to take the life of another human being.[144]

Killing Those We Love

Although Gandhi assumes the sanctity of life, he denies the priority of life, not because he does not value life but because he wants to celebrate a life that is honest to itself. He holds that nonviolent agents prefer their own death to "a life of falsehood" and would rather be killed than do "things unbecoming the dignity of a human being."[145] His commitment to the sanctity of an autonomous life leads him to show when killing another person is justifiable and indeed preferable to nonkilling.

> *Ahimsa* implies inability to endure other creatures suffering pain. From such inability arise compassion, heroism, and all other virtues associated with *ahimsa*. It is perverse logic to argue that we should be able to look on while others suffer. Again, it is not always true that death is more painful for human beings than anything they may suffer in life.[146]

Gandhi's rejection of perfectionism in regards to our relations with other human beings can be seen in his discussion about protecting our "wards," that is, individuals who are dependent on us and are entrusted to our care. Here, Gandhi takes up the issue of the conflict of good causes. It is good to protect the ward and it is good to be nonviolent. What should protectors do when the ward is threatened but do not know how to respond nonviolently? Given his reputation for nonviolence, Gandhi gives a surprising answer: "He who refrains from killing a murderer who is about to kill his ward (when he cannot prevent him otherwise) earns no merit but commits a sin: he practices no *ahimsa* but *himsa* out of a fatuous sense of *ahimsa*."[147] Gandhi extends this argument to a discussion of impending rapes. He holds that if a woman is threatened and her companion "does not believe in non-violence or cannot practice it, he must try to save her by using all the force he may have."[148]

These examples serve to emphasize the importance Gandhi gives to courage in the face of danger and how a violent response is preferable to passivity, even though inferior to a nonviolent one. What is Gandhi's response to those who are committed to nonviolence when someone in their care is violently threatened? He gives his answer when he relates a thought-experiment concerning his daughter. Gandhi asks what he will do if she "is threatened with violation and there is no way by which I can save her." In this narrative, Gandhi's daughter has not told her father what she would like him to do, so he must use his own best judgment. He concludes that "it would be the purest form of *ahimsa* on my part to put an end to her life and surrender myself to the fury of the incensed ruffian."[149] In this way, Gandhi believes, he protects his daughter's dignity which is more important than life itself, and he believes that this is what she would wish.[150] Two years earlier, he reveals that if one of his children were

attacked with rabies and there was no helpful remedy to relieve his agony, I should consider it my duty to take his life. Fatalism has its limits. We leave things to fate after exhausting all the remedies. One of the remedies and the final one to relieve the agony of a tortured child is to take his life.[151]

One startling feature about these last two cases is not merely that Gandhi allows that it can be justifiable to kill another person but that the killing is a sign of love. Moreover, the person doing the killing is Gandhi, and the persons killed are his own children. When we deliberately take the lives of those we love, Gandhi argues, it is because we want to assist them and not gain some good for ourselves. Such a disposition is less likely to occur with strangers; Gandhi's operative disposition here is not disinterest but love because only love can justify breaking the strong injunction against violence toward other human beings.[152] Related to this is the issue of fatalism. Gandhi is the consummate activist and repeatedly enlists his own energies against fatalism. He recoils at the idea that the intense suffering of those we love and for whom there is no hope should be fatalistically accepted. Gandhi's reasoning may not be ours. In the case of the impending rape of Gandhi's daughter, most of us would want to preserve her life, even if that meant she were raped, and then help her to put her life together as best she can. But Gandhi's anticonsequentialism offers a different response. He imagines the need to challenge the effort to humiliate, dominate, and violate by depriving the offender of his victim and preserving what Gandhi takes to be the dignity of the victim.

Gandhi continues his arguments on the permissibility of killing another human being in his discussion of other cases of taking a human life. In one, he has been asked to give his reaction to an elderly father who thought his own life was drawing to a close and took the life of his thirty-two-year-old, paraplegic, deaf daughter, expecting that no one would care for her after he died. Complaining that the father should have had greater confidence in the community to look after his daughter, Gandhi then observes that "such killing, if it is done bonafide, will certainly not count as *himsa* as defined by me."[153] On another occasion, he exonerates an actress who killed her lover at his request in order to relieve him of inordinate pain from a terminal illnesses.[154] Throughout his discussion of justifiable killing, he denies that anyone can take the life of another person "against his will."[155] In each case, Gandhi argues that when persons we love are deprived of their personhood and dignity, the usual restraints on nonviolence do not operate in the usual way. He explains that his examples show

> that refraining from taking life can in no circumstances be an absolute duty.
> The fact is that *ahimsa* does not simply mean non-killing. *Himsa*

means causing pain to or killing any life out of anger or from a selfish purpose, or with the intention of injuring it. Refraining from doing so is *ahimsa*.[156]

In taking up the issue of killing as a sign of ahimsa, Gandhi insists that it is "the highest duty of man to render what little service he can" to those in distress, even if this means taking another life on rare occasions and under exceptional conditions.[157] For him, the highest form of love is not expressed passively but actively. Gandhi is impatient with those who restrict ahimsa to "nonkilling," and not just because they allow suffering to proceed even though they could end it. He rebukes those whose rigid understanding of ahimsa shuts out other forms of suffering. Such a narrow outlook "has drugged our conscience and rendered us insensible to a host of other and more insidious forms of *himsa* like . . . the starvation and exploitation to which [many individuals] are subjected out of selfish greed, the wanton humiliation and oppression of the weak and the killing of their self-respect."[158]

Arguing that it is sometimes proper to take the life of someone we love, Gandhi returns to his opposition to a blind proceduralism: "Each such case must be judged individually and on its own merits. The final test as to its violence or non-violence is after all the intent underlying the act."[159] In probing the meaning and applicability of nonviolence, he requires people to examine their choices and not automatically apply principles without reflecting on why they act as they do. However, Gandhi always insists that, in most situations, nonviolence is the morally superior way.[160]

GANDHI, THE NAZIS, AND THE JEWS

Gandhi's reactions to the Nazis and recommendations to German Jews to engage in nonviolent civil disobedience present two special difficulties for his theory of nonviolence. One has to do with whether or not it is ever appropriate to use collective violence to forestall extraordinarily great harm. The other problem is whether Gandhi's methods are less universal than he claims. Is the efficacy of nonviolence dependent on context and on the participants?[161]

Gandhi continually insists that Nazism is evil and needs to be resisted.[162] In keeping with his commitments to satyagraha, he faults Allied military action against the Axis powers while condemning the Nazis: "If ever there could be a justifiable war in the name of and for humanity, a war against Germany, to prevent the wanton persecution of a whole race, would be completely justified. But I do not believe in any war."[163] Gandhi claims that nonviolence is a better route to take; he expects that through public suffering, the satyagrahi will touch those who employ violence and eventually convert them.[164] This is so, he thinks, because everyone possesses moral capacities that can be temporarily ignored but not permanently eliminated. For this reason, Gandhi wants the satyagrahi to be driven by trust even when one's opponent writes a record of deception and cruelty.[165] Gandhian trust in such cases represents an affirmation both in the principles of nonviolence as well as in the strength and courage of the satyagrahi who maintains integrity in the face of overwhelming violence.

Given his continued belief that civil disobedience will move opponents, Gandhi counsels German Jews to resist the Nazis publicly and nonviolently.[166] Sometimes he thinks that Hitler can respond to the nonviolent resistance of German Jews; at other times, he talks about how Jewish suffering can move the German public who will compel Hitler to change his policy or even replace him.[167] However, if one doubts that Hitler will be converted by the public, nonviolent resistance of Jews or that the German public will join Jews in opposing Hitler's policies, Gandhi's arguments for nonviolent resistance are suspect.

This is the reaction of several observers who argue that some situations simply do not lend themselves to nonviolent resistance.[168] They notice that Gandhi develops his theories out of his experiences with the British in South Africa and India and have gone on to observe that, for all of their faults, the British are not amenable to responding to Gandhi's politics with the methods of a Hitler or Stalin.[169] Many British are touched, others intimidated, and still others incensed by Gandhi's campaigns; but whatever their reactions, the British government and voters continue to value liberal goods, even if frayed, both in Britain and in India. When we turn to the Nazis, we find oppression and violence instead.

It appears that Gandhi's method is context-dependent. Some targets do not appear amenable to nonviolent resistance and will desist only when they face superior physical force. Even if such targets are open to change over time, the costs of waiting can be excessive. Without minimizing the great harm and domination that accompany British colonialism, there is a sharp difference between its evil and the evil of Nazism. In counseling nonviolent resistance to the Nazis, Gandhi writes as if they were British and as if their crimes were the crimes of the British. Yet he often acknowledges that the Nazis represent a heinous case of evil and violence. Writing in 1938, he sees the Nazis "showing how hideous, terrible, and terrifying [violence] looks in its nakedness."[170] What, then, are we to make of Gandhi's appeal to Jewish nonviolent resistance? To think about this question, it is helpful to reconsider Gandhi's own efforts to challenge violence and problematize nonviolence.

In previous sections of this chapter, I have argued that Gandhi shows there are situations when violence is appropriate: to protect the human dignity of those we love; to resist fatalism; to go on with the business of living (and thereby destroying lower forms of life); to defend one's own honor or the autonomy of a ward (in the case of an impending rape); and to respond to injustice violently rather than not respond at all.[171] What these cases demonstrate is a nonabsolutist position on Gandhi's part, and it is helpful to consider some additional situations where Gandhi is willing to accept violence, this time collective violence.

One such case emerges in Gandhi's reaction to the military defense of the Poles to Hitler's invasion of their country. He sees a courageous nobility in the Polish armed resistance and refuses to equate it with ordinary violence.

> If a man fights with his sword single-handed against a horde of dacoits armed to the teeth, I should say he is fighting almost nonviolently. Haven't I said to our women that, in defense of their honor they use their nails and teeth and even a dagger, I should regard their conduct non-violent. She does not know the distinction between *Himsa* and *Ahimsa* . . . . She acts spontaneously. In the same way, for the Poles to stand valiantly against the German hordes vastly superior in numbers, military equipment, and strength, was almost non-violence.[172]

In the case of the Poles, Gandhi emphasizes their spontaneity in the face of unprovoked, overwhelming violence aimed at defending their individual and national integrity. The Poles fight the Nazis knowing they are the far weaker party and will lose the battle, and Gandhi argues that their violence is an affirmation of their courage and a rejection of fatalism.

An additional case of Gandhi offering justifiable violence comes in his discussion of a community confronting a violent "madman" who is on a killing spree. Here, Gandhi claims that "Even manslaughter may be necessary in certain cases." We are told the madman

> runs amuck and goes furiously about sword in hand, and killing any one that comes his way, and no one dares to capture him alive. Any one who despatches this lunatic will earn the gratitude of the community and be regarded a benevolent man. From the point of view of ahimsa it is the plain duty of every one to kill such a man.[173]

In this case, we meet someone who seems unable to respond to either the head or the heart, and Gandhi invites us to protect our community. As in other cases where Gandhi justifies violence against persons, the damage threatened by inaction is immediate, consequential and irreversible,[174] and Gandhi assumes that the defenders do not know how to employ nonviolent alternatives. Gandhi, I think, would argue that he is not offering a string of exceptions to make the theory more palatable to skeptics but that these exceptions reflect the inability of ordinary human beings always to conceptualize nonviolent possibilities in every conceivable real-world situation where violence might assert itself.[175]

But would not this same reasoning apply to the Jews in Germany? Gandhi says no. One reason is that he wants to delegitimize the idea that Jews need to wait on violence or external forces to respond to the Nazis. He also seeks to take away the excuse of Germans who claim they do not know what is occurring. Public resistance exposes the injustice and violence of the Nazi regime and requires "ordinary" Germans to take a stand. He also wants to apply the same strict rules of nonviolence that he expects from Indians in their nonviolent resistance to British colonialism and a possible Japanese invasion.[176] Moreover, he wants to see a permanent change in the attitude of German officials; he wants a Germany where Jews will be safe and secure in the future and this requires, in Gandhi's account, conversion, not coercion.

Even so, one wonders why Gandhi does not extend his arguments for justifiable violence when he talks about Jewish resistance.[177] A problematized reading of Gandhi invites a different recommendation to German Jews than the one Gandhi himself gives. It moves away from a position that always denies the applicability of violence and invites a dialogue about specific, limited cases where violence may be appropriate to protect autonomy. Any conclusion about exceptions to nonviolence reached in such a dialogue does not falsify the theory but recognizes there are exceptional circumstances where violence might be appropriate.

EXPERIMENTING WITH THE TRUTH

Because violence is not completely avoidable but because it can be reduced, Gandhi wants to "experiment" with finding ways in which nonviolence can be effectively applied in diverse situations.[178] In undertaking these experiments, he seeks to show that violence is an inferior mode of proceeding and that violence, not nonviolence, needs to be justified. Gandhi works with several themes when he talks about experimenting with nonviolence. He wants to signal that nonviolence cannot be treated as a formula and approached dogmatically. What works in one situation may not be applicable in another, and what works for one person or group may not fit the requirements of others. Reflecting his commitment to plurality, Gandhi emphasizes that nonviolent action is open-ended and needs to be approached carefully. Believing that it is the most practicable way to achieve permanent change and overcome injustice, he wants nonviolent resistance to be more than a public affirmation of the moral principles of the resistor. He expects it to lead to an eventual change in the attitudes of the opponent and a commitment to eradicate both the practices and causes of injustice and violence. If nonviolence is only directed at changing policies, experimentation is less important than if it is directed at changing the attitudes of others.[179]

Gandhi knows, however, that many are passive in the face of domination; passive resistance is not contextually dependent because anyone can be passive in any situation. All that needs to happen is that the person disappears or acquiesces. The problem comes when we want to confront injustice actively and nonviolently with a view to changing matters.[180] At the heart of his "experiments with truth" lies his effort to understand how nonviolence can be applied under very different conditions. He reports that in working out his experiments, he "sometimes erred and learnt from my errors. Life and all of its problems have thus become to me so many experiments in the practice of truth and nonviolence."[181]

Because "truth has a primary and non-violence a derivative reality," it becomes necessary, Gandhi argues, to see how general principles that we take to be true are expressed in radically different situations by dissimilar people.[182] What emerges in Gandhi's experiments with nonviolence is an affirmation of the autonomy of everyone. Idealistic, even utopian, he offers a vision of men and women who settle their deep disagreements without violence or vengeance. In making his moves, he continually strives to open dialogue in order to find solutions that resist domination. Gandhian nonviolence is meant to introduce voices that have been mute and to fashion an agenda that speaks to their needs. In his repeated efforts to experiment with nonviolence, Gandhi seeks to translate his idealism into action.

NOTES

1. Reinhold Niebuhr, "What Chance Has Gandhi?" *Christian Century* 48 (1931), 1276.

2. *Young India,* June 1, 1921.

3. "My honor is the only thing worth preserving" (*Harijan,* October 15, 1938, in Iyer, *Writings:* 2, 487). In an earlier article, Gandhi writes that "a votary of truth would pray to God to give him death to save him from a life of falsehood. Similarly, a votary of *ahimsa* would on bent knees implore his enemy to put him to death rather than live a life of falsehood" (*Young India,* October 4, 1928, in Iyer, *Writings,* 2: 272).

4. In his Constructive Program, Gandhi makes civil disobedience part of his idea of service; it does not proceed or replace it. Also see "Speech," March 3, 1936, in Iyer, *Writings,* 3: 209–15.

5. See *Young India,* June 16, 1927.

6. See his dialogue with Indian terrorists in *Hind Swaraj,* ch. 15.

7. Nonviolence "is a conscious, deliberate restraint put upon one's desire for vengeance. But vengeance is any day superior to passive, effeminate, and helpless submission. Forgiveness is higher still. Vengeance too is weakened. The desire of vengeance comes out of fear of harm, imaginary or real." *Young India,* August 12, 1926.

8. See *Harijan,* February 1, 1935, and April 2, 1938.

9. *From Yervada Mandir,* 6. Gandhi holds that violence dehumanizes those who depend on it. The violent person believes the world is "at war with him and he has to live in perpetual fear of the world" (*Young India,* October 6, 1921). For Gandhi, persons who depend on violence brutalize themselves, separate themselves from society and build barriers to a full social life. See Ronald Terchek, "The Psychoanalytic Basis of Gandhi's Politics," *Psychoanalytic Review* 62, 2 (1975): 226.

10. Gandhi's argument parallels Simon Weil's claim that violence "turns anybody who is subjected to it into a *thing.*" For her, it "is as pitiless to the man who possesses it, or thinks he does, as it is to its victims: the second it crushes, the first it intoxicates." *The Iliad or the Poem of Force* (Wallingford, Pa.: Pendle Hill, 1956), 3, 11; italics in original.

11. *Young India,* May 21, 1925.

12. The problem of violence is compounded in the modern era where warfare becomes impersonal and technological. Stanley Milgram has shown that under experimental conditions, people are much more willing to impose pain when victims are physically remote than when they are close at hand. *The Individual in the Social World: Essays and Experiments* (New York: Addison-Wesley, 1977.

13. *Harijan,* March 30, 1947.

14. According to Gandhi, "the natural corollary to" the use of violence "would be to remove opposition through the suppression or extermination of the antagonists" (*Harijan,* May 27, 1939).

15. *Navajivan,* July 13, 1924, in Iyer, *Writings,* 3: 94.

16. He finds violence asserting itself not only in power politics and social practices but also in the household and community.

17. "Nonviolence is not meant merely for the *rishis* and saints. It is meant for the common people as well. Non-violence is the law of our species as violence is the law of the brute. . . . The dignity of man requires obedience to a higher law—to the strength of the spirit," something that Gandhi thinks is available to everyone. *Young India,* August 11, 1920; also see *Harijan,* September 5, 1936.

18. According to Gandhi, "No human being is so bad as to be beyond redemption, no human being is so perfect as to warrant his destroying whom he wrongly considers to be wholly evil." *Young India,* March 26, 1931.

19. For Gandhi, "Truth and non-violence are no cloistered virtues but applicable as much in the forum and the legislatures as in the market place." *Harijan,* May 8, 1937.

20. *Harijan,* July 21, 1940.

21. "Non-cooperation is not a passive state, it is an intensely active state,—more active than physical resistance or violence. Passive resistance is a misnomer" (*Young India,* August 25, 1920). In this connection, Joan Bondurant

observes, "It must be kept firmly in mind that *non-resistance* does not describe satyagraha" (*Conquest of Violence*, 36–37).

22. *Ahimsa* "does not mean helping the evil-doer to continue the wrong or tolerating it by passive acquiescence. On the contrary, love, the active state of ahimsa, requires you to resist the wrongdoer by dissociating yourself from him." *Young India*, August 25, 1920.

23. Also see Arendt, *The Human Condition*, 69–70. For her, "A comparatively small but well-organized group of men can rule almost indefinitely over large and populous empires, and it is not infrequent in history that small and poor countries get the better of great and rich nations." However, popular revolt often develops, sometimes forgoing "the use of violence in the face of materially vastly superior forces. To call this 'passive resistance' is certainly an ironic idea; it is one of the most active and efficient ways of action ever devised because it cannot be countered by fighting, where there may be defeat or victory, but only by mass slaughter in which even the victor is defeated, cheated of his prize since nobody can rule over dead men" (*Human Condition*, 200–1).

24. See *Indian Opinion*, February 22, 1908, in Iyer, *Writings*, 3: 33.

25. Letter, December 31, 1934, in Bose, *Selections from Gandhi*, 17.

26. "Our motto must ever be conversion by gentle persuasion and a constant appeal to the head and heart. We must therefore be ever courteous and patient with those who do not see eye to eye with us. We must resolutely refuse to consider our opponents as the enemies of the country." *Young India*, September 29, 1921.

27. He insists that his "method is conversion, not coercion" (*Young India*, January 12, 1928). Also see *Young India*, June 21, 1925 and *Harijan*, July 8, 1939, and February 10, 1946.

28. In many traditions, including Hinduism, suffering is something to be avoided or, as Margaret Chatterjee puts it, made it into "a practical problem" that should be eliminated. *Gandhi's Religious Thought*, 75.

29. *Young India*, November 5, 1931.

30. Chatterjee, *Gandhi's Religious Thought*, 80.

31. For those who find Gandhi's invitation to suffering esoteric and even perverse, it is helpful to recall that Machiavelli, Rousseau, and Lincoln insist the good citizen must sometimes be willing to sacrifice and suffer. John Diggins argues that Lincoln finds suffering is redemptive in *The Lost Soul of American Politics* (New York: Basic Books, 1984). In William Corlette's discussion of Lincoln, suffering is a sign of patriotism ("The Availability of Lincoln's Civil Religion" *Political Theory* 10 [1982]: 520–40).

32. *Young India*, November 5, 1931.

33. *Young India*, September 18, 1924.

34. "I have found that appeal to reason does not answer where prejudices are

agelong. . . . Reason has to be strengthened by suffering and suffering opens the eyes to understanding." *Political Philosophy of Mahatma Gandhi*, 131. Notice that neither "the heart nor the head" is sufficient by itself; Gandhi insists each is necessary and the way we reach reason is by disturbing settled routines and settled instrumental rationalities embedded in those routines through public suffering.

35. For a discussion of duragraha see Bondurant, *Conquest*, 42–44; Iyer, *Thought*, 310–12; and Terchek, "Gandhian Politics," 127–32.

36. Bondurant, *Conquest*, 43.

37. "Satyagraha—Not Passive Resistance," 1917, in Iyer, *Writings*, 3: 45.

38. See Gandhi's discussion of duragraha as a perverted form of nonviolence. It is for the "impatient" person filled with hatred (*Collected Works*, 14: 63–65; Nov. 3, 1917). Also see Dalton, *Mahatma Gandhi*, 40–46; and Terchek, "Gandhi and Moral Autonomy," *Gandhi Marg* 13, 4 (1992).

39. See Leo Kuper, *Passive Resistance in South Africa* (New Haven: Yale University Press, 1957), 80–81.

40. Bondurant, *Conquest*, 10–11. Also see Sharp, *Politics of Nonviolent Action*. Mill owners facing strikers organized by Gandhi, for example, do what most owners would in such a situation, that is, look for a way to resolve the conflict and get their mills operating again.

41. Bose, *Studies in Gandhianism* (Calcutta: India Associated Publishing Company, 1962), 116.

42. Niebuhr, "What Chance Has Gandhi?" 1275.

43. Parekh finds that Gandhi's satyagraha "was an ingenious combination of reason, morality and politics . . . and appealed to the opponent's head, heart, and interests." *Gandhi's Political Philosophy*, 156.

44. Gandhi appreciates the political nature of satyagraha when he observes, "Nonviolence presupposes an ability to strike." *Young India*, August 12, 1926.

45. See Parekh, *Colonialism, Tradition and Reform*, 108–12.

46. *Harijan*, December 8, 1946, in Iyer, *Writings*, 2: 262.

47. Gandhi reinterprets the Hindu tradition and insists that ahimsa is its central tenet. However, his reading is not the conventional one. Bondurant finds that " '*satyagraha*' was, indeed, familiar to the ear of the Indian" but Gandhi gives it a new meaning, projecting "the traditional ethical laws [of detachment] into the realm of social action" (*Conquest of Violence*, 110).

48. Letter to Narandas Gandhi, July 1930, in Iyer, *Writings*, 2: 230.

49. "On Ahimsa: Reply to Lala Lajput Rai," *The Modern Review*, October 1916, in Iyer, *Writings*, 2: 212.

50. According to Gandhi, "Ahimsa means 'love' in the Pauline sense" (*Harijan*, March 15, 1936, in Iyer, *Writings*, 2: 240). See also *Harijan,* March 24, 1936, in Iyer, *Writings*, 2: 140. Parekh argues that Gandhi's view of ahimsa as an

expression of active love runs contrary to conventional Hindu interpretations of ahimsa which hold that love is a passion and hence unreliable; as Parekh reads the Hindu tradition, detachment, not action, is necessary for the good life (Parekh, *Colonialism, Tradition, and Reform*, 113).

51. For all the many parallels between them, Gandhi and Buber part company over the fate of the Jews in Nazi Germany and the founding of a Jewish state in Israel. See Buber's "The Land and its Possessors: An Answer to Gandhi," in *The Writings of Martin Buber*, ed. Will Herberg (New York: Meridian Books, 1958), 281–86. Also see Dalton, *Mahatma Gandhi*, 135, 228.

52. Buber, *Writings*, 48.

53. Buber, *Writings*, 49.

54. Buber, *Writings*, 55.

55. For this reason, Buber rejects individualism which sees "man only in relation to himself" as well as collectivism which "does not see man at all; it sees society." *Between Man and Man*, 200, as cited in Herberg, *The Writings of Martin Buber*, 21.

56. Chatterjee finds that for Gandhi, "Love is the power which draws people closer together." *Gandhi's Religious Thought*, 89.

57. *Harijan*, July 21, 1940.

58. Aristotle, *Nicomachean Ethics*, ed. Terence Irwin (Indianapolis: Hackett, 1985), ch. 8.

59. See *Young India*, August 12, 1926.

60. See letter to Purushottam Gandhi, May 12, 1932, in Iyer, *Writings*, 2: 234. According to Gandhi, "where there is no compassion, there is no *ahimsa*. The test of *ahimsa* is compassion. The concrete form of *ahimsa* is compassion. Hence it is said there is as much *ahimsa* as there is compassion. If I refrain from beating up a man who comes to attack me, it may or may not be *ahimsa*. If I refrain from hitting him out of fear, it is not *ahimsa*. If I abstain from hitting him out of compassion and with full knowledge, it is *ahimsa*" ("*Ahimsa* v Compassion," March 31, 1929, in Iyer, *Writings*, 2: 225).

61. "*Ahimsa* and Truth are so intertwined that it is practically impossible to disentangle and separate them. . . . Nevertheless, *ahimsa* is the means and Truth is the end. Means to be means must always be within our reach, and so *ahimsa* becomes our supreme duty. . . . If we take care of the means, we are bound to reach the end sooner or later." Letter to Narandas Gandhi, July 31, 1930, in Iyer, *Writings*, 2: 230–31.

62. *Young India*, December 26, 1924.

63. *Young India*, July 17, 1924.

64. Note deleted in proofs.

65. See *Hind Swaraj*, ch. 7.

66. *Young India*, August 11, 1920. Martin Buber captures this view in his

observation to Christian missionaries, "It behooves both you and us to hold inviolably fast to our own true faith, that is, to our own deepest relationship to truth. . . . Our task is not to tolerate each other's waywardness, but to acknowledge the real relationship in which both stand to the truth" (*Israel and the World,* 40 as cited in Herberg, *Writings,* 37).

67. See Terchek, "Gandhi's Democratic Theory," 311–13; see also Parekh, *Gandhi's Political Philosophy,* 147.

68. *Harijan,* September 1, 1940. Gandhi goes on to argue that ahimsa "is also violated by our holding on to what the world needs. But the world needs even what we eat day to day. . . . What should we do then?" Letter to Narandas Gandhi, July 1930, in Iyer, *Writings,* 2: 230. In asking this question, Gandhi warns that ahimsa can never be total but should be approached as an ideal.

69. *Young India,* October 4, 1928. For Gandhi, "Perfect *ahimsa* is possible only in the *atman* in its disembodied state" (Letter to Purushottam Gandhi, May 12, 1932, in Iyer, *Writings,* 2: 235).

70. *Harijan,* September 1939.

71. Part of Gandhi's understanding of the human condition as struggle parallels Albert Camus' argument on behalf of struggle in *The Myth of Sisyphus.* See Dadhich, *Gandhi and Existentialism.*

72. "Pride is a monster that swallows" *ahimsa* because it refuses to acknowledge the worth and dignity of others. *Young India,* October 21, 1926.

73. "Man is a fallible being. He can never be sure of his steps. What he may regard as an answer to a prayer may be an echo of his pride. For infallible guidance, man has to have a perfectly innocent heart incapable of evil. I can lay no such claim. Mine is a struggling, striving, erring, imperfect soul." *Young India,* September 25, 1924.

74. See Gandhi, *My Religion,* ed. Bharatan Kumarappa (Ahmedabad: Navajivan, 1955), 62.

75. On Gandhi's account, "Any action that is dictated by fear or by coercion of any kind ceases to be moral" (*Ethical Religion,* ch. 3, 43). Gandhian courage is closely related to his conception of honesty and voluntary suffering as among the highest virtues.

76. Without courage, nonviolence is, at best, a tactic that people may find convenient when they are weak but discard when they think that they can strike without fear of retribution.

77. "Meaning of the *Gita,*" *Navajivan,* October 11, 1925, in Iyer, *Writings,* 1: 83.

78. "On Ahimsa," October 1916, in Iyer, *Writings,* 2: 213.

79. *Young India,* October 13, 1921.

80. "There is hope for a violent man to be some day non-violent, but there is none for a coward. I have therefore said more than once in these pages that if

we do not know how to defend ourselves, our women, and our places of worship by the force of suffering, i.e. nonviolently, we must, if we are men, be at least able to defend all these by fighting." *Young India,* June 16, 1927.

81. *Young India,* August 11, 1910, in Iyer, *Writings,* 2: 298. See also, *My Religion,* 62.

82. *Young India,* December 18, 1924.

83. *Harijan,* July 15, 1939.

84. For this reason, Gandhi holds that "Satyagraha is based on self-help." Gandhi, *Satyagraha in South Africa,* 282.

85. Bose, *Selections from Gandhi,* 162.

86. *Modern Review,* October 1916, in Iyer, *Writings,* 2: 214. Gandhi argues that we cannot claim to practice nonviolence when we leave it to others to protect us with their violence. He illustrates this in the story of a person who flees his village when a dangerous leopard arrives. "He will run away and when someone has killed the leopard, will return to take charge of his hearth and home. This is not non-violence. This is a coward's violence. The man who has killed the leopard has at least given proof of some bravery. The man who takes advantage of the killing is a coward. He can never expect to know true nonviolence." *Harijan,* June 9, 1946, in Iyer, *Writings,* 2: 257.)

87. "And so I am not pleading for India to practice non-violence because it is weak. I want her to practice non-violence being conscious of her strength and power." *Young India,* August 11, 1920, in Iyer, *Writings,* 2: 300.

88. *Hind Swaraj,* ch. 3.

89. *Young India,* October 1, 1931, in Iyer, *Writings,* 2: 294.

90. Gandhi holds that courage lays the grounding for civil disobedience: "We are restrained from violence through our weakness. What is wanted is a deliberate giving up of violence out of strength." *Young India,* August 22, 1929.

91. *Young India,* August, 11, 1920.

92. On Gandhi's account, "the weak can never forgive. Forgiveness is the attribute of the strong." *Young India,* April 2, 1931.

93. Arendt makes "the power to forgive" a miracle that is "within the reach of man." *Human Condition,* 247.

94. To dwell on the past and refuse to forgive increases the chance of future conflict. For his part, Gandhi repeatedly says that the British are welcome to remain in India after independence if they accept an independent India with its culture and its practices. On Gandhi's reading, nonviolence "does most emphatically exclude the possibility of future revenge after a successful termination of the struggle" (March 9, 1922, *Collected Works,* 23: 24–25). See also *Hind Swaraj,* ch. 20.

95. *Young India,* June 30, 1920; see also *Young India,* July 28, 1920.

96. "I believe, and everybody must grant, that no Government can exist for

a single moment without the co-operation of the people, willing or forced, and if the people suddenly withdraw their cooperation in every detail, the Government will come to a complete standstill." *Young India*, August 18, 1920.

97. See *Young India*, August 18, 1920.

98. *Young India*, September 22, 1920.

99. Gandhi extends his arguments about our complicity in violence to include those who agree with us and employ violence in our mutual cause. In condemning nationalist violence prior to Indian independence, he observes, "It has become the fashion these days to ascribe all such ugly manifestations to the activities of hooligans. It hardly becomes us to take refuge in that moral alibi. Who are the hooligans after all? They are our countrymen and, so long as any countryman of ours indulges in such acts, we cannot disown responsibility for them consistently with our claim that we are one people" (*Harijan*, April 7, 1946).

100. He holds that it is first necessary to obey valid law before undertaking to disobey unjust laws: "A *Satyagrahi* obeys the laws of society intelligently and of his own free will because he considers it to be his sacred duty to do so. It is only when a person has thus obeyed the laws . . . that he is in a position to judge as to which particular rules are good and just and which are unjust and iniquitous." *Autobiography*, 392; see also Bondurant, *Conquest*.

101. "I am resorting to non-co-operation in progressive stages because I want to evolve true order out of untrue order. I am not going to take a single-step in non-co-operation unless I am satisfied that the country is ready for that step, namely non-co-operation will not be followed by anarchy or disorder." *Young India*, August 18, 1920.

102. "I would be deeply distressed if on every conceivable occasion each one of us was to be a law unto himself and to scrutinize in golden scales every action of our future National Assembly. I would surrender my judgment in most matters to national representatives, taking particular care in making my choice of such representatives. I know that in no other manner would a democratic government be possible for one single day." Cited in Charles Andrews, *Mahatma Gandhi's Ideas* (New York: Macmillan, 1930), 144.

103. *Young India*, July 7, 1920. For Gandhi, social peace is a good, although hardly its highest expression.

104. As Tocqueville sees it, "When I refuse to obey an unjust law, I by no means deny the majority's right to give orders; I only appeal from the sovereignty of the people to the sovereignty of the human race. . . .

"If you admit that a man vested with omnipotence can abuse it against his adversaries, why not admit the same concerning a majority? Have men, by joining together, changed their character? . . . I will never grant to several that power to do everything which I refuse to a single man." *Democracy in America*, 250–51.

105. Sophocles, *Antigone* (Chicago: University of Chicago Press, 1954).

106. When a guard asks if he may "say something? Or just turn and go?" Creon answers, "Aren't you aware your speech is most unwelcome?" (315–316).

107. Haemon: I'd say it would be best if men were born / perfect in wisdom, but that failing them / (which often fail) it can be no dishonor / to learn from others when they speak good sense (720–23).

108. Creon exemplifies the arrogance of power when he asks "Am I to rule by other minds than mine?" (736).

109. Martha Nussbaum finds both Antigone and Creon are without love. *Fragility of Goodness, Luck and Ethics in Greek Tragedy and Philosophy* (New York: Cambridge University Press, 1986), 65. She goes on to argue that constraint and choice need each other but that both Antigone and Creon think only about choice and do not consider constraint, particularly self-constraint (81).

110. Locke's understanding of power is much more constrained than Gandhi's. Locke, for one, is prepared to accept the institutional arrangements in civil society as largely irrelevant to autonomy.

111. Locke's discussion of rebellion is found in his *Second Treatise of Government*, chs. 18–19.

112. Gandhi argues that "Civil Disobedience . . . becomes a sacred duty when the state has become lawless or, which is the same thing, corrupt. And a citizen who barters with such a state shares its corruption or lawlessness." *Young India*, January 5, 1922.

113. For this reason, Gandhian justifications for civil disobedience can be incorporated into minority movements, such as the civil rights movement in the United States, something Lockean justifications of resistance cannot do.

114. In addition to the disagreements discussed in this section, Gandhi categorically denies the inevitability of a class struggle or even that class is a particularly helpful way of understanding social relations. Moreover, Gandhi rejects Marx's optimism about the inevitability of progress and his faith that an industrial economy is liberating. For a further discussion of Gandhi and Marxism, see M. B. Rao, ed., *The Mahatma: A Marxism Symposium* (Bombay: Popular Prakashan, 1963).

115. On the avoidability of class conflict, see *Young India*, March 26, 1931; for Gandhi's view of "true socialism," see his *My Socialism* (Ahmedabad: Navajivan Publishing House, 1969). See also *Harijan*, September 28, 1934; on socialism as an ethical ideal that cuts across class lines, see *Harijan,* July 13, 1947.

116. According to Gandhi, "The expression [civil disobedience] was, as far as I am aware, coined by Thoreau to signify his own resistance to the laws of a slave State. He has left a masterly treatise on the duty of Civil Disobedience. But Thoreau was not perhaps an out and out champion of non-violence" (*Young*

India, March 23, 1921). Gandhi reports that he first read Thoreau's *Civil Disobedience* in 1907, when he "was in the thick of passive resistance" in South Africa (Letter to Henry Salt, October 12, 1929, in Iyer, *Writings*, 1: 102). For a recent comparison of Gandhi and Thoreau, see Naresh Dadhich and B. Arun Kumar, "Thoreau's Protest: A Means to Maintain the Ontological Essence of Man," *Gandhi Marg* 15, no. 3 (October 1993): 308–22. See also James Hunt, "Thoreau and Gandhi: A Re-evaluation of Their Legacy," in *New Dimensions and Perspectives in Gandhism*, ed. V. T. Patil (New Delhi: Inter-India Publications, 1988), 281–90.

117. Henry David Thoreau, *Walden and Civil Disobedience*, ed. Owen Thomas (New York: Norton Critical Editions, 1966), 225.

118. Thoreau, *Civil Disobedience*, 242.

119. Thoreau, *Civil Disobedience*, 228.

120. Thoreau, *Civil Disobedience*, 225.

121. Thoreau, *Civil Disobedience*, 230.

122. Thoreau, *Civil Disobedience*, 229–30.

123. For a discussion of Thoreau's democratic individualism, see George Kateb, *The Inner Ocean: Individualism and Democratic Culture* (Ithaca: Cornell University Press, 1992). Not everyone sees Thoreau as withdrawn. Nancy Rosenblum, for one, finds

> it soon becomes clear that Thoreau's hut at Walden Pond and *Walden* itself are designed to be provocative. His privatization is exhibitionist, a public act calculated to engage others. . . . Thoreau's main business in the woods, composing *Walden*, was ultimately directed to his Concord neighbors. He did not want to be left alone entirely and he certainly did not want to leave others be. He was a militant, not a quietest. *Another Liberalism* (Cambridge: Harvard University Press, 1987), 104, 112.

Although Thoreau clearly challenges his neighbors by his disobedience, he presents a limited view of social responsibility.

124. Contrast this with Gandhi's argument that "nonviolence is not a cloistered virtue to be practiced by the individual for his peace and final salvation, but a rule of conduct for society if it is to live consistently with human dignity." *Young India*, August 11, 1927.

125. For further discussions of Gandhi and King, see John Ansbor *Martin Luther King, Jr.: The Making of a Mind* (New York: Orbis, 1984); and Dalton, *Mahatma Gandhi*, 168–200.

126. King acknowledges his debt to Gandhi in several of his writings. See *Stride Toward Freedom* (New York: Harper and Row, 1958), 78–80; *Strength to Love* (New York: Pocket Books, 1968), 169; and *Where Do We Go from Here?* (New York: Bantam Books, 1968), 51–52. See also "My Trip to the Land of Gandhi," *Ebony*, July 1959, 84–92; and "More than Any Other Person in History," *Peace News*, January 1, 1958.

127. *Stride Toward Freedom*, 84.

128. *Why We Can't Wait* (New York: Signet Books, 1963), 82.

129. *Where Do We Go From Here?* 115–16.

130. "How can evil be cast out? Men have usually pursued two paths to eliminate evil and thereby save the world. . . .

"Man has subpoenaed nature to appear before the judgment seat of scientific investigations. . . . But in spite of [the] astounding new scientific developments, the old evils continue and the age of reason has been transformed into an age of terror. Selfishness and hatred have not vanished with an enlargement of our educational system and an extension of our legislative policies. . . .

"The second idea for removing evil from the world stipulated that if man waits submissively upon the Lord, in his own good time God alone will redeem the world. Rooted in a pessimistic doctrine of human nature, this idea, which eliminates completely the capacity of sinful man to do anything, was prominent in the Reformation" (*Strength to Love*, 146–48).

Here and elsewhere, King shows a greater affinity with Gandhi than simply a commitment to nonviolence. Like Gandhi, he offers an incisive critique of Enlightenment optimism as well as fatalism.

131. Surveying Christian liberalism and neo-orthodoxy as well as the Renaissance and Reformation, King holds that "each represents a partial truth" (*Strength to Love*, 147).

132. *Strength to Love*, 146.

133. Nonviolence "is not merely a personal virtue. It is also a social virtue to be cultivated like the other virtues. Surely society is largely regulated by the expression of nonviolence in its mutual dealings. What I ask for is an extension of it on a larger, national and international scale." *Harijan*, January 7, 1939, in Iyer, *Writings*, 2: 491.

134. Many of his early writings in South Africa are devoted to vegetarian topics. See also his *Autobiography*.

135. See *Young India*, November 11, 1928. Earlier, he writes "Taking life may be a duty. Let us consider this position. We do destroy as much life as we think is necessary for sustaining the body. Thus for food we take life, vegetable and other, and for health we destroy mosquitoes . . . , and we do not think that we are guilty . . . in doing so." *Young India*, November 4, 1926.

136. Gandhi holds that himsa consists not in merely taking life in anger, but in taking life for the sake of one's "perishable body." *Young India*, November 4, 1926.

137. See letter to Narandas Gandhi, July 31, 1930, in Iyer, *Writings*, 2: 230–31.

138. *Young India*, October 4, 1928.

139. "Ashram Observances," July 11, 1932, in Iyer, *Writings*, 2: 579.

140. "Ashram Observances," July 11, 1932, in Iyer, *Writings*, 2: 579.

141. "Ashram Observances," July 11, 1932, in Iyer, *Writings*, 2: 580; see also *My Religion*, 74–75.

142. "Ashram Observances," July 11, 1932, in Iyer, *Writings*, 2: 580.

143. *Harijan*, June 6, 1933; see also *Young India*, September 17, 1925. Gandhi's view of the universal applicability of his teaching can be seen in his arguments regarding ahimsa. He weaves a close relationship between ahimsa and Hinduism but does not mean to make ahimsa dependent on Hinduism in particular or religion in general. "It is not necessary to believe in an extra-mundane power called God in order to sustain our faith in *ahimsa*" (*Harijan*, September 5, 1936).

144. Life is not the highest good for Gandhi. He is prepared to sacrifice his own life in the service of the good, and he frequently counsels others to do the same.

145. *Young India*, October 4, 1928, in Iyer, *Writings*, 2: 272. As I indicated in the chapter on autonomy, Gandhi holds that "man does not live by bread alone. Many prefer self-respect to food" (*Young India*, February 5, 1925).

146. Letter to Purushottam Gandhi, May 12, 1932, in Iyer, *Writings*, 2: 235.

147. *Young India*, November 4, 1926.

148. *Harijan*, March 1, 1942.

149. *Young India*, October 4, 1928.

150. Responding to a correspondent who objects to his hypothetical argument for taking his daughter's life, Gandhi explains, "My reason for putting my daughter to death in circumstances mentioned by me would not be that I feared her being polluted but that she herself would have wished death if she could express her desire. If my daughter wanted to be put out of life because she was afraid of public scandal and criticism I would certainly try to dissuade her from her wish. I would take her life only if I was absolutely certain that she would wish it. I know that Sita would have preferred death to dishonour by Bavana." *Young India*, October 25, 1928, in Iyer, *Writings*, 2: 220.

151. *Young India*, November 18, 1926.

152. Responding to claims that it is sometimes permissible to take the life of an enemy in order to serve the best interests of the community, Gandhi insists that such an "act would still be spelt as *himsa* because it would not be altogether disinterested." *Young India*, November 18, 1928.

153. *Young India*, December 9, 1926.

154. *Young India*, December 30, 1926. Gandhi makes it clear that "in practice, however, we do not cut short the sufferings of our ailing dear ones by death because as a rule we have always means at our disposal to help them and because they have the capacity to think and decide for themselves. But supposing that in the case of an ailing friend I am unable to render any aid whatever and recovery is out of the question and the patient is lying in an unconscious state in the throes of fearful agony, then I would not see any *himsa* in putting an end to his suffering by death" (*Young India*, November 18, 1926).

155. *Young India*, November 1, 1928, in Iyer, *Writings*, 2: 280. With the great advances made in modern medicine and public health, many more people are living longer today than in the past. However, many become comatose and this often raises troubling decisions for members of their family. Gandhi joins a debate in medical ethics about the status of life at the intersection between the loss of human dignity and the maintenance of biological life. His arguments do not provide a formula as much as they question the position that biological life is so sacred it can never be taken, even at the expense of denying dignity to the dying person.

156. *Young India*, November 4, 1926.

157. *Young India*, October 11, 1928.

158. *Young India*, October 4, 1928.

159. *Young India*, October 4, 1928.

160. "I do not mean to suggest that violence has no place at all in the teaching of the *Gita*. The *dharma* which it teaches does not mean that a person who has not yet awakened to the truth of non-violence may act like a coward. Anyone who fears others, accumulates possessions and indulges in sense-pleasures will certainly fight with violent means, but violence does not, for that reason, become justified as his *dharma* . . . . But this *dharma* does not under any circumstances countenance running away in fear. In this world which baffles our reason, violence there will then always be. The *Gita* shows the way which will lead us out of it, but it also says that we cannot escape it simply by running away from it like cowards. Anyone who prepares to run away would do better, instead, to kill and be killed." "Meaning of the *Gita*," *Navajivan*, October 11, 1925, in Iyer, *Writings,* 1: 83.

161. Considering the universal applicability of nonviolence as an effective mode of responding to injustice and transforming relationships, Rajni Kothari finds that "Gandhi was quite unrealistic in his belief in the inevitability of" nonviolence (*Footsteps into the Future*, 98). For a further criticism of the universability of Gandhian nonviolence, see Parekh, *Gandhi's Political Philosophy.*

162. Speaking of World War II, he reports, "My sympathies are wholly with the Allies. Willynilly, this war is resolving itself into one between such democracy as the West has evolved and totalitarianism" (*Harijan*, September 30, 1939). A month later, he records his "sympathy for the cause of the Allies . . . must not be interpreted to mean endorsement, in any shape or form, of the doctrine of the sword for the defence of even proved right" (*Harijan*, October 14, 1939). On another occasion, he argues that "it is permissible for, it is even the duty of a believer in *ahimsa* to distinguish between the aggressor and the defender. Having done so, he will side with the defender in a non-violent manner, i.e. give his life in saving him" (*Harijan*, October 21, 1939).

163. Tendulkar, *Mahatma*, 4: 312.

164. Gandhi reports that his "belief in non-violence is based on the assumption that human nature in essence is one and therefore unfailingly responds to the advances of love." *Harijan*, December 24, 1938.

165. "A *satyagrahi* bids goodbye to fear. He is therefore never afraid of trusting the opponent. Even if the opponent plays him false twenty times, the *satyagrahi* is ready to trust him for the twenty-first time, for an implicit trust in human nature is the very essence of his creed." *Satyagraha in South Africa*, ch. 22, 246.

166. *Harijan*, November 26, 1938.

167. Hitler "would be a spent force if he had not the backing of his people. . . . I must refuse to believe that the Germans as a nation have no heart or markedly less than the other nations of the earth. They will some day rebel against their own adored hero, if he does not wake up betimes." *Harijan*, January 7, 1939.

168. Several scholars and sympathetic observers of Gandhi have taken his response to German Jews as defective. See, for example, Dennis Dalton who observes, "A government's capacity for ambivalence must matter because it gives a resistance movement license to mobilize or to publicize its cause. Hitler's willingness and ability to use state power in an unrestrained extermination process precluded organized non-violent action" (*Mahatma Gandhi*, 137).

Joan Bondurant takes the opposite position and holds that "the chances for success" of a Jewish satyagraha campaign in Germany "are certainly as great as are the chances for violent revolution under the modern police-state system. Satyagraha may, in fact, be the only possibility open to an oppressed people in this age of highly technical means of oppression." One consequence of nonviolent Jewish resistance, according to Bondurant, is that world opinion would have mobilized "much more rapidly than it did" (*Conquest of Violence*, 227).

169. Consider Karl Jasper's observation, "It was only under the British, and only under their attempt at liberal rule which is unique in the history of empires, that Gandhi could succeed." *The Future of Mankind* (Chicago: University of Chicago Press, 1961), 38.

170. *Harijan*, November 26, 1938.

171. See *Young India*, August 11, 1920. The same month, he allows that he "would risk violence a thousand times than the emasculation of a whole race" (*Young India*, August 4, 1920). In each of these pieces, he goes on to insist that nonviolence is the preferred way of responding.

172. *Harijan*, August 25, 1940.

173. *Young India*, November 4, 1926.

174. In this way, he parallels John Stuart Mill's argument concerning "otherregarding" action. It is behavior that threatens immediate, irreversible, and consequential harm to others.

175. In the case of the person who "runs amuck" and is on a killing spree,

Gandhi allows that there is "one exception" to the duty of ordinary people to kill the mad killer. This is the "*yogi* who can subdue the fury of this dangerous man. . . . But," Gandhi continues, in the case at point, "we are not dealing with beings who have almost reached perfection; we are considering the duty of a society of ordinary erring human beings" (*Young India*, November 4, 1926).

176. *Harijan*, March 16, 1942.

177. Why not extend the advice he gives to women in India during the post-independence communal rioting? In each community, there is widespread abuse and rape, and Gandhi tells women that it is appropriate to resist violently. What he has in mind is physical resistance: biting, scratching, and other forms of physical defense or mass suicide (which he thinks will so disgrace the rapists, they will relent). Whatever one thinks of these recommendations, each involves a form of violence.

178. The subtitle of Gandhi's *Autobiography* is *The Story of My Experiments with Truth*.

179. For a further discussion of the role of experiments in Gandhi's theory, see Power, *Meanings of Gandhi*, 93f.; and Fox, *Gandhian Utopia: Experiments with Culture*.

180. Even though he believes people are naturally nonviolent, Gandhi also holds that people need training in the spirit and methods of nonviolence when they move into political activity.

181. *Harijan*, March 28, 1936. However, Gandhian nonviolence does not mean that individuals should confront every evil without first weighing the consequences of their actions. Gandhi admits that he himself acts precipitously when one of his nonviolent campaigns against British colonialism results in violence on both sides. Mass civil disobedience campaigns in particular require discipline to sustain the nonviolence of the participants throughout the campaign, even when provoked. See *Young India*, February 27, 1930.

182. Gandhi finds that the "nonviolence of two persons occupying different positions will not automatically take the same shape." Gandhi, *Law of Love*, ed. Anand Hingorani (Bombay: Bharatiya Vidya Bhavan, 1970), 48.

7

GANDHI IN THE
TWENTY-FIRST CENTURY

The opinions I have formed and the conclusions I have arrived at
are not final. I may change tomorrow; I have nothing new to teach
to the world. Truth and nonviolence are as old as the hills. All I
have done is to try experiments in both on as vast a scale as I could
do. In doing so, I have sometimes erred and learnt by my errors.
Life and its problems have thus become to me so many experiments
in the practice of truth and nonviolence.[1]

O n its face, Western democratic societies have seldom been
stronger. Their dangerous totalitarian opponents have been van-
quished; their technology continues to move at a dizzying pace; their
citizens are living longer, are more literate, and generally enjoying a
higher standard of living than earlier generations; their models of the
economy and polity have become dominant; and their culture is becoming globalized. The West has put its stamp on the world: modernity and
modernization provide the standards by which we understand success
and failure. But the themes of several recent books published in the West
signal that for some, at least, all is not well. Agnes Heller writes about
the dissatisfied society; Jeffrey Goldfarb offers us *The Cynical Society*;
Daniel Bell detects the cultural contradictions of capitalism; Norbitto
Bobbio talks about the broken promises of democracy; David Marquand
finds *The Unprincipled Society*; Ronald Beiner asks, *What's the Matter with
Liberalism?*; and Alan Bloom laments *The Closing of the American Mind*.[2]
There are other signs of trouble and discontent. Political participation is
declining while cynicism is increasing; hard choices assert themselves
between full employment and a generous state; drugs and crime climb
to troubling levels; the family is under siege; people live longer but many

seem neither secure nor satisfied; and the environment is degraded while the world's population increases.

Special problems await the two largest groups in the world, the young and the poor. The young are likely to have some education, live in urban areas, move away from the traditions of their parents, accept cosmopolitan norms of identity and of the good, be less deferential to authority, and be part of a changing, mobile environment. At the same time, very large numbers will be underemployed or unemployed, finding that the promises of modern culture have been broken and that they have no worth in their own society.[3] Where this leads is uncertain. Strong, disciplinary governments may check unrest with harsh police measures that are not respecters of basic rights; political leaders may manipulate loneliness and frustration into ugly, violent, nativist movements; crime and social disorganization may intensify; internal civil strife may explode; or the poor may be intimidated and humiliated in the harsh realities of their urban slums. From a Gandhian perspective, such outcomes are neither imaginary nor inevitable. They are not imaginary because severe dislocations, the intense demands of individualism, a decayed tradition, a continued devaluation of persons in the economy, and a host of other dislocating moves are bound to have an effect, sometimes leading to violence, always involving some measure of domination, and invariably sacrificing autonomy. However, Gandhi thinks this state of affairs can be challenged in two different but related ways. In the first place, he wants to show that injustice can be confronted nonviolently. Secondly, he insists that a different imperative—one that emphasizes the cosmological interdependence of everyone—and different institutional arrangements can foster (though not guarantee) a society that resists these assaults on autonomy. In this way he speaks to those at the margin, admonishing them to discard their lethargy, reject fatalism, and claim their own dignity through public, nonviolent assertion.

I have argued that one of Gandhi's great contributions as a political theorist of the twentieth century comes with his invitation to think freshly about the future, and he does this by reaching for both the past and present. If the future is as menacing as Gandhi fears it can become, then his importance increases with his reminders of what we risk losing and his claim that people can nonviolently challenge modern versions of fatalism.

His sweeping challenge to modern expressions of fatalism makes

Gandhi distinctive in the late-modern era. By questioning the inevitability and intractability of modernity, he wants to expose it as a construction that can be resisted. He is not interested in replacing everything that is modern, but in contextualizing the modern temper within a cosmological framework that guards autonomy. Moreover, he sets out to defend and nourish local traditions where individuals live and work and which, Gandhi believes, provide them with purpose and dignity. To do this, he confronts modern versions of fatalism; some hold that we cannot escape complexity, that we cannot avoid centralization, that we cannot resist the globalization of modern culture, that we cannot repeal the inevitability of violent conflict, or that we cannot challenge the growing impersonality of a world that judges the good in terms of its economic contribution.

Although it is impossible to return to an earlier cosmos, Gandhi means to fill in some of the blank spaces left by modernity. He does this by continually applying ethical standards to contemporary practices and institutions. For him, the earlier cosmic harmony promised that the autonomy of everyone would be assured, and he wants to make this the ultimate standard for judgment in the modern world. Therefore, he constantly asks about the status of autonomy and all that he thinks autonomy requires.

Gandhi challenges the contemporary tendency to see modernity embodying progress, reason, and liberation and to believe that alternative standards and practices that stand in its way can be eliminated without costly consequences. Should this attitude prevail, Gandhi fears that an increasing number of persons will become obsolescent, seen as having no worth and nothing to contribute in the modern world. For him, the modern tendency to make economic criteria the standard for judging persons and institutions reduces human beings to means; with such an outlook, talk about their dignity is beside the point.

As society becomes increasingly complex, there is an accelerating tendency for greater centralization, coordination, and hierarchy and the increasing dominance of the specialist. Deeply troubled by these encroachments on autonomy, Gandhi is especially alarmed at the prospect of the centralized state. His specific proposals for the panchayat raj may not offer much guidance in the crowded polity of the late modern world, but his political critique signals what has traditionally been at the heart of the democratic project, namely that people ought to govern themselves. Accordingly, he wants to show the dangers of concentrated power and the need to disperse power and encourage participation throughout society.

Gandhi warns about the globalization of the modernized economy, not only because of its economic effects but also because it is accompanied with the globalization of culture. He continually celebrates the diversity he sees in India and fears that such globalization is reducing what is distinctive and fostering what is uniform. Local cultures are critical to Gandhi's project because he sees each providing a concrete, not abstract, sense of identity and meaning apart from productivity and consumption. To defend autonomy and resist domination, Gandhi argues that persons must be equipped with a standard and that standard typically comes from tradition. However, one cannot rely on a tradition that has grown tired and corrupt, and so Gandhi continually revisits tradition and, where he finds it necessary, challenges it. For him, a revitalized and reformed tradition represents the best moral resource to question the efficiencies of the age.

GANDHI'S CIVIC REALISM

Although it seems strange to think of Gandhi as a political realist, much of his work is infused with a rich understanding of power and he shares much with conventional political realists, such as Machiavelli[4] in the West and Kautilya in India. In the realist account, power is unavoidable, seductive, and important. Whether we like it or not, power surrounds us; for realists, including Gandhi, the issue is not whether we can avoid power by ignoring it but how we understand and respond to its nature and uses. Realists share the views that power cannot be completely tamed, that it frequently carries dangerous consequences, and that it can never be fully exonerated by a comprehensive morality. To the realist, power itself is ubiquitous, unpredictable, and often hazardous. It provides us with the means to achieve some goal or overcome obstacles, but our quest for power often blinds us to its dangers. Realists see us frequently inflating our capacity to direct and control power and failing to appreciate its limits. Entering the fluid, unpredictable world of power, we frequently harm others and unintentionally injure ourselves.

For all of the problems associated with it, realists find people continually searching for more power, often to keep pace with their competitors.[5]

For someone such as Machiavelli, the power of any person or state is always problematic, subject to the wiles of *fortuna*. Even though one actor has ostensibly greater power than its opponents at any given moment, it can be undermined by unexpected changes or unconventional power.[6] One reason is that power takes many forms, and what seems to be an overwhelming expression of power in a particular setting can be inexplicably undermined by alternative modes of power.[7]

Gandhi's realism follows from his reading of power as unavoidable, dangerous, and coveted. For him, power needs to be understood more expansively than it generally is, not to repackage in new containers that deny its hazards or inevitability, but to show people its many locations and forms. Although Gandhi does not hold the bleak view of conventional realists that people are constantly driven by ambition and ready to dominate others, he finds that any society is open to this possibility. For this reason, Gandhi wants to domesticate power by dispersing it throughout society to avoid monopolistic or oligopolistic concentrations.

Gandhi's civic realism departs from conventional realism in several important ways. One reflects his argument that politics is about more than power and must address the purposes for which it is employed and how it is used. He intends to direct it in ways that speak to the dignity, freedom, and equality of persons. For him, the way power is applied has profound effects, and often unintended ones. In arguing that violent applications of power undermine even generous principles, Gandhi insists that people pay attention to the kind of power they employ and the means they use to mobilize it. If the purpose of power is to foster mutuality and autonomy, he means to show that violence only subverts these goals.

Gandhi's civic realism is also reflected in the attention he gives to the institutions of civil society which are critical to his understanding of power. The ways they organize and distribute power serve to facilitate or diminish individual self-governance, and he calls attention to the ways that institutions reward, ignore, and penalize particular forms of behavior. Some arrangements signal to people that they can protect their own economic well-being and security only by transferring their self-governance elsewhere. For these reasons, Gandhi leaves a conventional political realism that is preoccupied with state power and moves to a wider understanding of power which pays attention to how civil society is organized and what happens there.

The very features of politics that Gandhi makes a central part of his understanding of power and politics, namely love and conversion, seem to disqualify Gandhi as a realist, but I think not. He finds that lasting change does not come through coercion; that support born of good economic times often falters when the economy grows sour; that appeals to conscience often have a profound effect—if not immediately, then over time; and that some of the most intractable issues are not settled by violence but require dialogue and understanding. He takes his readers beyond conventional meanings of power to show what an expanded version can accomplish. Gandhi's civic realism, for all of its emphasis on love, speaks more directly to power than a political realism purporting to be scientific, a realism trying to mimic economic markets, or a realism that makes efficient management its center. In presenting a multidimensional understanding of power and its effects on individuals, Gandhi leaves a crude realism and attempts to teach a civic realism in order to reach ethical conclusions about political life.

GANDHI'S FUTURE

Although many support autonomy and decentralization and the postmodernist impulse to question is extensive, these positions—along with Gandhi's—do not seem to be the priorities of the late modern world. It is not so much that the twenty-first century promises to be hostile to Gandhi's theories and his idiom; more likely, it will be unconcerned. The metaphors of the future are apt to revolve around globalization and its kin uniformity; the market and its kin consumerism; instrumental rationality and its kin order and predictability; and none of these metaphors has need of Gandhi. Where Gandhi wants diversity, modernity covets regularity; where he sees politics as struggle, it sees politics as administration; where he looks to a reformed tradition, it concentrates on current satisfactions; where he reaches for localism, it revels in universalism; and when he joins his voice with the periphery, it is indifferent. Gandhi's walk into the twenty-first century, then, may be a lonely one.

Although the modern temper is preoccupied with matters far removed from much that Gandhi promotes and although some of his specific proposals are anachronistic in our complex, troubled society, his ideals continue to speak to the late modern world. It is a world that seems fragmented and incoherent and where control seems elusive, and Gandhi means to challenge this state of affairs. Tying together disparate themes, he abandons the usual specializations that conventionally mark modern thinking. Politics, economics, morality, religion, tradition, and the household are interwoven into his frame of thinking in an effort to see how they can cohere in ways that speak to freedom and equality.

In his efforts to recover coherence and control, he raises questions to unsettle and disturb both those who carry formal power and those who do not in order to challenge the former and energize the latter. In upsetting what has been thought to have been decided in the modern era, he seeks to show his readers that they do not have to assume the world can be no other way than it is now; that current standards used to judge success and failure are constructions which do not necessarily speak to the best in them and sometimes address the weakest in them. For him, politics, economics, and tradition are not separate, discrete phenomena but are interlocking and carry significant consequences for men and women.

Even though Gandhi's call to limit wants may seem utopian and the likelihood of its being accepted remote, the urgency of his message becomes all the more pressing with each passing year. The environment is degraded, waterways assaulted, nonrenewable resources depleted, and the atmosphere corrupted. Today's consumer society has little sense of obligation to the environment, and Gandhi wants to challenge this kind of moral apathy. He finds that modern consumption rests on a hubris that threatens to destroy both consumers and those who serve them. However, the ethic of limited consumption Gandhi wants to encourage seems to have little prospect of succeeding today. Recognizing the magnitude of the task, he believes a voluntary limitation of consumption is more likely to thrive if people have a cosmological outlook rather than a narrowly individualistic one. Persons who see interconnectedness and interdependency are more likely to recognize the need to limit their consumption than someone whose sole point of reference is the isolated, "independent" self.

Another area of concern in the late modern world that Gandhi addresses is violence. Although the great threat of global thermonuclear destruction has lessened in the post-Cold War period, other forms of armed conflict continue unabated, and the traffic in weapons intensifies. In this setting, Gandhi is a clear voice about the dangers of accepting violence as inevitable, whether local or international. He invites us not only to address the ways conflict can be settled without violence but also to see how civil society, with its patterns of domination and humiliation, can be reconstituted in order to avoid the conditions that give rise to violence in the first place.

If Gandhi speaks to the future, what political language is equipped to translate his teachings to the modern ear? The twenty-first century is likely to be a time when some form of liberalism is the dominant language of politics. What should be noticed is that there is not a single liberalism but many forms, and some are more open to much that Gandhi says just as some are antagonistic. Gandhi's frequent attacks on many basic principles in much liberal thinking should not obscure his many affinities with liberalism. True, he is impatient with a liberalism that spawns a narrow individualism, disregards tradition and community, and equates economic growth with morality. At the same time, he borrows heavily from a liberalism that speaks of civil liberties, the need to separate church and state, and representative democracy. To acknowledge Gandhi's kinship with aspects of a generous liberalism that raises questions about poverty, racism, sexism, and violence and that celebrates autonomy is to make him accessible and familiar to liberals who share his distemper with violence and domination and his commitment to self-governance.

PROBLEMATIZING GANDHI

Reading Gandhi as a problematizer of violence and modernity also serves to problematize Gandhi. The defender of tradition turns out to be one of its harshest critics; his self-conscious attacks on modernity cannot conceal his own reliance on many of its central concepts, such as equality, freedom, and reason; his assault on modernization is always coupled with a sense of what it promises and what it fails to deliver; and his opposition to violence is accompanied by repeated calls for struggle and resistance. Gandhi's harsh criticisms of tradition, violence, modernity, and modernization are not meant to offer a metanarrative of despair, and his morality tales about a simple economy and polity are not presented as a metanarrative of nostalgia. If Gandhi has something to say to the late modern world, it is surely not found in his specific proposals for spinning or a rural economy. His legacy comes with the issues he raises about autonomy, democracy, economic security, participatory communities, and the nonviolent resolution of conflict. For Gandhi, these issues need a home in the late modern world and ought not become remainders.

He is particularly concerned about the ways efforts to dominate continue to appear and reappear in any society. Fearing that many individuals often accept domination as necessary, as beyond challenge, or even as legitimate, Gandhi sees people becoming complicit in the way power is employed. Should we expect Gandhi to offer more than struggle to live an autonomous life? Although he continually holds out ideals and repeatedly talks about the need to find a harmony in one's life and community, in the end he thinks that such goods can only be approached through struggle. Efforts to picture him building a regime and community that are perpetually peaceful and harmonious misread Gandhi.

If Gandhi is to have a voice in the twenty-first century, then not all of his texts can be approached literally. Texts do not entirely speak for themselves, particularly those that teach and admonish, often by reaching to practices, problems and opportunities whose original home is much different than that of later readers. In responding to his own immediate world, Gandhi not only calls up specific solutions that do not address the late modern world, he also reaches for resources—such as a rural economy and a simple society—that have weakened in our own time. Anyone in the late modern world who is interested in addressing the issues Gandhi raises earlier about autonomy and nonviolence needs to interrogate him to understand how his commitments are transported to a different world and translated into their own idiom.

Because this often means accepting Gandhi's invitation to experiment and because the results are unpredictable, many find this is one of the most discordant aspects of his theories.[8] They lead, as Joan Bondurant observes, "to solutions as yet unknown."[9] And they must, given Gandhi's views that no one possesses the whole truth, that truth emerges in the encounters agents have with one another, and that to approach the truth, struggle is often necessary.

NOTES

1. Gandhi, *Harijan*, March 28, 1936.

2. See Agnes Heller and Ferenc Feher, *The Postmodern Political Condition* (Cambridge: Polity Press, 1988); Jeffrey Goldfarb, *The Cynical Society* (Chicago: University of Chicago Press, 1991); Daniel Bell, *The Cultural Contradictions of Capitalism* (New York: Basic Books, 1976); Bobbio, *Future of Democracy*; David Marquand, *The Unprincipled Society* (London: Fontana Press, 1988); Ronald Beiner, *What's the Matter with Liberalism?* (Berkeley: University of California Press, 1992); and Alan Bloom, *The Closing of the American Mind* (New York: Simon and Schuster, 1987).

3. I am indebted to Rajni Kothari's discussion of the impact of the consequences of a blind technological imperative. See his *Footsteps into the Future*, particularly 90–94.

4. See Anthony Parel, "Gandhian *Satyagraha* and Machiavellian *Virtu*" in *The Meanings of Gandhi*, ed. Paul Powers (Honolulu: University Press of Hawaii, 1971).

5. To temper the destructive aspect of pride, Kautilya and Machiavelli counsel prudence; for Niebuhr, the solution comes with humility.

6. Gandhi also recognizes that power does not necessarily respond to our rational plans or best efforts.

7. Gandhi works with this kind of reasoning to mobilize unconventional power from below in order to confront formal, institutional power with his civil disobedience.

8. Those who particularly value order find remarks by Gandhi on experimentation disturbing. "Evolution is always experimental. All progress is gained through mistakes and their rectification. . . . This is the law of individual growth. The same law controls social and political evolution also. The right to err, which means the freedom to try experiments, is the universal condition of all progress." Gandhi, *Truth Is God* (Ahmedabad: Navajivan Publishing House, 1990), 135.

9. Bondurant, *Conquest of Violence,* 194.

Appendix

SELECTIONS FROM THE *GITA*
DISCOURSE III[1]

The following are verses 4 to 8.

Not by nonperformance of actions does a man attain freedom from action; nor by mere renunciation of actions does he attain his spiritual goal.

For no one, indeed, can remain, for even a single moment, unengaged in activity, since everyone, being powerless, is made to act by the disposition of matter.

Whoever having restrained his organs of action still continues to brood over the objects of senses—he, the deluded one, is called a hypocrite.

But he who, having controlled the sense-organs by means of the mind, O Arjuna, follows without attachment the path of action by means of the organs of action—he excels.

Do your allotted work, for action is superior to nonaction. Even the normal functioning of your body cannot be accomplished through actionlessness.

. . . .

The following is verse 16.

Whoever, in this world, does not help in the rotating of the [cosmic] wheel thus set in motion—he is of sinful life, he indulges in mere pleasures of sense and he, O son of Pritha, lives in vain.

. . . .

The following is verse 20.

For, verily, by means of work have Janaka and others attained perfection. You should also do your work with a view to the solidarity of society.

NOTE

1. *Sources of Indian Tradition*, translated by R. N. Dandekar, 283–84. I have chosen this translation over Mahadev Desai's translation of Gandhi's in *The Gospel of Selfless Action or the Gita According to Gandhi* (Ahmedabad: Navajivan Publishing House, 1946). Gandhi translated the *Gita* into Gujarat and Desai offers us that translation into English. The Dandekar version seems more accessible to the modern reader and is one translation rather than the two we have with Desai.

BIBLIOGRAPHY

Ackerman, Bruce. *Social Justice and the Liberal State*. New Haven: Yale University Press, 1980.

Adler, Lisa, and L. H. M. Ling. "From Practice to Theory: Towards a Dissident-Feminist Reconstruction of Nonviolence." *Gandhi Marg* 16, 4 (January 1995): 462–80.

Ambedkar, B. R. *What Congress and Gandhi Have Done to the Untouchables*. Bombay: Thacker and Co., 1946.

Ambler, Rex. "Gandhi's Concept of Truth." In *Gandhi's Significance for Today*, edited by John Hick and Lamaont Hempel. New York: St. Martin's Press, 1989.

Ames, Robert, Wimal Diossanayake, and Thomas Kasulis. *Self as Person in Asian Theory and Practice*. Albany: State University of New York Press, 1994.

Ananthanathan, A. K. "The Significance of Gandhi's Interpretation of the *Gita*." *Gandhi Marg* 13, 3 (October 1991): 302–15.

Andrews, Charles. *Mahatma Gandhi's Ideas*. New York: Macmillan, 1930.

Ansbor, John J. *Martin Luther King, Jr.: The Making of a Mind*. New York: Orbis, 1984.

Appleby, Joyce. *Liberalism and Republicanism in the Historical Imagination*. Cambridge: Harvard University Press, 1992.

Arendt, Hannah. *Between Past and Future*. New York: Viking, 1961.

———. *The Human Condition*. Chicago: University of Chicago Press, 1958.

Aristotle. *Nicomachean Ethics*. Indianapolis: Hackett, 1985.

———. *The Politics*. Chicago: University of Chicago Press, 1984.

Arrow, Kenneth. *Social Choice and Individual Values.* New Haven: Yale University Press, 1951.

Ashe, Geoffrey. *Gandhi.* New York: Stein and Day, 1980.

Augustine. *City of God.* New York: Random House, 1950.

Aurobindo, Sri. *The Foundations of Indian Culture.* Pondicherry: Sri Aurobindo Ashram, 1988.

————. *The Renaissance of India,* 4th ed. Pondicherry: Sri Aurobindo Ashram, 1951.

Baird, Robert. *Religion in Modern India.* New Delhi: Manohar, 1989.

Baker, J. I. "Gandhi and the *Gita*: Sanskrit and Satyagraha." *Gandhi Marg* 15, 1 (April 1993): 39–61.

Bandyopadhyaya, Jayantanuja. *Social and Political Thought of Gandhi.* Bombay: Allied Publishers, 1969.

Bentley, Arthur. *The Process of Government.* Evanston: Principia Press, 1908.

Barry, Brian. "Circumstance of Justice and Future Generations." In *Obligations to Future Generations,* edited by R. I. Sikora and B. Barry. Philadelphia: Temple University Press, 1978.

Bhattacharya, Buddhadeva. *Evolution of the Political Philosophy of Gandhi.* Calcutta: Calcutta Book House, 1969.

Bhattacharyya, Sailendr. *Mahatma Gandhi: The Journalist.* Bombay: Times of India Press, 1962.

Bloom, Alan. *The Closing of the American Mind.* New York: Simon and Schuster, 1987.

Bobbio, Norberto. *The Future of Democracy.* London: Polity Press, 1987.

Bondurant, Joan V. *Conquest of Violence.* Berkeley: University of California Press, 1967.

Bose, Nirmal Kumar. *My Days with Gandhi.* Calcutta: Nishana, 1953.

————, ed. *Selections from Gandhi.* Ahmedabad: Navajivan Publishing House, 1957.

————. *Studies in Gandhianism.* Calcutta: India Associated Publishing Company, 1962.

Brown, Judith. *Gandhi: Prisoner of Hope.* New Haven: Yale University Press, 1989.

Buber, Martin. *The Writings of Martin Buber,* edited by Will Herberg. New York: Meridian Books, 1958.

Buck, Lucien. "Gandhi and Jefferson on Democracy and Humanism," *Gandhi Marg* (July 1995): 175–92.

Canovan, Margaret. *Hannah Arendt.* Cambridge: Cambridge University Press, 1992.

Chatterjee, Margaret. *Gandhi's Religious Thought.* London: Macmillan, 1983.

Chatterjee, Partha. *Nationalist Thought and the Colonial World: A Derivative Discourse.* Delhi: Oxford University Press, 1986.

Chaudhury, P. C. Roy. *Gandhi and His Contemporaries.* New Delhi: Sterling, 1972.

Connolly, William. *IdentityDifference: Democratic Negotiations of Political Paradox.* Ithaca: Cornell University Press, 1991.

————. *Political Theory and Modernity.* Oxford: Basil Blackwell, 1988.

Corlette, William. "The Availability of Lincoln's Civil Religion." *Political Theory,* 10 (1982): 520–40.

Dadhich, Naresh. *Gandhi and Existentialism.* Jaipur: Rawat, 1993.

————, and B. Arun Kumar. "Thoreau's Protest: A Means to Maintain the Ontological Essence of Man." *Gandhi Marg* 15, 3 (October 1993): 308–22.

Dahl, Robert. *Dilemmas of Pluralist Democracy.* New Haven: Yale University Press, 1982.

————. *Who Governs?* New Haven: Yale University Press, 1961.

Dallmayr, Fred. *Beyond Orientalism.* Albany: State University of New York Press, 1996.

————. "Toward a Comparative Political Theory." *Review of Politics* 59, 3 (Summer 1997).

Dalton, Dennis. "The Ideology of Sarodaya: Concepts of Politics and Power in Indian Political Thought." In *Political Thought in Modern India,* edited by Thomas Pantham and Kenneth Deutsch. New Delhi: Sage, 1986.

————. *The Indian Idea of Freedom.* Gurgaon: Academic Press, 1982.

————. *Mahatma Gandhi: Nonviolent Power in Action.* New York: Columbia University Press, 1993.

Dan, Alice. *Reframing Women's Health: Multidiciplinary Research and Practice.* Thousand Oaks: Sage, 1994.

Datta, D. M. *The Political Philosophy of Mahatma Gandhi.* Madison: University of Wisconsin Press, 1953.

Desai, Mahadev. *Diary of Mahadev Desai.* Ahmedabad: Navajivan, 1953.

————, ed. and translator. *The Gospel of Selfless Action of the Gita According to Gandhi.* Ahmedabad: Navajivan Publishing House, 1984.

de Smet, Richard. "Towards an Indian View of the Person." In *Contemporary Indian Philosophy*, edited by Margaret Chatterjee. London: George Allen, 1974.

de Tocqueville, Alexis. *Democracy in America*, edited by J. P. Mayer. New York: Harper & Row, 1966.

Deutsch, Kenneth. "Sri Aurobindo and the Search for Political and Spiritual Perfection." In *Political Thought in Modern India*, edited by Thomas Pantham and Kenneth Deutsch. New Delhi: Sage, 1986.

Dhawan, G. N. *The Political Philosophy of Gandhi*. Bombay: Popular Book Depot, 1946.

Diggins, John. *The Lost Soul of American Politics*. New York: Basic Books, 1984

Downs, Anthony. *An Economic Theory of Democracy*. New York: Harper and Row, 1957.

Dunn, John. *The Political Thought of John Locke*. Cambridge: Cambridge University Press, 1975.

————. *Western Political Theory in the Face of the Future*. Cambridge: Cambridge University Press, 1979.

Dworkin, Gerald. "The Concept of Autonomy." In *The Inner Citadel*, edited by John Christman. New York: Oxford University Press, 1989.

Dworkin, Ronald. *Taking Rights Seriously*. Cambridge: Cambridge University Press, 1978.

Edleman, Murray. *Constructing the Political Spectacle*. Chicago: University of Chicago Press, 1988.

————. *The Symbolic Uses of Politics*. Urbana: University of Illinois Press, 1967.

Edwards, Michael. "The Irrelevance of Development Studies." *Third World Quarterly* 11, 1 (January 1989): 116–35.

Embree, Ainslie. *Sources of Indian Tradition*. New York: Columbia University Press, 1988.

Feinberg, Joel. *Harm to Self*. New York: Oxford University Press, 1986.

————. "The Moral and Legal Responsibility of the Bad Samaritan." In *The Spectrum of Responsibility*, edited by Peter French. New York: St. Martin's Press, 1991.

Fisher, Louis. *Gandhi: His Life and Message for the World*. New York: New American Library, 1982.

————. *The Life of Mahatma Gandhi*. New York: Harper and Row, 1981.

Foucault, Michel. *The Birth of the Clinic*. New York: Pantheon Books, 1973.

———. *Discipline and Punish: The Birth of the Prison*. New York: Vintage, 1979.

———. "Of Other Spaces." *Diacritics* (Spring 1986): 22–27 (translated by Jay Miskiewic).

———. *Power and Knowledge*, edited by Colin Gordon. New York: Pantheon, 1980.

Fox, Richard. *Gandhian Utopia: Experiments with Culture*. Boston: Beacon Press, 1989.

Frankfort, Harry. "Alternate Possibilities and Moral Responsibility." In *The Spectrum of Responsibility*, edited by Peter French. New York: St. Martin's Press, 1991.

———. *The Importance of What We Care About*. New York: Cambridge University Press, 1988.

Gandhi, M. K. *All Men Are Brothers*, edited by Krishna Kripalani. New York: Columbia University Press, 1958.

———. *An Autobiography or the Story of My Experiments with Truth*. Ahmedabad: Navajivan Publishing House, 1972.

———. *Bread Labour*. Ahmedabad: Navajivan Publishing House, 1960.

———. *Collected Works*. 90 vols. Delhi: Publications Division, Ministry of Information and Broadcasting, 1958–84.

———. *Constructive Programme*. Ahmedabad: Navajivan Publishing House, 1941.

———. *Democracy, Real and Deceptive*. Ahmedabad: Navajivan Publishing House, 1961.

———. *Diet and Diet Reform*. Ahmedabad: Navajivan Publishing House, 1949.

———. *Discourses on the Gita*. Ahmedabad: Navajivan, 1946.

———. *Ethical Religion*. Madras: Ganesan, 1922.

———. *For Pacifists*. Ahmedabad: Navajivan Publishing House, 1938.

———. *From Yeravda Mandir*. Ahmedabad: Navajivan Press, 1932.

———. *Health Guide*. Trumansburg, N.Y.: Crossing Press, 1978.

———. *Hind Swaraj*. Ahmedabad: Navajivan Publishing House, 1938.

———. *Hindu Dharma*. Ahmedabad: Navajivan Publishing House, 1950.

———. *India of My Dreams*. Ahmedabad: Navajivan Publishing House, 1959.

————. *Industrialize and Perish.* Ahmedabad: Navajivan Publishing House, 1966.

————. *Law of Love,* edited by Anand Hingorani. Bombay: Bharatiya Vidya Bhavan, 1970.

————. *My Religion,* edited by B. Kumarappa. Ahmedabad: Navajivan Publishing House, 1955.

————. *My Socialism.* Ahmedabad: Navajivan Publishing House, 1969.

————. *Nonviolence in Peace and War,* edited by Bharatan Kumarappa. 2 vols. Ahmedabad: Navajivan, 1942–1949.

————. *Panchayat Raj.* Ahmedabad: Navajivan Publishing House, 1959.

————. *Rebuilding Our Villages.* Ahmedabad: Navajivan Publishing House, 1952.

————. *Satyagraha in South Africa.* Ahmedabad: Navajivan Publishing House, 1950.

————. *Socialism of My Conception.* Bombay: Bharatiya Vidya Bhavan, 1957.

————. *Spinning and Khadi.* Lahore: Gandhi Publications League, 1943.

————. *Trusteeship.* Ahmedabad: Navajivan Publishing House, 1960.

————. *Truth Is God.* Ahmedabad: Navajivan Publishing House, 1990.

Gier, Nicholas. "Gandhi, *Ahimsa,* and the Self." *Gandhi Marg* 15, 1 (April 1993): 24–38.

————. "Gandhi: Pre-Modern, Modern, or Post-Modern?" *Gandhi Marg* 18, 3 (October 1996): 261–281.

Glendon, Mary. *Rights Talk: The Impoverishment of Political Discourse.* Cambridge: Harvard University Press, 1991.

Green, Martin. *Tolstoy and Gandhi.* New York: Basic Books, 1983.

Harding, Sandra. *Racial Economy of Science.* Bloomington: Indiana University Press, 1993.

Hayek, Friedrich. *The Political Order of a Free People.* Chicago: University of Chicago Press, 1973.

Heller, Agnes. *A Philosophy of History in Fragments.* Oxford: Blackwell, 1993.

Henry, Garojini. "Social Ethic of Mahatma Gandhi and Martin Buber." *Journal of Dharma* 16, 4 (1991): 375–386.

Herman, A. L. *A Brief Introduction to Hinduism.* Boulder: Westview, 1991.

Hick, John, and Lamaont Hempel. *Gandhi's Significance for Today.* New York: St. Martin's Press, 1989.

Hirsch, Fred. *The Social Limits of Growth.* Cambridge: MIT Press, 1976.

Hobbes, Thomas. *Leviathan*, edited by C. B. Macpherson. Harmondsworth, Middlesex: Penguin, 1968.

Hunt, James. "Thoreau and Gandhi: A Re-Evaluation of Their Legacy." In *New Dimensions and Perspectives in Gandhism*, edited by V. T. Patil. New Delhi: Inter-India Publications, 1988, 281–90.

Iyer, Raghavan N. *Moral and Political Thought of Mahatma Gandhi*. New York: Oxford University Press, 1973.

————, ed. *The Moral and Political Writings of Mahatma Gandhi*. Oxford: Clarendon Press, vols. 1 & 2, 1986, and vol. 3, 1987.

Jasper, Karl. *The Future of Mankind*. Chicago: University of Chicago Press, 1961.

Karunakaran, K. P. *New Perspectives on Gandhi*. Simla: Indian Institute of Advanced Study, 1969.

Kateb, George. *The Inner Ocean: Individualism and Democratic Culture*. Ithaca: Cornell University Press, 1992.

Kertzer, David. *Ritual, Politics and Power*. New Haven: Yale University Press, 1988.

King, Martin Luther. "More than Any Other Person in History." *Peace News*, January 1, 1958.

————. "My Trip to the Land of Gandhi." *Ebony*, July 1959, 84–92.

————. *Strength to Love*. New York: Pocket Books, 1968.

————. *Stride Toward Freedom*. New York: Harper and Row, 1958.

————. *Where Do We Go from Here?* New York: Bantam Books, 1968.

————. *Why We Can't Wait*. New York: Signet, 1963.

Kothari, Rajni. *Footsteps into the Future*. New York: Free Press, 1974.

————. *Poverty*. Atlantic Highlands, N.J.: Zed Books, 1993.

Kuntz, Paul Grimley. "Gandhi's Truth." *International Philosophy Quarterly* 22 (Summer 1982): 141–55.

Kuper, Leo. *Passive Resistance in South Africa*. New Haven: Yale University Press, 1957.

Lindbloom, Charles. *Politics and Markets*. New York: Basic Books, 1977.

Locke, John. *Two Treatises of Government*, edited by Peter Laslett. Oxford: Oxford University Press, 1988.

Lowi, Theodore. *The End of Liberalism*. New York: Norton, 1969.

Machiavelli, N. *The Prince and Discourses*. New York: Random House, 1940.

MacIntyre, Alasdair. *After Virtue*. Notre Dame: Notre Dame University Press, 1981.

Macpherson, C. B. *The Political Theory of Possessive Individualism*. Oxford: Oxford University Press, 1962.

Matthews, Richard. *The Racial Politics of Thomas Jefferson*. Lawrence: University Press of Kansas, 1984.

Mehta, V. R. *Foundations of Indian Political Thought*. New Delhi: Manohar, 1992.

———. *Ideology, Modernization, and Politics in India*. New Delhi: Manohar, 1983.

Milgram, Stanley. *The Individual in the Social World*. New York: Addison-Wesley, 1977.

Mill, John Stuart. "On Liberty." In *Collected Works*, vol. 18. Toronto: University of Toronto Press, 1977.

Naess, Arne. *Gandhi and the Nuclear Age*. Totowa, N.J.: Bedminister Press, 1965.

Nanda, B. R. *Gandhi and His Critics*. Bombay: Oxford University Press, 1985.

———. "Gandhi and Religion." *Gandhi Marg* 12, 1 (April 1990): 5–23.

———. *Gokhale, Gandhi, and the Nehrus*. New York: St. Martin's Press, 1973.

Nandy, Ashis. *At the Edge of Psychology: Essays in Politics and Culture*. New Delhi: Oxford University Press, 1980.

———. "Culture, Voice and Development: A Primer for the Unsuspecting." In *The Changing Structure of World Politics*, edited by Y. Sakamoto. Tokyo: Iwanami Shoten, 1989.

———. "Shamans, Savages, and the Wilderness." Paper for the Workshop on the Coming Global Civilization, Moscow, October 1988.

———. *Traditions, Tyranny and Utopias*. Delhi: Oxford University Press, 1987.

Naravane, V. S. *Modern Indian Thought*. Bombay: Asia Publishing House, 1967.

Nehru, Jawaharlal. *The Discovery of India*. Oxford: Oxford University Press, 1946.

Niebuhr, Reinhold. *Moral Man and Immoral Society*. New York: Scribners, 1932.

———. "What Chance Has Gandhi?" *Christian Century* 48 (1931); 1274–76.

Nietzsche, Friedrich. *The Genealogy of Morals*, translated by Walter Kaufmann and R. I. Hollingdale. New York: Vintage, 1989.

————. *The Portable Nietzsche.* New York: Penguin, 1976.

Norgaard, Richard. *Development Betrayed.* London: Routledge, 1994.

Nussbaum, Martha. *Fragility of Goodness, Luck and Ethics in Greek Tragedy and Philosophy.* New York: Cambridge University Press, 1986.

Oakeshott, Michael. *Rationalism in Politics and Other Essays.* Indianapolis: Liberty Press, 1962.

Offe, Claus. *The Contradictions of the Welfare State.* Cambridge: MIT Press, 1984.

Organ, Troy Wilson. *Hinduism.* Woodbury, N.J.: Barron's, 1974.

Pandiri, Ananda M. *A Comprehensive, Annotated Bibliography on Mahatma Gandhi.* Vol. 1. Westport, Conn.: Greenwood Press, 1995.

Pantham, Thomas. "Gandhi's Intervention in Modern Moral Political Discourse." In *Gandhi and the Present Global Crisis.* Shimla: Indian Institute of Advanced Study, 1996.

————. "Gandhi, Nehru, and Modernity." In *Crisis and Change in Contemporary India,* edited by Upendra Baxi and Bhikhu Parekh. New Delhi: Sage, 1995.

————. "Indian Secularism and Its Critics." *Review of Politics* 59, 3 (Summer 1997): 523–40.

————. "On Modernity, Rationality, and Morality: Habermas and Gandhi." *Indian Journal of Social Science* 1, 2 (1988): 187-208.

————. *Political Theories and Social Reconstruction.* New Delhi: Sage, 1995.

————. "Post-Relativism in Emancipatory Thought: Gandhi's Swaraj and Satyagraha." In *Multiverse of Democracy,* edited by D. C. Gheth and Ashis Nandy. New Delhi: Sage, 1997.

————. "Thinking with Mahatma Gandhi: Beyond Liberal Democracy." *Political Theory* 11, 2 (May 1983): 165–88.

————, and Kenneth Deutsch, eds. *Political Thought in Modern India.* New Delhi: Sage, 1986.

Parekh, Bhikhu. *Colonialism, Tradition, and Reform.* New Delhi: Sage. 1989.

————. *Gandhi.* Oxford: Oxford University Press, 1997.

————. *Gandhi's Political Philosophy.* Notre Dame: Notre Dame University Press, 1989.

————. "Some Reflections on the Hindu Tradition in Political Thought." In *Political Thought in Modern India,* edited by Thomas Pantham and Kenneth Deutsch. New Delhi: Sage, 1986.

Parel, Anthony. "Gandhian *Satyagraha* and Machiavellian *Virtue.*" In *The Meanings of Gandhi*, edited by Paul Power. Honolulu: University Press of Hawaii, 1971.

―――. "Gandhi's Idea of Nation in *Hind Swaraj.*" *Gandhi Marg* 13, 3 (October 1991): 261–81.

―――. "Introduction." In *Hind Swaraj*, edited by A. Parel. Cambridge: Cambridge University Press, 1997.

Patil, V. T. "Gandhi and His Ideas on Religion and Politics." In *New Dimensions and Perspectives in Gandhism*, edited by V. T. Patil. New Delhi: Inter-India Publications, 1989.

―――, ed. *New Dimensions and Perspectives in Gandhism*. New Delhi: Inter-India Publications, 1989.

―――. ed. *Studies on Gandhi*. New Delhi: Sterling, 1983.

―――. ed. *Studies on Nehru*. New Delhi: Sterling, 1987.

―――, and S. T. Kallapur. "The Paradoxical Element in Gandhi." In *Studies on Gandhi*, edited by V. T. Patil. New Delhi: Sterling, 1983.

Pocock, J. G. A. *The Machiavellian Moment*. Princeton: Princeton University Press, 1975.

Power, Paul, ed. *The Meanings of Gandhi*. Honolulu: University Press of Hawaii, 1971.

Prabhu, R. K., and Vavindra Kelker, eds. *Truth Called Them Differently (Tagore-Gandhi Controversy)*. Ahmedabad: Navjivan, 1961.

Prabhu, R. K., and U. R. Rao. *The Mind of Mahatma Gandhi*. Oxford: Oxford University Press, 1945.

Rao, M. B. *The Mahatma: A Marxist Symposium*. Bombay: People's Publishing House, 1969.

Rawls, John. *Theory of Justice*. Cambridge: Harvard University Press, 1971.

Ray, Stephen. "Jain Influences on Gandhi's Early Thought." In *Gandhi, India, and the World,* edited by Stephen Ray. Bombay: Nachiketa Publishers, 1976. ·

Raz, Joseph. *The Morality of Freedom*. Oxford: Clarendon, 1986.

Redclift, Michael. *Sustainable Development: Exploring the Contradictions*. London: Methuen, 1987.

Riessman, Catherine Kohler. "Women and Medicalization: A New Perspective," *Social Policy* 14 (Summer, 1983): 3–18.

Rolland, Romain. *Mahatma Gandhi*. London: Allen and Unwin, 1924.

Rosenau, Pauline M. *Post-Modernism and the Social Sciences*. Princeton: Princeton University Press, 1992.

Rosenblum, Nancy. *Another Liberalism*. Cambridge: Harvard University Press, 1987.

Rothurmund, Indira. "The Gandhian Pattern of Mass Communication." *Gandhi Marg* 8, 12 (1987).

———. *The Philosophy of Restraint—Mahatma Gandhi's Strategy and Indian Politics*. Bombay: Popular Prakashan, 1963.

Rousseau, J. J. *Government of Poland*. Indianapolis: Library of Liberal Arts, 1972.

———. *Social Contract and Discourses*. London: Dent, 1983.

Roy, Ramashray. *Self and Society: A Study in Gandhian Thought*. New Delhi: Sage, 1985.

Rudolph, Lloyd. "Contesting Civilizations." *Gandhi Marg* 13, 4 (January 1992): 419–31.

———, and Susanne Hoeber Rudolph. *The Modernity of Tradition*. Chicago: University of Chicago Press, 1967.

Said, Edward. *Orientalism*. New York: Pantheon Books, 1978.

Sandel, Michael. *Liberalism and the Limits of Justice*. New York: Cambridge University Press, 1982.

Sassen, Saskia. *Losing Control? Sovereignty in an Age of Globalization*. New York: Columbia University Press, 1996.

Schattschneider, E. E. *The Semisovereign People*. New York: Harcourt, Brace, Jovanovich, 1975.

Schumpeter, Joseph. *Capitalism, Socialism, and Democracy*. New York: Harper & Brothers, 1942.

Sen, Sachin. *The Political Thought of Tagore*. Calcutta: General Printers and Publishers, Ltd., 1947.

Sharp, Gene. *The Politics of Nonviolent Action*. Boston: Porter Sargent, 1973.

Sheean, Vincent. *Lead Kindly Light*. New York: Random House, 1949.

Shklar, Judith. *The Faces of Injustice*. New Haven: Yale University Press, 1990.

Singh, Ajai, and Shakuntala Singh, "The Tagore-Gandhi Controversy Revisited." *Indian Philosophical Quarterly* 19, 4 (October 1992): 265–82.

Sinha, Uttam. "Gandhi's Attitude Towards Labour-Capital Relations." *Gandhi Marg* 15, 4 (January 1994): 426–42.

Smith, Adam. *Theory of Moral Sentiments*, edited by D. D. Raphael and A. L. Macfie. Oxford: Oxford University Press, 1976.

Smith, Steven. "Gandhi's Moral Philosophy." In *Gandhi's Significance for Today*, edited by John Hick and Lamaont Hempel. New York: St. Martin's Press, 1989.

Sommleitner, Michael. "Gandhi and God: The Personal and Impersonal." *Gandhi Marg* 16 (April 1995): 67–83.

Sophocles. *Antigone*. Chicago: University of Chicago Press, 1954.

Southard, Barbara. "The Feminism of Mahatma Gandhi." In *New Dimensions and Perspectives in Gandhism*, edited by V. T. Patil. New Delhi: Inter-India Publications, 1989.

Tagore, Rabindranath. *Towards Universal Man*. London: Asia Publishing House, 1961.

Taylor, Charles. *Sources of the Self*. Cambridge: Cambridge University Press, 1989.

Tendulkar, D. G. *Mahatma: The Life of M. K. Gandhi*. New Delhi: Ministry of Information and Broadcasting, 1961.

Terchek, Ronald. "Gandhi and Moral Autonomy." *Gandhi Marg* 13, 4 (March 1992): 454–65.

———. "Gandhian Politics." In *New Perspectives and Dimensions on Gandhi*, edited by V. T. Patil. New Delhi: Inter-India Publications, 1989.

———. "Gandhi's Democratic Theory." In *Political Thought of Modern India*, edited by Thomas Pantham and Kenneth Deutsch. New Delhi: Sage of India, 1986.

———. "The Psychoanalytic Basis of Gandhi's Politics." *The Psychoanalytic Review* 62, 2 (Summer 1975).

———. *Republican Paradoxes and Liberal Anxieties: Retrieving Neglected Fragments in Political Theory*. Lanham, Md.: Rowman and Littlefield, 1996.

Thoreau, Henry David. *Walden and Civil Disobedience*, edited by Owen Thomas. New York: Norton Critical Editions, 1966.

Toinnes, Ferdinand. *Community and Society*. East Lansing: Michigan State University Press, 1957.

Touraine, Alain. *What Is Democracy?* Boulder: Westview Press, 1997.

Truman, David. *The Governmental Process*. New York: Knopf, 1951.

Varma, V. P. *Modern Indian Political Thought*. Agra: Lakshmi Narain Agarwal, 1967.

Varna, S. P. "Social and Political Thought of Gandhi in the Perspective of Contemporary Thinking on Democracy." *Gandhian Studies* 1, 2 (July 1996): 7–45.

Walzer, Michael. *Spheres of Justice*. New York: Basic Books, 1983.

Weber, Max. *From Max Weber*, edited by H. H. Gerth and C. Wright Mills. New York: Oxford University Press, 1958.

————. *The Interpretation of Social Reality*. London: Eldridge, 1971.

————. *The Protestant Ethic and the Spirit of Capitalism*, translated by Talcott Parsons. New York: Scribners, 1958.

Weil, Simon. *The Iliad or the Poem of Force*. Wallingford, Pa.: Pendle Hill, 1956.

Williams, Bernard. *Problems of the Self*. Cambridge: Cambridge University Press, 1973.

Wilson, Boyd. "Ultimacy as Unifier in Gandhi." In *Religion in Modern India,* edited by Robert Baird. New Delhi: Manohar, 1989.

Wolin, Sheldon. *The Presence of the Past*. Baltimore: The Johns Hopkins University Press, 1989.

Wong, Huiyun, "Gandhi's Contesting Discourse." *Gandhi Marg* 17, 3 (October 1995): 261–85.

Yack, Bernard. *Longing for Total Revolution*. Princeton: Princeton University Press, 1986.

Young, Robert. "Autonomy and the 'Inner Self.' " *Ethics* 17 (1980).

Zolo, Danilo. *Democracy and Complexity*. University Park: The Pennsylvania State University Press, 1992.

GLOSSARY

ahimsa: nonviolence, nonkilling, absence of harm or injury, rejection of intent to injure; Gandhi often uses the term interchangeably with love.

artha: money, wealth.

ashram: a community united by spiritual goals.

atman: the soul.

brahmacharyashram: a student; first of four stages of life, requiring celibacy.

brahmin: the first of the four castes, popularly known as the priestly caste.

charkha: spinning wheel.

crore: ten million.

dharma: duty, natural law, right conduct.

duragraha: stubborn persistence; usually associated with self-serving uses of nonviolent civil disobedience.

Gita: an episode set before an impending battle in the epic *Mahabharata;* a philosophical and theological discussion about faith and the duty to act according to what is right regardless of the consequences to the self.

grihastha: a house-holder. The second stage in the life of caste Hindu as spouse and parent.

Harijan: Gandhi's term for the untouchables; literally child of God.

hartal: work stoppage, strike, usually for political rather than economic purposes.

himsa: violence, injury; intent to harm.

karma: law of ethical causality; action; service.

khadi: hand-spun cloth.

kshatriya: the second of the four castes, warriors.

lakh: a hundred thousand.

Mahabharata: a sacred, ancient epic ostensibly about war but seen by Gandhi as about the conflict between good and evil.

Mahatma: great soul.

moksha: freedom from worldly attachments; salvation.

panchayat: popularly elected village council.

raj: rule.

ryot: peasant; tenant farmer.

samaj: an organization or association.

sannyasis: ascetics who have abandoned worldly ties.

sarvodaya: good or welfare of all.

sat: truth.

satyagraha: truth-force; nonviolent resistance; usually associated with Gandhi's civil disobedience campaigns.

satyagrahi: one who practices satyagraha.

shudra: laborers; lowest caste.

smritis: sacred texts based on memory, authoritatively below the Vedas.

sutras: ancient, sacred rules or aphorisms.

swadeshi: traditional way of life; self-reliance; a product made in one's own country.

swaraj: self-rule; independence; used by Gandhi to mean both national or political independence and the self-rule of individuals.

tapas: penance; self-sacrifice.

Upanishads: sacred texts written at the close of the Vedic period; an important concept taken from them by Gandhi is the relationship between human beings and the cosmos.

vaishya: the third caste, merchants.

vanaprastha: the third stage of life, characterized by leaving the traditional household.

varna: traditional caste; often used by Gandhi to refer to an idealized ancient caste system before its present form developed.

varnadharma: the duties and relationships of the four castes. Ideally, each has a specific social duty: the brahmin, exercising spiritual authority; the kshatriya, administering temporal power; the vaishya, managing economic activities; and the shudra, contributing manual labor.

Veda: literally, knowledge; earliest Hindu scriptures.

yajna: sacrifice; as used by Gandhi the term refers to the sacrifice that one makes for the good of the community or its most vulnerable members.

zamindar: landlord class.

INDEX

ABOUT THE AUTHOR

Ronald J. Terchek is professor of government and politics at the University of Maryland at College Park. He is the author of *Republican Paradoxes and Liberal Anxieties* (Rowman and Littlefield) and coeditor of *Foreign Policy as Public Policy*. He has published numerous articles and lectured extensively on liberal-democratic theory, theories of autonomy, and the political theory of Mahatma Gandhi in the United States, Canada, Europe, and India. He is a member of the editorial advisory board of the *Journal of Gandhian Studies*.